Learning Trajectories, Violence and Empowerment amongst Adult Basic Skills Learners

I0896279

Learning Trajectories, Violence and Empowerment amongst Adult Basic Skills Learners offers deep insights into the lives of marginalised communities and the link between learning, literacy and violence, not previously carried out in-depth in a small scale study. It breaks the negative stereotypes of adults who struggle to read and write, who are often labelled and stigmatised by dominant discourses, and in doing so exposes why and how Basic Skills learners often find themselves in marginal positions. The structural inequalities many face from childhood to adulthood across the private and public domains of their lives are revealed and probed, thus challenging neo-liberalism claims of an apparently egalitarian social field. The learners' narratives expose the contradiction, complexities and ambivalences they experience in their daily lives, and how they try to make sense of them from their structural positioning as basic skills learners in a society based on inequality of opportunity and choice.

Applying a feminist, qualitative, longitudinal, ethnographic and participatory approach, the book offers a critical perspective, drawing on Bourdieu's work as the theoretical framework, as well as using a range of feminist, sociologists of education, literature on the ethics of care and critical literacy pedagogy, including the New Literacy Studies. The author's personal position as an 'insider' with 'insider knowledge' of marginalised communities is also woven throughout the chapters and offers insights into the struggles, conformity and resistance faced by the participants in the study.

The book contributes to the debate on the impact of violence on learning and its link to class, gender and basic skills as well opening up a discussion on the power of a critical curriculum to empower people across the domains of their lives. It will be valuable reading for trainee teachers, teachers, education and sociology students, postgraduate students, as well as literacy specialists, researchers, academics, policy makers and managers of public services.

Vicky Duckworth is Senior Lecturer and MA co-ordinator in Post Compulsory Education and Training (PCET) and Schools' University Lead at Edge Hill University, UK.

'Through an in-depth exploration of the lives of sixteen learners, Duckworth offers her readers valuable insights into the complex interplays between literacy, learning, violence, gender and social class. The richness of the data and the insightful analyses make for a fascinating read. This is an important book that will appeal to a wide audience, including teachers, researchers and policy makers.'

—Professor Carolyn Jackson, Department of Educational Research, Lancaster University, UK

'Whilst this book offers poignant insight into the lives of some adult basic skills learners, it is no less a landmark in "rich" and critical life/story methodologies. It will be required reading for all my post-graduate students, from any sector, working to create biographies sociologically.'

—Honorary Professor Peter Clough, The University of Sheffield, UK

'This is a hugely engaging book about adult literacy – and much more. It uses Bourdieusian ethnographic research and personal reflection to explore the lives of working class adult learners. Interwoven into the text is the author's narrative, her experience as a literacy teacher and the recent social history of Oldham. This book will inspire education researchers and reflective practitioners with an interest in learning and empowerment. I thoroughly recommend this book.'

—Professor Liz Thomas, Edge Hill University, UK

'*Learning Trajectories, Violence and Empowerment amongst Adult Basic Skills Learners* is a passionate and powerful account of the struggles faced by learners in marginalized communities. It provides a gripping picture of the complexities and contradictions that shape their lives, and attests to the enduring power of feminist ethnography to illuminate the workings of class and gender in education.'

—Professor Diane Reay, University of Cambridge, UK

Routledge Research in Lifelong Learning and Adult Education series

Books in this series:

Learning Trajectories, Violence and Empowerment amongst Adult Basic Skills Learners
Vicky Duckworth

Routledge Research in Lifelong Learning and Adult Education series

Learning Trajectories, Violence and Empowerment amongst Adult Basic Skills Learners

Vicky Duckworth

Routledge
Taylor & Francis Group
LONDON AND NEW YORK

First published 2014
by Routledge

2 Park Square, Milton Park, Abingdon, Oxon OX14 4RN
711 Third Avenue, New York, NY 10017, USA

Routledge is an imprint of the Taylor & Francis Group, an informa business

First issued in paperback 2016

British Library Cataloguing in Publication Data
A catalogue record for this book is available from the British Library

Library of Congress Cataloging in Publication Data
A catalog record for this book has been requested

ISBN: 978–0–415–82872–7 (hbk)
ISBN: 978–1–138–28291–9 (pbk)

Typeset in Galliard
by Swales & Willis Ltd, Exeter, Devon

This book is dedicated to my daughters,
Anna and Niamh Ludlow

Contents

Figures

Acknowledgements

I would especially like to thank Mary Hamilton, who has provided me with on-going support, encouragement and inspiration throughout the duration of the research.

What is important is that this research would not have been possible without the strength, generosity and inspiration of the 16 learners whose narratives form the soul of this study. Special thanks go to all these learners in sharing their time, energy and words which provided the material for this study as well as nourishing my enthusiasm in continuing the study and belief that we could make a difference.

My thanks go to the following women: Mam, Ann Duckworth (nee Macauley); Nana, Johanna Duckworth (nee Kippax); Anne Beeley (nee Duckworth); Amy Robinson, Marie Ludlow and Maxine Williamson. Not forgetting the men: my dad and three brothers, Ant, James and Matt.

A special thanks to all my family for their support and love, especially my husband Craig for his patience and encouragement.

I would also like to thank Peter Clough, Murray Saunders, Paul Trowler, Carolyn Jackson, Ann-Marie Houghton, Diane Reay, Liz Thomas, all at Lancaster University, Yvon Appleby, Jonathan Tummons, Catherine White, Sandra Varney and Steve Ingle; and special thanks to Paula Bithels, Mike Austin, Sharon Fitzpatrick, Sandra Robinson and my soul-sister, Michelle Stephens, for being there from the beginning. Thanks to Robert Smedley, Margaret Postance, The PCET team and all my colleagues at Edge Hill University. And finally thanks to all the team at Routledge for their patience and support: Clare Ashworth, Eleanor Rivers, Rebecca Wilford, Julie and Richard Willis and Kristin Susser.

Acknowledgements

Chapter 1

Overview of the book

This book seeks to highlight how 16 former Basic Skills learners have been shaped by the public domain and the private domain of their lives. It is based on a six-year qualitative, longitudinal, ethnographic and participatory approach. The learners were all enrolled on basic skills courses at a Further Education College based in the North of England. This book explores how they arrived at their current position, and seeks to highlight the learners' perception of their reality, unscrambling the links between their past, present and future while striving to highlight the intersection of class and gender on their pathways onto basic skills programmes and their subsequent trajectories.

The interpretation uses a critical perspective drawing on Bourdieu's work as the theoretical framework, as well as using a range of feminist work, sociologists of education, literature on ethics of care and critical literacy pedagogy, including New Literacy Studies.

Bourdieu's notion of habitus, with modifications, is used to explore the historical, present and emergent character of the learners' trajectories. Further to this, the concepts of capitals and their relationship to the learners' trajectories are also employed. This illuminates the objective and subjective dimensions of identities across the domains the learners travel, together with how they inform and transform the habitus and their changing interplay between classed and gendered processes over the learners' life-course.

My positioning

My personal position as an 'insider' with 'insider knowledge' of marginalised communities was a key motivation to becoming a basic skills tutor and becoming involved in this study. For example, my own life-history has greatly influenced the commitment I have for finding opportunities to enable others to take agency and aspire to reach their potential. I was born and brought up in the same community as the learners, attended the local state school and was the first generation of my family to enter college and university; my subsequent trajectory has also contributed to this commitment.

Further to this, involvement in this research was driven by my experience as a tutor and programme leader delivering literacy in a college of Further Education based in the North of England. With an increasing move towards performance via target setting, results and accountability, like many tutors I felt a great deal of my time and energy was beginning to be governed by a managerial driven system based on close scrutiny of my paperwork, rather than my practice in the classroom. Avis (2005: 212) identifies how this shift towards performance management is at odds with the rhetoric of the knowledge economy, which places an onus on a non-hierarchical approach based on trusting and respectful relationships between teams. With the managerialist discourse, where managers claim the right to manage and where professional judgements are under intense surveillance, notions of 'trust' can be something of an illusion. A blame culture can be the result of such approaches whereby accountability becomes a means by which the institution can call staff to account. In an age of insecure employment and redundancies the pressure to conform to a management agenda can work to erode a practitioner's autonomy and undermine their professionalism.[1] Within this context, the space I had for critical reflection and innovative practice was very limited. Critical autonomy and deep forms of intrinsic motivation were essential in sustaining this research. My drive came from the knowledge that education can be truly life enhancing and transforming if appropriate mechanisms are put in place to push open spaces that create a meaningful enquiry into the learners' lives.

So, with no monetary assistance from the Further Education College (funding in the latter stages was supported by the Higher Education I work at) and a full teaching time-table which relied heavily on emotional labour (see Hochschild 1983; James 1989) and 'underground working' (see Gleeson 2005), my drive was the commitment to expose and address issues relating to the myriad of complexities of working with basic skills learners.

Throughout the book I have embedded my own and the learners' poetry, narratives and photographs into the study to show ' *another person* how it is to feel something' (Richardson 2003: 190, my emphasis). In doing so I aim to celebrate the creative voice of the learners and do what Richardson refers to as showing rather than telling through creative expression.

Finding a critical space

I wanted to carry out an inquiry which opened a meaningful 'space' to develop a teaching and learning culture which moves towards a research based approach to Best Practice. As a critical educator/researcher, I sought to develop my practice through this research and reflect a critical pedagogy, providing a curriculum which is culturally relevant, learner driven, and socially empowering (Freire 1996; Barton et al. 2007).

I began with an interest in the class and gender issues that affect learning and have found that Bourdieu's work offers an appropriate and illuminating theoretical frame for my work. The theme of violence (both physical and symbolic), emerged strongly from participant accounts of their experience and has become a central focus of my analysis. The symbolic and institutional violence that shaped students' understanding of themselves within the educational context and the creation of a critical education provided a space which enabled the learners and me to explore and transcend the internal and external influences and violence that shape the learning experience.

Communities of practice

My progression through the research was also supported by the community of practice (Lave and Wenger 1991; Wenger 1998; Wenger et al. 2002) in which I was involved. This included: Research and Practice in Adult Literacy (RaPAL) and North West dialogue. I was also North West Convener for the Learning and Skills Research Network (LSRN) and continue to be a member. It also embraced interactions in the construction of values and identity, for example, the sharing of values in the RaPAL community includes sharing more critical approaches to teaching basic skills and thereby encourages people to reclaim their own learning processes by building their own learning from their own experiences. Each of the communities has supported and contributed to my knowledge and practice, offering a critical space to reflect and develop my own professional practice and identity as a teacher, activist and researcher.

Practitioner Action Research (PAR) has been a key part in driving my practice forward: for example, rather than presuming to know what the learners want to learn and what type of resources are best, I began to listen more closely to the learners' voices, letting their needs, aspirations and dreams shape the lessons (Hamilton et al. 2007).

I would also add that my study offered opportunities to work closely with the learners to develop a framework and tools to empower them and their communities to share their stories in the public and private domain (see Figure 4.1).

Initial research questions

The research question I started with in this study was how 16 former Basic Skills learners have been shaped, their whole being influenced by and responding to the public domain of schooling, college and work and the private domain of family, friends and home. I wanted to explore the learners' perceptions of their reality in these domains while seeking to address in what ways their past, present and future have been influenced by class and gender, and how this has impacted on their pathways and subsequent trajectories.

From my experience of living and working with learners from disadvantaged backgrounds, I felt that the notion of neo-liberalism (and its implication that an individual is free to determine their own pathway) is limited by the impact of structural and historical inequalities: gender, race and class and other markers of identity that shape the learners' educational journeys (Leathwood 2006). One way in which this happens is that learners from disadvantaged backgrounds are not considered to have the right attributes to progress (Archer et al. 2003;

Burke 2006). Indeed, many of the participants in this study are faced with cultural as well as national exclusion where choice for the 'excluded poor/dispossessed working class is, mostly, a myth' (Byrne 2005: 141). I wanted to add original evidence exploring these dimensions of learners' experiences.

The research group included 16 informants from across my Adult Basic Skills part-time day and evening class together with the New Deal full-time group. Their gender, age, occupation, ethnicity and social class are illustrated in Table 1 (Appendix 1). The New Deal course is aimed at supporting the participants back into employment. Their motivations for enrolling on the course and the impact of this will be fully explored in the study. Three of the initial research group, names listed in italics, left the course at differing stages and therefore could not be contacted through to the end of the study. Robert, engaged in the research social events but did not want his personal accounts revealed in the study.

Participation in the research group was voluntary. I informed each of my classes about the project and asked those who were interested to let me know after class. For those who voiced their interest I had a further meeting with them outside the lesson. I explained what the research would involve, which included interviews, collecting information about their life story and working together as a research group to make sense of the findings. From the beginning I was keen not to put any pressure on the group to say yes, so I asked them to think about it and let me know at a later date. I also wanted to make it clear it would be a collaborative study, where they had choice and power. This power included telling them they could set dates and places for interviews, they could also leave the study at any point and ask me any questions just as I asked them. I assured them that I would be willing to place my own narrative with theirs.

Following in the narrative tradition used by Walkerdine et al. (2001), Luttrell (1997) and Skeggs (1997), the main research tool chosen to collect life-history was semi-structured interviews. This was utilised to help the interviewees feel more confident and comfortable with the process and to facilitate the learners' stories to follow their chosen direction.

The semi-structured interviews were initially conducted utilising a series of questions, in bold, in Table 2 (see Appendix 2). The topics were chosen from my own learning journey and personal experience and used as a start point due to their 'broadness', with a view that most or all of them would be discussed by each member of the study group. This, I envisaged, would promote a participant-led approach insomuch as further themes would be generated which could then act as a focus of the subsequent interview sessions. These generated themes/topics, that are explored in this study.

Broad sociological overview

Oldham, a provincial northern town, poor and thinly populated in pre-industrial times, metamorphosed to become both nationally and internationally known in the Industrial Revolution. Oldham is now a tapestry of cultures and ethnic groups. Most of today's Muslim population arrived in England in the 1950s and 1960s in large numbers from the Indian sub-continent. Arriving in Oldham, they worked in the cotton mills where there was ample work and demand for labour was very high. These immigrants were willing to work long hours and undertake menial jobs for low pay. Many of the factories they worked in, now derelict, initially brought people to the area for work and helped cement the community. With the demise of Oldham's textile industry, since the mid-20th Century, the town has seen hard times for the indigenous, the Indian, Pakistani, Bangladeshi and Caribbean Community.

Indeed, high unemployment, poverty and a lack of morale was manifested in the Race Riots, which hit Oldham hard in May 2001. The riots followed a long period of inter-racial tensions and attacks in Oldham. This fight to be heard may be compared with the protests of the Peterloo radicals, only this time the ethnic and white communities were hitting out at a system which they felt had abandoned them. Youths that were previously hidden from the public domain began to be heard. They gathered on the streets near the college where I taught. Many were former learners and told me about the unrest and unease they felt, but they were also keen to stress that this may get them heard and change the 'shit' in their lives. The Ritchie Report (2001) blamed deep-rooted segregation which authorities had failed to address for generations, together with poverty and lack of opportunity.

Threaded together

The historical thread and geographical landscape links the learners and me to each other through the sharing of location and history. Resistance, conformity and struggle that the learners and I faced and in some instances continue to face, are threaded through our historical narrative into the fabric of our lives; shaping both myself and the learners, and the lens through which we look when exploring our lives.

Oldham is where the learners and I grew up (although I was born a stone's throw away in North Manchester). We went to the local schools and as kids roamed the streets looking for adventure among the rows and rows of terraced houses, estates and rise of factories. In the centre of Oldham, yesteryear's workhouse[2] – now The Royal Oldham Infirmary – is where my three younger brothers were born (one under the care of the famous Dr Steptoe[3]) and it is where I gave birth to my daughters Anna and Niamh, and where the learners in the study had their children.

The changing face of Oldham

With childhood now behind the learners and me, many of the factories still fill our view as they spike Oldham's skyline. Some are skeletons of their former industrial glory, hiding places for kids on adventures and dumping grounds for residents' rubbish, rusty bikes and broken shopping trolleys. A scattering of crammed bin liners are left rotting where machines once churned and chimneys thickened the air with smog, (which locals still call pea soup). Others have metamorphosed into other businesses, such as bakeries and play centres.

Across the town, to what many consider the more salubrious 'Saddleworth' these broken skeletons have been mended and flesh laid on their bones; modernised as upmarket apartments laboured on by the working classes to fulfil the bourgeoisie taste for urban living.

Our lives in the factories

It is these factories, which fed my own and the learners' family trees, both historically and recently. Shammy's father travelled from Uganda in the 1950's and, setting up home in Oldham, found work in the local factory. Rachel and Craig's fathers also worked in the local factory. Following his father's footsteps Craig left school to start work on the factory floor before moving up to management and an office. Joanne and Tracy also left school at 15 to work in a factory; Joanne working as sewing machinist, while Tracy worked on a production line. Stella's mum laboured in a factory, Stella following her to take up a job as a cleaner. My maternal grandmother, Evelyn, worked in a bottle factory in Gorton, Manchester; while my paternal grandparents, Joan and Harry worked in a mill that changed into a supplier of coats, in the 1960s and 1970s.

Figure 1.1 Danimac, Hollinwood. The top two photographs are of the local industrial landscape, the bottom is Danimac.

The great escape from factory work

While Joanne, Tracy, Stella and Craig continued to work in a factory until their 30s, it was surrounded by the red brick of Danimac (see Figure 1.1) that I found my great escape. At 16 I'd left behind the local comprehensive school where I'd spend most of the day staring out at the clueless sky. I couldn't wait to be grown up, working and earning. The school bell ringing for the last time sees me and my mates breaking free, as we run through the green gates. Full of laughter and screams, we chase one another across the school fields, egging[4] each other's white shirts. Excited to be leaving the classroom behind, I didn't realise back then that I'd never see some of those kids that I'd grown up with again. Our lives would fork in different directions, like the signs that took us on bus routes in and out of town.

On leaving school my first two jobs were at a local factory on a Youth Training Scheme[5] paying 25 pounds a week. No more laughs with my class mates; no more promising skies to stare at, only the tapping away of time and hope. I was aware that certain people had power, which was usually male managers, and others (mainly women), appeased them and did the clerical work. Unlike the laughs and shouts I'd hear from the men on the factory floor, there was also an expectation that us women would work in silence and only speak to bosses when spoken to.

I was no better or worse than any of the women around me but I couldn't accept my lot without a fight. Rather than the factory becoming a way of life, it offered me resistance and a determination to challenge being unskilled and without qualifications. Starting at the local Further Education College was liberating and filled me with endless possibilities.

When I reflect now on my own experiences as a young woman growing up in this environment, I realise how these fit with the analysis offered by Skeggs (1997, 2004); Walkerdine (1989, 2001) and the concepts of Bourdieu (1993). My move away from the workplace was collecting an initial identity and then when I went to college, a collective identity away from the men who managed the spaces in which I worked, and the women who were subservient to them. In many ways, the conditions of oppression and work (although manifesting in different forms) remains as it did in the Industrial Revolution, a model where there are those who give orders (have power) and those who obey (become powerless).

Book structure

In this book, I bring a critical perspective to the accounts of the 16 learners who provided me with narratives of their lived experiences from childhood to adulthood in the public and private domains of their lives. I explore how they perceive their home, education and work life; their interpretations of their situations, their experiences of navigating across these domains, which include resistance, conformity and struggle and their subsequent trajectories. Throughout the study, I offer personal reflections, woven throughout the narratives of the learners (at their request) which offer transparency to my changing position across the domains of my life and the lens through which we explore the research.

In addressing the principal research question, 'How have 16 former basic skills learners been shaped by the public domain of schooling, college and work and the private domain of family, friends and home?' the central tenet of this study revolves around accounts from learners gathered in semi-structured interviews and a range of data collection strategies. It is important to note that, in striving to reach an understanding of this material, I analysed the interview material which required me to contextualise the interviewees' accounts and materials necessitating a strong awareness and familiarity with the historical conditions and context of the learners' lives.

In Chapter 3, I outline the theoretical framework developed through the study. I employ and develop theoretical concepts from a range of critical education studies and Bourdieu (for example, 1977, 1986, 2001). It is suggested that applying the notions of capitals within a Bourdieuian framework opens up a way to theorise class and gendered processes, which permits the complexity of relations and merging between these categories. The research also employs and develops the notion of habitus, partaking in recent debates which have used its value in exploring the unpredictability of the habitus (Reay 2004a). This book examines concerns over whether the concept implies a deterministic interpretation of action, as well as exploring habitus resistance and compliance.

Chapter 4, explores the research design methodologies, including participatory action research and feminist standpoint theory, while also drawing on life history, literacy studies and ethnographic approaches to exploring social practices.

Chapter 5, through to Chapter 8 establishes the core of this study. Within these chapters I offer an analysis and interpretation which addresses both the gendered and classed dimensions of the accounts offered by the learners. I have organised these chapters according to domain and chronology of time, commencing with the site of schooling.

In Chapter Five, I discuss how the learners are positioned in the field of schooling and how this is influenced and changes in relation to the flow or lack of flow of capitals. It explores how they navigate through these flows and the impact of this on their constraints, resistance, possibilities, disempowerment and empowerment. It is suggested that schooling can act as a constraint that prevents learners from achieving their potential because they do not have what is deemed by those with symbolic power (teachers and peers) as having legitimate capitals that are valued. A tension which runs through the chapter is how schooling is a site for symbolic, embodied and physical violence and how the learners struggle against this by resistance and conforming.

In Chapter Six, I draw out the learners' experience of childhood violence and trauma in the domain of family and home and its impact on learning. I suggest that within the limited forms of capital available and carried by them, learners struggle with limited movement through social space. However, they are not passive in their struggle, they resist disempowerment by subverting the 'violence' and 'trauma' they have experienced in the public domain of schooling and private domain of home into a 'resistance capital'. For example, they take agency by turning the violence and trauma into street-credibility, respect, optimism and opportunities for employment.

In Chapter Seven, I explore the learners' experience of violence and trauma, as adults, in the public field of the workplace and their resistance, conformity and struggle when faced with these experiences. I have taken the view that adulthood is not distinct from childhood, but an extension of it, whereby the habitus shaped in childhood is taken into the field of adulthood. I suggest that the violence and trauma experienced by learners in both childhood and adulthood can influence the way they view themselves and the choices they make, whether these be about the form of employment or no employment they enter into and the reasons they make these choices.

In Chapter Eight, I explore the learners' experience of violence and trauma, as adults, in the private domain of the home. I suggest that the violence and trauma in the learners' lives both in childhood and adulthood can influence the way they view themselves, the choices they make in the relationships they form, the reasons they make these choices and their views of motherhood, fatherhood and the family. This entails, for example, taking seriously the learners' accounts from the private domain – which have the potential to uncover the violence and trauma the learners in the study have experienced – and recognising the barriers that learners face in pursuit of their aspirations and dreams.

In Chapter Nine, I explore the learners' experience of literacy in relation to shame, blame and respectability. I suggest that that tutors, PAR and the strong caring bonds formed between the teacher and the learners can help address and challenge these emotions, by developing and delivering more egalitarian approaches to pedagogy based on care and mutual respect. This entails exploring how critical reflection and dialogue can facilitate the move from a competence-based model to a holistic approach, which I suggest empowers the learners and their communities. I also explore how creativity in the curriculum, community projects, dissemination of the research in the local, national and international domain and consciousness raising can engage learners and communities in mutual learning and development of knowledge, which offers the potential for raising hope and working towards social justice.

In the final chapter, I draw together the main conclusions of the study. I show the way the habitus is socially constructed by class and gender as well as highlighting the processes for potential change and transformation in the habitus over the learners' life-course. I demonstrate the means in which symbolic and physical expressions of violence are used to reinforce the dominant class and gender norms that participants struggle against across the domains of their lives. I suggest the ways in which the inequalities of opportunities and choices are viewed across the learners' lives concern interacting processes of (mis)recognition and (mal)distribution. I have explored the struggle to transform habitus, despite neo-liberalist claims of an apparently egalitarian social field. To conclude, I offer suggestions for future research.

Notes

1 This pervasive culture is now permeating through Higher Education. Jane Thompson, national industrial relations official at the University and College Union, blames rising levels of stress on the shift from a collegiate to a managerial culture. In addition, the Research Assessment Exercise has led to increased internal competition and micro-management, she says. 'Feedback from members suggests that it's probably getting worse.' Job insecurity, prompted by the economic climate, adds to the problem. She says, 'This is shown to be one of the main sources of stress, especially for researchers, who are often on short-term contracts.' See: http://www.researchresearch.com/index.php?option=com_news&template=rr_2col&view=article&articleId=1068500.

2 The Royal Oldham Hospital is formed by a collection of buildings built in succession since 1851 along Rochdale Road. Its earliest parts exist from the site's time as a local workhouse, having been named *Oldham Union Workhouse*.

3 Patrick Steptoe, the 'test tube' baby pioneer.

4 Bringing eggs in on the last ever day of school was a tradition. We would chase and be chased as we smashed eggs onto each other's white school shirts never to be worn again.

5 The Youth Training Scheme (YTS) was the former name in the United Kingdom of an on-the-job training course for school leavers aged 16 and 17, managed by the Manpower Services Commission.

Chapter 2

Social class, gender and basic skills revisited

In this chapter I draw on a number of bodies of literature in order to place the study in a historical, social and political context and identify how the issues raised relate to my own research. The key literature will cover issues related to class and gender and the background of adult literacy, educational achievement, empowerment and learning and violence.

Literacy practices

In order to address issues related to class, gender, literacy and empowerment it is helpful to consider 'literacy' both in the realms of how it is defined and how it is positioned as an ideological discourse. The notion of what constitutes 'literacy' has shifted over time, from meaning the de-coding of words – where it is placed in the realm of *an individual, cognitive skill* – to that of literacy as a *social practice* (Barton 1994; Barton and Hamilton 1998; Gee 1996; Street 1984). Literacy practices shape the way we relate to and interact with literacy and are interwoven with our identity and practices. It is important to recognise that literacy is not value free; it is not neutral but deeply political. Gee (2000) explores how discourses offer us markers of identity which can shift from one context to the next. For example as my daughter calls out, 'what are we having for tea?' I write a note to remind myself I need to buy potatoes, milk and fish – I am writing as a mother, a carer; placing the note on top of my books I begin to type once again. Now I am a research practitioner and writing this monograph. These changing discourses, in which I write as a teacher, a mother, a wife, a sister, a friend, a student are mediated through the literacy I use. These literacy events[1] (see Heath 1983; Street 1984; Barton 1994) have unequal power and value when framed against the dominant ideologies of literacy.

The scribbled note, full of abbreviated words (*pots* for potatoes, *br* for bread) are what Barton and Hamilton (1998) describe as a vernacular (everyday literacies) and what I will describe as 'domestic literacy'.

The 'domestic literacy', which has been traditionally carried out by women, seldom enters the public domain and often remains invisible and unrecognised. Literacy's ideological role of supporting women's subordinate position due to structural inequalities and unequal distribution of power within society has been explored by, for example, Horsman 1991; Rockhill 1993.

The second activity is a dominant literacy (institutional), which leads to the monograph I now write. This may be perceived as putting me (and those who achieve it) in a position of power. From this position, the 'dominant' written word can be used to influence others actions, behaviour and attitudes. Historically this 'institutional knowledge' has been the privilege of men and equated with logic, mind and power.

'Institutional literacies' are often viewed as the basis of educational progress and deemed to be more important than 'vernacular literacies'. In my study, I will explore how 'dominant literacies' equate to linguistic capital, different amounts allowing entry to different positions in the hierarchy of the labour market (unskilled, skilled and professional); while 'vernacular literacies' equate to private, community and informal practices in all domains, for example workplace, domestic literacies, hobbies. Both vernacular and dominant literacies can offer an insight into the many aspects of the world that affect us, and through this and the reflective process, offer the means to act upon the world itself, and take agency as a drive to implement change (see Freire 1996).

At a personal level literacy lies in the development of self-identity; in our social, cultural and emotional life, happiness and well being. For the male and female learners in this study, returning to education was a means for them to develop their literacy skills. Literacy was very much linked with their subjectivity and how they viewed their self worth in the public and private domains of their lives. When considering the vernacular literacies the learners brought to the classroom, they were united in what Shirley Brice Heath (1983) describes as their 'way with words' which did not privilege their literacy practices at school or within the Lifelong Learning Sector (LLS). This influenced their experience at school, the 'choices' they had or did not have and their subsequent trajectories as adults. As their teacher I looked for meaningful approaches and strategies to link with 'their way with words' and empower the learners to reach their goals.

Empowerment and literacy

There is a fruitful educational tradition of literacy and empowerment. Paulo Freire's (1996) seminal text *The Pedagogy of the Oppressed*, addresses who and what education is for and whose group interests are promoted. Linking literacy with critical pedagogy, he examines the ideologies of classroom practice and the 'banking theory' of knowledge. Within this theory, he argues, traditional pedagogical practice is a means to fill the learners with information/knowledge that serves to maintain the status quo of structural inequalities and unjust hierarchies of power. The learners come to be passive receivers of information, and accepting of the dominant hegemony (I employ Antonio Gramsci (1891–1937), a leading Marxist thinker, who used the term hegemony to signify the power of one social class over others, for example, the bourgeois hegemony. It embodies not only political and economic control, but also the ability of the dominant class to assign its own way of viewing the world so that those who are subordinated by it accept it as 'natural'. Gramsci's ideas have influenced popular education practices which I draw on; these include the adult literacy and consciousness-raising methods of Paulo Freire in his *Pedagogy of the Oppressed* (1996) and methods of participatory action research (PAR)) which, rather than empowering working-class students, works to demoralise and label them as unknowing (Freire 1993: 64).

In Freire's challenge to the 'banking' system, he recommended a critical pedagogy model for teaching adult literacy. Educationalist theorists have developed this approach (see Giroux 1997; Lankshear and McClaren 1992; Lankshear 1993; Shor 1992, 1993). They have challenged prescriptive approaches to curriculum designs which do not take into account the history or background and needs of learners. These non-critical curriculums place dominance on an instrumental approach, ignoring the political, social and economic factors that have conspired to marginalise the learners and the communities in which they live. Having been born and brought up in, and still living in the emotional and geographical landscape of the learners, I am immersed in their communities. This immersion allows me, as a practitioner, a critical positioning whereby I have insider knowledge of their lives, motivations, pressures, hopes and dreams (see Giroux 1997; Macedo 1994; Shor 1992). It is from this position that the critical model moves towards the learner being the co-producer of knowledge. In doing so it shifts away from teacher-directed, top-down, commonly imposed and standardised assessments that prescribe the same for all students, regardless of their ability, values, ethnicity, history, their community requirements or their specific contexts. Instead it takes an egalitarian approach, whereby there is a sharing of power between the teacher and the student in learning, the curriculum, its contents and methods. Freire (2006) proposed to do this via 'culture circles'. A 'culture group' is a discussion group in which educators and learners use codifications to engage in dialectic engagement for consciousness raising, liberation, empowerment and transformation. Education for liberation provides a forum open to the empowerment of learners, teachers and the community, while also providing opportunities for the development of those skills and competencies without which empowerment would be impossible.

Such emancipatory practices encourage autonomy and critical thinking, opening up spaces where learners and communities can ask questions, analyse and subsequently work through effective and meaningful strategies to enhance their situation. Rather than being pawns of the system, they have the opportunity to be actors of their future and active members of their communities.

In order to develop these skills, linking with NLS offers a socially situated model which, like the Freirian 'culture circle' challenges dominant models of literacy, for example replacing the economic driven model associated with workforce training, productivity and the notion of human capital[2] (institutional literacies) with a socio-cultural model which includes vernacular literacies. It recognises that literacy practices are formed in a number of contexts and domains, for example the private domain of home and the public domain of schooling. In their book *Local Literacies* Barton and Hamilton (1998) explore the many literacy activities people are involved in across the different domains of their life. A key aspect of their findings is that people have 'ruling passions' which can be a key into where, why and what literacy practices matter to them. As a tutor, knowledge of learners' 'ruling passions' offers a means to recognise and celebrate the learners' practices. Whether the practice is drawing, words, poetry or photographs like the 'Culture Circles', NLS draws on the literacies from the learners' lives. These artefacts are a way to develop a dialogue, leading to an analysis of the concrete reality represented by the learners and facilitating them to address inequalities in their lives.

In the context of literacy, sociologist Geoff Payne (2006: 220) highlights that the rise of NLS (see Heath 1983; Street 1984 and Barton and Hamilton 1998) has seen a push to address issues of gender, class and ethnicity, and to recognise that 'lack of literacy wastes human potential, which is both individually damaging and socially inefficient'. He asserts, however, that British sociology has given matters of the sociology of literacy and its impact only passing attention. The article is contentious because Payne fails to recognise the degree to which socio-literacy studies have helped cross-disciplinary contributions to the socio-cultural study of language and literacy. For example, academics operating within philosophy, classical studies, anthropology, history and linguistics greatly influence the development of literacy studies (for example, see Bernstein 1971a; Street 1984; Gee 1996). It does, however, recognise how low levels of literacy are clasped to other forms of social inequality. The link with social injustice in its various forms will be explored in this study. Feeley (2007: 88), for example, identifies how learners' self-esteem is influenced by perceptions of 'fast' and 'slow' readers and how these relate to educational inequalities.

The politics of literacy and its link to learner identity and empowerment is explored in my study, from the standpoint of how the learners' everyday lives have been shaped by the lack of and development of literacies. Part of the praxis of the research is to draw on participatory and democratic pedagogical practices as a way of countering the dominant models while questioning how power and knowledge are valued, what counts as literacy and what does not, who benefits from this and who is marginalised. The impact of dominant literacies on the learners' trajectories and the use of socially situated models in my practice are unpicked as I explore how a critical curriculum can empower the learners and lead to emancipation and transformation in their personal and public trajectories (McNamara 2007; Duckworth 2009).

The changing tradition of class analysis

An overview of the political climate and key policies is helpful in placing the literature in a political context. Since the 1980s, research and debates surrounding class may be seen as being side-lined in political discourse. Indeed, notions of class loyalty and solidarity were in many ways torn apart under Thatcherism.[3] In 1997 New

Labour came into power. Under this party a re-invigoration of conservatism and the notion of a classless society was seen and heard in their rhetoric of meritocracy and equal opportunities. Individualism and self-improvement were driven under this premise, as were ideas that talent was based on ability rather than privilege. These ideologies were deeply embedded in the neo-liberalist rhetoric of 'choice for all'. There is overwhelming evidence, however, that in economically unequal societies, only those with enough resources/capitals can make choices and those who are at a structural disadvantage, such as being poor, have no choices at all (Gewirtz et al. 1995; Whitty et al. 1998; Lauder et al. 1999, 1998; Archer et al. 2003; Lucey and Reay 2002; Reay & Lucey 2003; Reay 2004b; Ball et al. 2000; Ball 2010).

Over ten years ago, *The Learning Age* document supported Britain's drive for business and commerce, noting that: 'Learning will be the key to a strong economy and an inclusive society' (DfEE 1998: 3). Four years later, another key government policy document, *Success for All*, stated how the government's goals should be 'social inclusion and economic prosperity' (DfES 2002: 9). The rhetoric being used in these policies and reports correspond to an instrumental model with a drive towards employability in the labour market as the key to social inclusion. With this in mind, employability has acquired a central role within policy, strategy and the student curriculum.

Globalisation, competition and the rapid progress of technology have also caused a shift in the nature and patterns of working life and employment. The current plans for the UK remain ambitious (UK commission 2010: 6).

Due to shifts in working patterns of employment, many people do not have the same stability of employment or the same length of service with a single employer. The concept of a 'job for life' now seems a thing of the past to many people, many of whom are being displaced from traditional to new forms of work. A good example of this is in the implementation of ICT across many industrial sectors. Previously labour-intensive processes have been automated, with ICT changing the nature of work, speed and volume of communication, information and working practices. In 2008, a report by the Teaching and Learning Research Programme (TLRP) identified how the 'demand for knowledge workers rises exponentially in the knowledge economy [and] has resulted in a shift from mechanical Taylorism to digital Taylorism, so that knowledge work becomes portable working knowledge' (Brown et al. 2008: 1).

Under the premise of a 'knowledge economy' one of the most significant duties given to education is to provide a flexible, adaptable and skilled workforce to make countries competitive in the globalised economy. It focuses on education for work positions and education as a commodity, and pays no regard to issues of economic, political and social equality. For example, learners from socio-economically deprived areas may not have the same access to opportunities as those who live in more affluent areas who would be more able to attend high achieving state schools or receive a private education (see Figures 3.1a and b). Thus, school success may be seen as linked by 'the amount and type of cultural capital inherited from the family milieu rather than by measures of individual talent or achievement' (Reay et al. 2005: 19). For the children who face such structural inequalities, the choices they have on leaving school or college can be limited and can affect their life chances, opportunities for future education or training and future employment.

The notion that class identities have diminished in significance over recent decades is also a key feature of contemporary social theory. This may be seen as a result of the cultural shifts aligned with individualisation, de-traditionalisation and post-modernisation (for examples, see Beck 1992; Giddens 1991; Bauman 1987, 1998). The idea of class going out of fashion fitted with post-modern thought, which viewed the world as transcending economic and social relations to life chances, and in turn educational success. This study argues that class is still relevant and aims to follow the thread of academics such as Skeggs (1997); Walkerdine (2001); Luttrell (2005) and Horsman (1999) and more recently Reay and Ball (2005) who challenge the trend of academic dismissal of class and labour to fix its oppressive state and thus attempt to surmount the situation of oppression critically with a view to facilitating its transformation (Freire 1996).

There are a number of recent basic skills learner studies that have come from the National Research and Development Centre (NRDC) (for example, Bynner and Parsons 1997, 2003, 2008; Bynner et al. 2001, 2006; Barton et al. 2006; the Basic Skills Agency (BSA) Parsons and Bynner 1997, 2002, 2005a; Parsons 2002; Bynner and Steedman 1995; and the Scottish Executive 2001). The 1958 and 1970 British birth cohort studies, known respectively as the National Child Development Study (NCDS) and the 1970 Cohort Study (BCS70), contain key information about the role of literacy and numeracy in adult lives. Members of this cohort have been surveyed in 1975, 1980, 1986, 1991, 1996, and 2000. Some 11 000 of the original cohort are still involved. Bynner and Parsons make use of the data, reanalysing the data about these individuals, including tests of their levels of literacy and numeracy, to show how these affect their life-course and life-chances.

Traditionally, there has been a long academic trend of both class analysis and the school debate (for example, see Hargreaves 1967; Bowles and Gintis 1976, 1982; Willis 1977; Goldthorpe et al. 1986, Goldthorpe 1996; Heath 1981; Ball 1981, 2003, 2008, 2010, Ball et al. 1995, 2000; Reay 1997, 2003, 2005, 2007; Reay et al. 2002, 2005; Savage 2000, 2003). These are part of the relevant literature that informs, complements and reinforces the findings of this research from the perspective of large scale surveys. In Britain, prior to the late 1970s, most research sought to investigate the relationship between social class origins and educational outcomes, producing an important body of work often informed by a conflict view of society. It was a body of work, however, that I would argue was limited by its positivism and tendency to disregard matters within the school itself. A few early exceptions were studies by Hargreaves (1967) and Lacey (1970, 1976). Drawing on ethnographic studies they considered factors such as streaming in schools. Following on from Willis' seminal text (1977) there has been an increased importance of ethnographic methodology for the study of teachers and teaching. This is reflected in the publication of classics such as *Beachside Comprehensive* (Ball 1981) and *Two Cultures of Schooling* (Hargreaves 1986).

Paul Willis' seminal 1977 book *Learning to Labour* argues that the function of education in society is to satisfy the demands of capitalism and prepare working-class children for a life of labour intensive jobs. It is an ethnographic study which includes combined observations with discussions, case study work and interviews which offer an in-depth, descriptive and often brutally honest understanding of the 12 working-class 'lads' from a school in Birmingham. The study was conducted between 1972 and 1975 and aimed to uncover the question of how and why 'working-class kids get working-class jobs' (1977: 1). Many sociological writers such as Bowles and Gintis (1976) believe the unintentional purpose of education and schooling is to find one's place in society. Therefore, by rejecting their schooling it may be argued that the boys in Willis' study have inadvertently placed themselves in the 'working-class' bracket. The education system is thus a method of 'working-class reproduction'. While Willis recognises the conflict within the educational system, however, he refutes the notion that education is an entirely successful agency of socialisation as suggested by Marxists such as Bowles and Gintis (1976). He also rejects the view that there is a simple deterministic relationship between the economy and the way the educational system operates. This is where it is worth considering the fundamental difference between classical Marxism and Neo-Marxism, the former premised on economic determinism, the latter on a broader consideration of social and intellectual influences that perpetuate the oppression of the working class. In brief, he believed that education can have unintended influences on pupils who make conscious decisions themselves. Willis ultimately suggests that the resistance of the working-class 'lads' in his study functioned as a reinforcement of their social class position. This is not without agency as they consciously and 'actively' made decisions about resisting the school culture. In this way, he engaged himself to the debate of the relationship between structure and social actors, the object and the subject respectively. His neo-Marxist approach moves from the economic determinism and positivism of classical Marxist theories, instead incorporating other sociological views developed after Marx to provide a more holistic view of social class structures and dynamics with a focus more on society than the economic system alone. It is this approach that, like Skeggs (1997) and other sociologist and educationalists before me, I draw upon in my study.

If we compare the choices the school leavers had in Willis' study to today's school children, it may be argued that little has changed, apart from the discourses being used. The rhetoric of the 'third way' places neo-liberalism at the centre of education and positions individuals as entrepreneurs, managing their own lives and responsible for their success or lack of it. In this climate, learners are expected to succeed against the odds and if they do not, the fault is their own, rather than being down to the structural inequalities many encounter at each step of their learning journey (and indeed life). The themes Willis raises (which include anti-school subcultures and resistance, and the 'hidden curriculum') were built upon and explored in this study. The classed nature of education will also be explored, along with education's role in reproducing inequalities through formal and informal structures which work together to establish a system which has no relevance to the histories and lives of working-class children (Whitty 1985; Plummer 2000; Walkerdine et al. 2001).

Both Stephen Ball and Diane Reay's work may be seen as being influenced by Paul Willis' research. Like Willis' (1977) study they explore how learners' 'choices' or lack of them still reflects a distinctive cultural pattern of social reproduction. Ball (2008), in his recent book, and Reay (2006) discuss the impact of globalisation on education, noting that society's notion of 'choice' is flawed and not all social groups have the same advantages. They challenge New Labour's rhetoric of 'choice for all' whereby education is viewed as meritocratic and provides equal opportunities. Instead education is geared for preparing learners for work as a commodity (much like the working-class reproduction in Paul Willis' study), paying no regard to issues of economic, political and social equality. I draw on their work and on the impact of structural inequalities in shaping the choices my learners had on leaving school and how this affected their life chances, opportunities for future education or training and future employment. As such my research views 'choice' as inseparable from wider social relations, structural inequalities and the identities of the learners, as a course of action which is value-laden and culture-specific, leading to the social legitimisation of some choices over others.

Formations of class and gender

By the early 1980s, British sociologists of education were modifying class analysis to incorporate gender inequality. A number of influential anthologies were published in this decade that included both empirical studies and theoretical analyses of gender (for example, see Arnot and Weiner 1987). A decade later Skeggs' (1997) longitudinal, ethnographic study of 83 white working-class women in the North of England resulted in the key text, *Formation of Class and Gender*, being published. Skeggs argues that for the young women in her study 'without understanding the significance of class positioning, many of the women's movements through social place, education, families, labour markets and in particular, the production of subjectivity, could not be understood'. In the same way that Willis' (1977) text was heavily criticised for equating working-class 'kids' with working-class boys, Skeggs' qualitative studies parallels with Willis' gendered approach in its focus on working-class girls. Skeggs' research may have benefitted from the inclusion of males from vocational Further Education courses, allowing for a comparative exploration of gendered production of subjectivity, trajectories and notions of respectability. My study includes both male and female learners and explores the learners' lives, as well as capital transfer, gendered trajectories and what it means to be poor and working class.

Skeggs examines how subjectivity is produced through class, gender and sexuality and seeks to explain how working-class women inhabit and occupy social and cultural positions. Many of the women in her study did not see themselves as working class, they disassociated from it. For Skeggs this was not about them lacking awareness, but was instead a strategy for survival in the face of a culture which equates working-class (and under-class) women with derogatory labels such as 'slags'. They sought to avoid being pathologised by derogatory and gendered labels and instead looked at ways they could find value in who they were and how they were positioned in the class system. My study will also explore how learners sought to avoid being pathologised in the private and public domains of their life, and builds on notions of 'respectability' in relation to learners who struggle to read and write.

Building on from Skeggs' work, bound up in this reality are the issues Walkerdine et al. (2001) explore; for example, the way that globalisation and economic rationalism shape the labour market which the young women in their study enter. It explores 'how working-class people manage their daily lives, how they cope, and the practices through which their subjectivity is produced' (Walkerdine et al. 2001: 14). In this context it unpicks how these young women's subjectivity is formed within education and working practices and seeks to highlight how class influences this subjectivity. It is this subjectivity, inextricably embedded in class, that will be examined in my book, as well as exploring the way both men and women, at different stages in their life, survive in the new social, economic and political system which has seen a changing work culture, based on an economy driven by technology, the service sector and communication.

Further to this, there will be an exploration of how 'jobs for life' have been replaced by 'lifelong learning' (see Walkerdine et al. 2001) and how a new 'flexible, lifelong learner is articulated by policy in relation to the knowledge economy' (Ball 2008: 39) where the meaning of education and what it means 'to be educated' are constantly changing. The idea that knowledge plays an important role in the economy is not new. All economies, however simple, are based on knowledge, for example in a rural community; this knowledge may be about farming. Indeed we only need to consider the knowledge needed in the Industrial Revolution to see this is not a new idea. Today, however, a so-called 'knowledge economy' is emerging from the increasing need for knowledge in order to participate in a globalised economy.[4] The other main driver of the emerging knowledge economy is the rapid globalisation of economic activities. In the knowledge economy there are new ground rules. These rules affect people and their lives. Being successful in the knowledge economy requires being skilful in a wide variety of knowledges and competencies.

People must be able to apply these skills effectively to successfully partake in the ever-changing knowledge economy. This means lifelong learning to constantly 'up-skill', whereby a person must expect and make ready for transitions in her or his life (Field 2000, 2008; Field et al. 2009). These include basic skills and new and emerging technology. The study will explore how having or not having these skills affected the learners' lives. The notion of 'self-invention', 'transformation' (Walkerdine et al. 2001) and 'bettering oneself' through adult education will also be considered (Luttrell 1997).

Movement from traditional discourse

In order to address the issues raised above, this study moves away from traditional discourses where working-class practices are not fully acknowledged or understood. It challenges what was viewed as pathology in working-class homes by middle-class observers, whom I would argue have minimal experience of 'working-class life' and consequently 'know very little about working-class culture and practices' (see Walkerdine et al. 2001: 83). It unpacks these negative assumptions, based on dominant discourses of the middle class, together with what I consider the normative culture, grounded in ontological assumptions, which pathologises gender and class (see Skeggs 1997) and women's and working-class experience (see Walkerdine et al. 2001; Skeggs 2004; Lawler 2005).

The inclusion of the men in my study was essential in recognising that 'women do not inhibit a single-sexed universe' (Stanley and Wise 1991: 44). Further to this, it opens up an approach that explores men's narratives in relation to class and race and exposes how this has affected their trajectories. One key theme that emerged was that violence was experienced by both men and women in this study, although enacted in different ways across the domains; the research also explores the strategies they employed to deal with it or not (see Owen 1996) and how it has shaped their trajectories. As identified by Horsman (1999) the debate of violence needs to be opened up in literacy, with men's experience of violence and abuse also being heard.

Learning, violence and trauma

Violence emerged as a theme in my research. Other studies which have found violence in adult learners include the Adult Learners' Lives project (2004). Together with the initial findings of the Adult Learners' Lives project, I draw on the later findings in the book *Literacy, Lives and learning* (Barton et al. 2007). They argue that even when learners have been in vulnerable situations, facing domestic violence or other social or emotional difficulties, adult literacy education can often be a critical space to support and empower learners to take agency, no matter what their trajectory so far. In building on their work, I will explore the link between both adult literacy and PAR as a dialogic space to develop a critical space both in and out of the classroom and examine issues related to and experiences of violence and trauma.

Jenny Horsman's (1999) book *Too Scared to Learn* explores the impact of violence and trauma on the life of adult learners. She uncovers how violence can affect learning and silence learners in a cloak of shame. This silence and shame stops a dialogic engagement with both the teacher and the means to provide a critical space which would facilitate learners to give voice to their histories of violence and trauma. The text reveals strategies a teacher can use to create a classroom based on respect and recognition of the learner as a whole person,[5] whereby learners can begin to heal and hope to reach their potential. This is supported by the source book *Take on the Challenge* by Morrish et al. (2002). Its critical approach links with a Freirian model where literacy is a means to develop pedagogy for empowerment and transformation. I draw on Horsman's study and egalitarian approaches as a means to empower the learners who have experiences of violence. I also use the approaches to explore strategies for classroom praxis based around developing, implementing and evaluating resources which recognise and address the violence that learners experience. I seek to find meaningful ways which encourage learners to share their experiences and look for strategies for consciousness raising and moving forward.

Maggie Feeley's PhD (2007) offers insights into how literacy learning in survivors of institutional abuse is linked to equality and care. Her three year ethnographic study explored the role of care in learning literacy. This notion of 'care' or 'lack of care' is useful in exploring the lives of the learners in this study and its impact on their trajectories. Further to this, I explore how a caring, egalitarian classroom helped to heal learners' experiences of violence and trauma to facilitate transformation and empowerment.

For a wider sociological engagement with issues of violence I draw on the following literature: Brownridge (2009); Skinner et al. (2005) and Wykes and Welsh (2009). Brownridge's study offers an intersectionality-based approach recognising multiple oppressions as shaping women's experiences, and how different structures intersect in women lives and impact on women who experience violence. Skinner (2005, 2009) offers insights into the work she has done with survivors of violence, which include carrying out the research in sensitive ways. Wykes and Welsh (2009) offer accounts of how violence is kept secret within the family and out of the public domain. All three of these studies show the many aspects of gendered violence and how structural inequalities such as class impact on the women over the course of their life, and how they find ways to survive.

I have chosen the words 'violence and trauma' as the central premise for the learners' stories, because the former relates to the immediate impact, while the latter recognises both the short- and long-term impact. In this study, physical, psychological and symbolic violence and trauma will be explored across the domains of their life.

In identifying 'gender violence' as a theme experienced by females and males it is important to recognise 'different vulnerabilities and understand why some groups are more vulnerable to violence than others' (Brownridge 2009: 12). This study unpacks this from the perspective of the participants and explores it fully in the study.

The family and friendships

In the face of violence in the public and private domains of the learner's lives, I will explore who the learners turn to for strength to come to terms with and help overcome experiences of violence and trauma. Roseneil and Budgeon et al. (2006), address issues related to the changing face of what constitutes a family and how to answer the questions: 'if the family today is not what it was, where do people find their intimacy and care? Are friends the new family? Is friendship increasingly significant and are people's ideas of who really matters in their personal life changing?'

Granovetter (1973) published his seminal paper based on the concept that society is cemented by *weak* and *strong* bonds that exist between people. I would also suggest that rather than this position being fixed and binary the ties were fluid; they are neither weak nor strong but a continuum of both over a given time and space. Granovetter was aware that his paper did not address the content of the ties, only their strength; this is where the concept needs to be elaborated upon.

Further to this, the bonds which were formed through classroom engagement and PAR will be explored. These friendships will be examined in the context of what Giddens (1992) sees as friendships that are the relational type, and thus most suited to a contemporary world of what he considers individuality, equality, mobility and choice. Beck (1992) and Giddens (1992) discuss the move from traditional relational customs to 'de-traditionalisation' and individualisation whereby people are free from historically significant customs such as marriage, or staying in a marriage which is unfulfilling. They argue that class, gender, family and religion are fading into the history books, so much so that tradition is being replaced by individualisation and personal fulfilment in relationships. I would argue this is a simplistic notion, and structural inequalities such as class and gender continue to shape people's lives and trajectories. Notions of freedom of choice and individualisation are problematic, for example for many women it is difficult to leave a bad marriage when they do not have the financial means to take care of themselves and their family. I would also argue, however, that family structure today is very fragile and, for many, fractured. Without this support mechanism, friends can be seen as a substitute for support and personal fulfilment.

Drawing on Stuart (2006) and Reay (2001), I will further explore how friendship can be seen as social capital. The research also aims to explore family, friends and emotions which include grief and pain in relation to 'trigger events' which are the catalyst to returning to education (see Mezirow 1991, 2000).

Conclusion

It needs to be recognised that although my political standpoint begins with feminism, it is also deeply grounded in the notion of working-class self-determination. In order to engage in a struggle for collective working-class self-determination I embrace feminism, as that becomes the vehicle by which I position myself as a female in the centre of the struggle, which encompasses the intersection between gender and class. In this capacity there is an understanding of domination with a critique of domination in all its forms. As such, this study, which includes females and males, hopes to drill down into how gendered and classed domination has an impact on the learners' lives.

Notes

1 A literacy event can be viewed as any occasion/activity where the written text is essential to the activity being carried out, for example, consider the note I wrote to remember what I needed to buy from the supermarket and the writing of this study needed to recognise the research, in terms of receiving a qualification, from the world of academia.

2 Human capital may be viewed from a micro-perspective, for example, the way the accumulation of knowledge and skills, such as literacy practices enables learners to increase their productivity and their earnings and macro, and how this has an impact on the productivity and wealth of the communities and societies they live. The dominant model of institutional literacies derives human capital from economic returns, such as employability.

3 For example, the break-up of the unions and an emphasis on 'individualism' over 'collectivism'.

4 Globalisation in the 1950s and 1960s was driven by the global spread and development of Taylorism, but is now post-Taylorist, in the form of flexible organisations that drive and shape globalisation.

5 **Spirit** Violence convinces us that we are worthless, and that our own knowledge is not worth believing and growing. We can find ways to let our strong spirit help us learn. **Emotions** Violence makes us angry, sad, afraid and confused. We can find ways to use our emotions to help us learn. **Body** Injury and illness is caused by violence. We can find ways to use our bodies to help us learn. **Mind** We are not stupid. We are experts on ourselves as learners. We learned to survive and we can learn new things and change.

Chapter 3

Theoretical framework

People say forget the past,
it's time to let it go.
Sometimes thinking of the past,
Is the reason I get through.
By Carol

Introduction

To offer a theoretical structure for the book, in this section I will explain the basic concepts of Bourdieu's theory, and show – through examples from my data – how these ideas can offer a useful framework for analysing the learners' narratives of their lives and encounters with education. The study aims to analyse inequality in both the public and private domains. To do this I draw on Bourdieu's theory 'The forms of capital' (1986) as a framework, providing the tools for understanding how the learners' narrative accounts of their educational and personal journey from childhood to Basic Skills Learner and beyond have been shaped. Bourdieu explains the production of inequality within society via the forms of capital: economic capital, social capital, cultural capital and symbolic capital. Cultural capital can be broken down into three categories: 1) an embodied state of mind and body (see Reay 2005); 2) objectified; and 3) institutionalised (see Bourdieu 2001a). Bourdieu's concept of cultural capital is vital in exposing the transmission of wealth and power, and incorporating ideas about how those in a position of power – whom Puwar (2004) describes as 'insiders' – reproduce and maintain their domination. In unfolding the learners' narratives, my overarching aim is to recognise and understand their narratives against the backdrop of wider socio/economic/political and historical contexts (Goodson and Sykes 2001; Goodson 1992). Bourdieu's fields of social, cultural and economic power overlap and feed into each other; separately and together, they offer a valuable framework for understanding the historical formation and reproduction of the research group in this study. Critical education offers me the opportunity to expand on Bourdieu's concept by including this as a lever for change and increasing the potential for learner empowerment.

Capitals

When considering the fields the learners cross and inhabit the research will explore changes within the varied flow of capitals, and what impact this has on the learners' possibilities. Cultural capital is Bourdieu's most well-known concept. This concept may be defined as:

1 Economic capital (income and wealth),
2 cultural capital (for example, educational qualifications)
3 social capital (networks of connections across different sites, for example, friends at the gym, colleagues at work, and so on).

Importantly, capitals do not stand alone but function in conjunction with other forms of capital. For example, economic capital earned from employment can be spent buying/experiencing cultural capital, such as purchasing pieces of art, or visiting the theatre to watch a show. On visiting the theatre the person may take the opportunity to acquire social capital, perhaps meeting new friends and new people. Capitals also have symbolic significance and power, for example, the purchase and ownership of art can be deemed as having distinction, distinction being legitimate value in the dominant ideology of culture and taste.

Bourdieu and Wacquant (1992: 14) define social capital as:

> The sum of the resources, actual or virtual, that accrues to an individual or a group by virtue of possessing a durable network of more or less institutionalised relationships of mutual acquaintance and recognition.

To explore the nature of these resources I draw on the work of Granovetter (1973) who published his seminal paper based on the concept that society is cemented by *weak* and *strong* bonds that exist between people. Strong ties are the relationships between close friends and family while weak ties are more remote and serve a function, for example, colleagues or friends whom we encounter through our everyday activities. For parents weak ties could also include contact with other parents in the school playground. The stronger ties are considered to provide emotional support systems, but this is based on the premise that more time, energy and commitment are invested into them.

The connections made in social networks will be explored through the different bonds (social capital) the learners forge on their life journey. This, for example, gives confidence for people to enter new social situations, since a common barrier to entering higher education is the reluctance of people to engage in unfamiliar situations. Particularly as a number of the learners in the study are following non-traditional pathways and have previously experienced symbolic violence in the domain of education, I will explore the impact of bonds made to ease the transition and support the journey through the field of higher education.

Cohen and Prusak (2001: 4) describe social capital as a:

> stock of active connections among people: the trust, ***mutual understanding***, and ***shared values*** and behaviours that bind members of human networks and communities and make cooperative action possible.
>
> (My emphasis)

I will also explore social capital as the sharing of values. In juxtaposition to this, the strengthening and weakening of previous and new social networks/bonds will be explored as the learners' position changes in the field of education and work and their values and understandings shift. A comparison may be made between moving from one community of practice to another (see Lave and Wenger 1991).

I seek to understand how membership in new groups creates new social capital and has an impact on and flow to other capitals (see Bourdieu 1986; Coleman 1988). Further to this, I will explore how the support networks the learners form support and facilitate their progression in the face of structural inequality and symbolic, psychological and physical violence.

Fields

This study asks why and how structures of inequality and domination are reproduced across the public and private domains of the learners' lives. To probe these structures, Bourdieu uses the concept of 'field'. Bourdieu and Wacquant (2002: 76) point out that:

> The field of power is a *field of forces* defined by the structure of the existing balance of forçes between forms of power, or between different species of capital. It is also simultaneously a *field of struggles for power among the holders of different forms of power*. It is a space of play and competition in which social agents and institutions, which all possess the determinate quantity of specific capital (economic and cultural capital in particular) sufficient to occupy the dominant positions within their respective fields [the economic field, the field of higher civil service or the state, the university field, and the intellectual field, confront one another in strategies aimed at preserving or transforming this balance of forces . . . This struggle for the imposition of the dominant principle leads, at every moment, to a balance in the sharing of power, that is, to what I call a ***division of the work of domination***. It is also a struggle over the legitimate principle of legitimation and the legitimate mode of reproduction.

Fields are domains where human action occurs in a struggle for capital (for example the cultural and social capital discussed earlier), with each player hoping to distinguish themselves from the others by building up forms of capital. It is not only individuals, but institutions and other agents who compete for power in the field. Bourdieu commonly adopts the metaphor 'the game' to describe the field. At first glance, this is a seemingly innocent metaphor but on deeper probing it reveals how these fields are sites controlled by the dominant class. The game is a means to win advantage – but not always fairly – and in doing so, players pass on their capital to the next generation and the ball rolls on to the next, and the next.

Grenfell and James (2004: 510) discuss the nature of fields, as being bounded and as such:

> Within a field at any given moment, there are elements that are passing through quickly and those with established, semi-permanent positions.

Recognition of the changing face of the field in which the learners are located is vital for reflexivity and also for exploring resistance and challenges within these sites of symbolic power.

Family as a field

Bourdieu places the family at the centre of social capital. The field of family is not homogenous, however. The notion of 'family' and what a family constitutes has different meanings depending of the make-up of the field. The changes that have taken place in the formation and behaviour of 'the family' are reflected in the wider changes seen in society. The functionalist sees the family as being a vital component to maintaining the order of society. For example, Murdock (1949) argues that there are four main functions of the family: sexual, reproduction, socialization and economic. While exploring idealistic notions of marriage Wykes and Welsh (2009) draw on Giddens (1992) to examine how this disguised its practical role of preserving family capital and power:

> The spread of ideals of romantic love was one factor tending to disentangle the marital bond from wider kinship ties and give it a special significance. Husbands and wives increasingly became seen as collaborators in a joint emotional enterprise, this having primacy even over their obligations towards their children. The 'home' came into being as a distinct environment set off from work; and, at least in principle became a place where individuals could expect emotional support, as contrasted with the instrumental character of the work setting.
>
> (Giddens (1992) cited in Wykes and Welsh 2009: 93)

This picture of the 'especial significance' of enduring marriage for both emotional support and the securing of capital is contrasted by the landscape of many of today's families. For example, in England and Wales the rates of marriage have lowered while divorce rates have risen from 1,346.2 in 1996 to 1,739.2 in 2006. The number of divorces in the Northwest in 2006 was: 7,469.9 (ONS 2009). These statistics have an impact on the number of children living in 'alternative' rather than 'traditional' family settings (Nicholson 1997). The Office of National Statistics states that:

> The number of dependent children living in married couple families in the UK fell by 1.0 million between 1998 and 2008. This was equivalent to a fall of 7 percentage points in the proportion of dependent children living in married couple families, from 70 per cent to 63 per cent.
>
> In contrast, the number of dependent children living with cohabiting couples and lone parents both increased, by 0.6 and 0.1 million respectively. The proportion of dependent children living with cohabiting couples rose from 8 per cent to 13 per cent, and the proportion of dependent children living with lone parent families rose from 22 per cent to 23 per cent. These changes were driven by changes in family formation and separation, as well as an increase in the proportion of births outside marriage.
>
> (Source: Office of National Statistics, 2009)

The formation of the family can influence the amount of capital the family has or does not have. For example, lone parents are at a higher risk of poverty than families with two parents present. To say that lone parenting is a sole cause of poverty is problematic, however, as other factors also influence how children develop in single-parent families, including the parent's class, education level and occupation, the family's income and the support structure of friends and extended family members. Therefore, rather than it being the status of being a single parent, much like the 'traditional' family, structural inequalities such as class have a profound influence on poverty or wealth. Three of the learners in this study had been brought up in lone parent households, while six were lone parents themselves and struggled with poverty.

It is important to highlight that what constitutes a 'family' varies depending on the lens viewing it. When viewed from the dominant, middle class lens, the symbolic power of a two parent family is vastly different to that of the pathologised single teenage mother (for example, see McRobbie 2000b). The media and internet sites serve to establish and re-enforce this negative labelling. McRobbie (2006) notes that the internet site 'Popbitch' labels teenage mothers with derogatory terms such as 'pram face' with, 'the face of impoverished, unkempt, slovenly maternity and restigmatised single motherhood (www.guardian.co.uk/world/2006/mar/02/gender.comment).

This stigmatising of young mothers signifies deep and cruel class distinctions targeted at impoverished teenage girls, who are deemed to lack respectability and distinction (Skeggs 1997) both as teenagers and mothers.

This study will also explore the impact of social capital or lack of social capital in the field of family. Bourdieu (1986: 249) describes it thus:

> Social capital is the aggregate of the actual or potential resources which are linked to possession of a durable network of more or less institutionalised relationships of mutual acquaintance and recognition.

This study recognises that childhoods are experienced differently depending on the different capitals (including social capital) the family has. As Franklin (1995:

7) states, childhoods are varied and are 'social constructs formed by a range of social, historical and cultural factors.' These factors include the type of family (field) they live in and how this is shaped by and shapes their experiences, choices and identity. For example, homes and family may appear to be neutral, but through symbolic representation, the cultural capital a middle class child brings from home (knowledge of books, experience of going to the theatre) to achieve success in the accruing of qualifications can be seen as 'natural' rather than the result of them transferring this 'inherited' cultural capital into academic success, 'qualifications', and cultural capital, whilst the street capital a child brings to school (being able to take care of themselves, strength, and street savvy, cook, clean, look after siblings, and so on) is deemed redundant and not of equal parity at school, although it nevertheless provides them with survival tools on the streets. Therefore, the notion of what constitutes valuable capital will be explored in relation to how it is viewed in the social context of the learners' lives and by the dominant middle-class lens.

The field of the workplace

The learners' experience of crossing the field of school to employment or unemployment will be unpacked, together with examining how childhood and adulthood violence and trauma shape the capitals, or lack of capital, and their flow in the field of work. Bourdieu describes how fields are all connected to economic power. This study will examine how capitals influence the learners' choices, or lack of choices, on leaving school and how this shaped how they viewed themselves. These capitals will also include the importance of linguistic capital needed for entry into the field of work, for example, the meta-language needed in the field of health and nursing.

When considering the females in the group, and linking their struggles with basic skills and employment, it is worth looking at Parsons and Bynner's (2007: 21) NRDC study which highlights:

> full-time employment, starting almost as soon as it had begun in their teens. Around four-fifths of women with Level 1 or higher skills were in paid employment from age 23, compared with around two-thirds of women with Entry 2 numeracy and just half of women with Entry 2 literacy. Women with Entry 2 literacy had experienced almost twice as much unemployment as women with Entry 3 skills and nearly four times as much as women with Level 1 or higher skills. Many women with Entry 2 skills had spent at least twice as much time in a full-time home-care role as women with Level 1 or higher skills by age 34.
>
> (Parsons and Bynner 2007: 21)

They also identified (Bynner and Parsons 2006: 29) how:

> For women, poor educational achievement underpins poor employment prospects, especially in the non-manual office jobs that young women tend to favour. In contrast to men in this situation, the outcome for low-skilled women is frequently early partnership and parenthood, offering the alternative career path of mother and carer. Though such young women – particularly following partnership breakdown – may be isolated and stressed through poverty and ill health, they are often more able to cope with the help of other women in comparable situations.

The findings demonstrate that a lack of basic skills had an impact on the women's choices (or lack of choices), health and well-being. My study will explore how different capitals, accrued at home and in their communities, influence gendered trajectories on leaving school. For example the male learners transferring 'muscle capital' into manual work needing strength, and the female learners trading in 'caring' and 'domestic' capital for caring and cleaning work. I also explore both resistance to and alternative routes into employment, for example choosing motherhood, rather than work; choosing to return to college rather than continue in unemployment, and choosing the informal economy rather than the dominant legitimate economy.

Education as a field

School, with its own rules and regulations, may be deemed a field. Fields are sites of power struggles where cultural capital (qualifications) can be exchanged. Cultural capital (such as having knowledge of literature and the arts) may be seen as giving people a feel for the 'game'. The symbolic power embedded within the field and the possession of legitimate cultural capital can lead to differential access to advantages and education being misrecognised in terms of individual natural abilities and effort, rather than in terms of unequal distribution of inherited cultural capital among the social classes, which offers the recipient a better feel for the game (see Figures 3.1a and b). If a student feels that they do not fit in, that their social and cultural practices are inappropriate and that their tacit knowledge is undervalued, they may be more inclined to withdraw early. This can be contrasted to a student from the dominant social class who, in Bourdieu's words, 'encounters a social world of which it is a product, it is like a "fish in water": it does not feel the weight of the water and it takes the world about itself for granted' (Bourdieu and Wacquant 1992: 127). Bourdieu locates the education system as the most important player in the unequal distribution of cultural and linguistic capital. This is manifested through its curriculum (see Bowles and Gintis 1976; Willis 1977; Walkerdine et al. 2001; Skeggs 1997; Luttrell 1997; Horsman 1999) which legitimises the imposition of the 'cultural arbitrary', put plainly, the values and meanings of the dominant culture. The institution of education continues to be a conservatising force, within which teachers bring to the classroom the dominant cultural values and symbolic power related to their legitimate authority.

In this capacity the school system serves to reproduce a middle-class discourse (Bourdieu 1984), and all the assumptions, standards and values of middle class ideologies (Apple 2000).

Culturally different children (see Willis 1977; Bourdieu 1977) are at a disadvantage because educational success depends upon possession of the cultural capital which the teachers value; schools fulfil a political agenda of providing an education to working class which reproduces existing relations of educational consumption. Reay (1997: 227) identified that:

> Even when class is not overt and articulated in people's decoding of the social world, it is still there as part of the implicit, taken-for-granted understandings they bring to their relationships with others.

In order to understand how social class and gender impact on education, this study examines the links between schools and families of different social classes. It recognises that standards of the field are always shifting and changing and this includes the educational field (Bourdieu 1994; Bourdieu and Wacquant 1992). Bourdieu's theoretical model provides the means to explore the diverse cultural practices in these changing fields and society. It offers an approach to exposing how some practices pathologise the working class as 'other', and avoids a deficit model where the families of the middle class are idealised and working class 'othered'.

The study will also explore the learners' journey into the fields of Further and Higher Education. These fields will be unpicked against the backdrop of such documents as The *Learning Age* document. The aim of this was to support Britain's drive for business and commerce stating that: 'Learning will be the key to a strong economy and an inclusive society' (DfEE, 1998: 3) while the document *Success for All* states how the government's goals are 'social inclusion and economic prosperity' (DfES 2002: 9). This study explores the Labour Government's notion of 'Individualism' and the rhetoric being used in related policies and reports. This corresponds to an instrumental model to drive towards employability in the labour market, which has impacted on the learners' experiences and choices in education.

The discourse of a neo-liberal approach to learning societies which privileges individual over collective learning will be explored. I will also discuss education as a commodity which pays no regard to issues of economic, political and social equality. The main role given to education is to provide a flexible, adaptable and skilled workforce to make countries competitive in the globalised economy. Ten adults in this study were unemployed and were identified as being socially excluded. Of these ten learners, five attended a mandatory New Deal programme at college. The drive behind the New Deal curriculum was to get them to re-enter the workforce. The onus was on them to acquire the skills to enter the work force. The New Deal curriculum is based on an 'instrumental model' which places an emphasis on equipping them with employability skills, rather than critical literacy pedagogy, which would encourage learners to increase their knowledge and skills, thus enabling them to develop a critical view of society and culture (Freire 2004). The curriculum which I was expected to deliver linked literacy closely with job-seeking skills; education for fun, personal development and self-fulfilment were not viewed by the college as of primary importance. The subversion of this model and the development of a critical curriculum linked to praxis will be explored.

School success

Having considered the field of schooling, I will now further explore how a learner's positioning is influenced by capitals and the symbolic power they represent. In this study, access to different capitals and how this influences the learners' choices/or lack of choice, struggles, conformity, resistance, identities and trajectories at school and beyond is explored. Bourdieu's concept of cultural capital and symbolic violence offers a frame to explore how schooling is part of symbolic process of cultural and social reproduction (Bourdieu and Passeron 1977). For example, schools appear to be neutral, but through symbolic representation, the cultural capital a middle class child brings from home to achieve success in accruing of qualifications can be seen as 'natural' rather than the result of them transferring this 'inherited' cultural capital into academic success 'qualifications' and cultural capital. Reay et al (2005: 19) highlight how school success is linked by 'the amount and type of cultural capital inherited from the family milieu rather than by measures of individual talent or achievement'. She draws on Bourdieu's concept of cultural capital as 'breaking with the received wisdom that attributes academic success or failure to natural aptitudes such as intelligence and giftedness'. This concept of 'natural' ability relates with the idea of IQism where 'ability is a fixed and definable and measurable quality of individual students' (Ball 2008: 180). What it fails to recognise is the unequal distribution of cultural capital transferred through the family network (Robbins 1991) and brought from the home to school; its legitimisation in the school curriculum serves to reproduce the dominant interests of society at a cultural and social level.

This research aims to explore the learners' forms of capital and its impact on their educational journey, which includes both the first steps and often the last steps of schooling before entering the field of Further Education. In doing so, I am seeking to further the research of Walkerdine et al. (2001); Skeggs (1997) and Luttrell (1997) based around the impact of the learners' lives on their learning and the notion of their 'worth'. It also explores how those who teach have the power to transmit their values, their world visions, their ideologies and prejudices; this makes the teaching–learning process a non-neutral one. It is positioned by the subjectivities of those who are involved in it and by the symbolic–cultural determinations that are representative of the educational system, constructed from a privileged logic where those in a position of power (having the valued forms of capital) can determine whether the capitals the learners possess are legitimate or illegitimate.

Habitus

Bourdieu (1987a: 10) asserted that:

> Any theory of the social universe must include representations that agents have of the social world and, more precisely, the contribution they make to the construction of the vision of that world, and consequently, to the very construction of the world.

This concept was defined as the habitus. My study works with Bourdieu's concept of the habitus, as it offers a valuable tool for highlighting the ways experience is both classed and gendered. The habitus recognises that people are born into different circumstances (for example, into wealth and poverty) and the ways in which these different types and amounts of capital shape the learners' lives. Bourdieu argues that the combination of economic, social, cultural and symbolic capital constitutes a habitus. In this vein Skegg (1997: 8–9) observes capitals, or access to capital as varying depending on:

> inherited social space from which comes access to and the acquisition of different amounts of capital assets. From being born into gender, class and race relations we occupy the associated social positions such as woman, black, working class (Moi 1991). We also inherit ways of understanding; we inherit the meanings associated with social positions and positions in knowledge.

This is further elaborated upon by Reay (2004a: 434) who notes that Bourdieu theorises that:

> A person's individual history is constitutive of habitus, but also is the whole collective history of family and class to which they belong.

The above quote highlights the part collective history plays in locating the individual in society (consider the learner's positioning in the field of family, work and education), in terms of the influence of their class positioning (a signifier of legitimate capitals accrued or not accrued) and how their positioning and capitals shape individual habitus. When considering the aforementioned it is important to highlight that central to Bourdieu's methodology is the structural constructivist theory. This theory addresses issues related to the definitions of a person as active agent at one end and as a product of external structures at the other. He highlights how social practices are more structured than free will, but less controlled than simply a response. Bourdieu (1987b: 12) describes how:

> The habitus entertains with the social world which has produced it a real ontological complicity, the source of cognition without consciousness, of an intentionality without intention, and a practical mastery of the world's

> regularities which allows one to anticipate the future without even needing to posit it as such.

In applying this lens, he rejects the view that people neither have free will nor are passive victims, noting:

> Any theory of the social universe must include the representations that agents have of the social world and, more precisely, the contribution they make to the construction of the vision of that world, and consequently, to the very construction of that world.
>
> (Bourdieu 1987c: 10)

Bourdieu (1977) views human behaviour deterministically in that it is always conditioned by the habitus. The habitus becomes almost intuitive and as such is carried out without conscious awareness. Different classes, he argues, have a different habitus and therefore different perceptions, aspirations, dispositions, tastes and concepts of cultural values, and so on. This is demonstrated in everyday human behaviour such as 'blowing of the nose', gait and attitudes. On a symbolic level it is visible in the way a person dresses, the make-up they wear, the haircut they have, and so on. It is not, however, a matter of everyone being different but having equal footing in the field. For example as noted earlier, the most important institution may be deemed the field of education, and the symbolic power it brings, from the accruing of qualifications, progression into professional occupations and the capitals this can offer. Access to this symbolic power, however, may vary depending on opportunities to attend, for example, what may be considered 'better' high achieving schools (Ball et al. 1995) perhaps located outside the catchment area of the child and deemed too 'posh' by working class parents to send their children to (Reay 1998b) even if they offer their child the best opportunities for academic success. This lack of opportunity is two-fold.

The habitus may be viewed as guiding the parents to opt for certain choices. These 'choices' are not viewed as a power relation between the classes, but by symbolic identification, as legitimate demands for obedience, a value judgment becoming a 'cultural arbitrary' (Moore 2004). Therefore, symbolic power leads to advantages in the field of education, generated through advantage, with the dominant classes (middle classes) always winning.

Reay and Ball (1998) referred to parents as either 'insiders' or 'outsiders' within the educational field. Figures 3.1a and b below illustrate symbolic power and symbolic violence. The 'insiders' are represented by the wheel of symbolic power, 'the outsiders' by the wheel of symbolic violence. The figures highlight how symbolic violence and symbolic power evolve over time, with each successive deprivation or enrichment of capital having an impact on the next and strengthening it across the learners' trajectory from education to work.

The cycles perpetuate disadvantage and deprivation (see Figure 3.1b) and advantage and success (see Figure 3.1a); this cycle presents little opportunity for

Wheel of Symbolic Power (a)

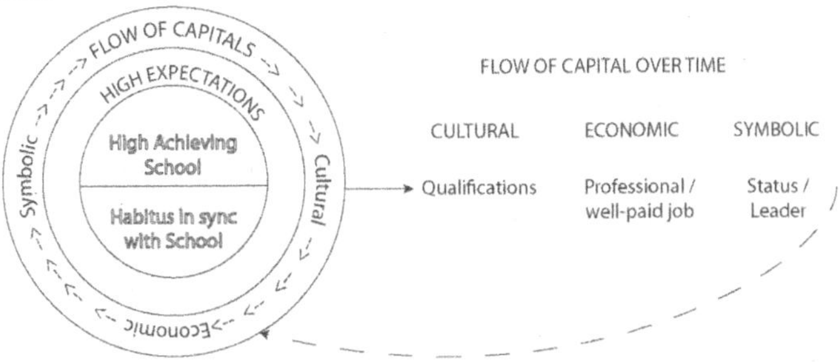

The wheel of symbolic power evolves over time, each capital feeding into the next and strengthening the symbolic power.

Wheel of Symbolic Violence (b)

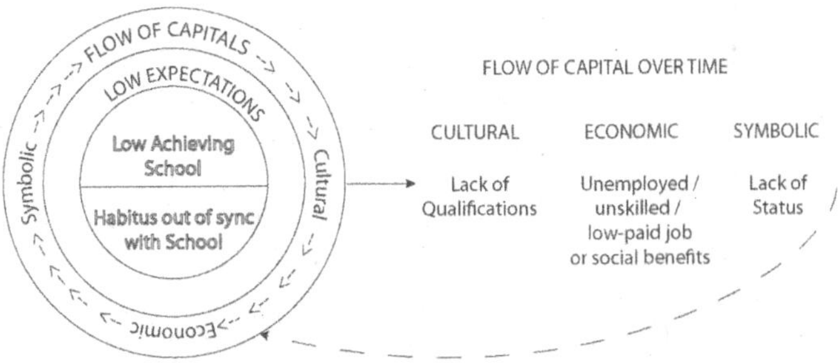

The wheel of symbolic violence evolves over time, each deprivation of capitals impacting the next and strengthening the symbolic violence.

Figure 3.1 Wheels of symbolic power and violence

breaking out. The system organising actions, perceptions and judgments (in this case the institution of education) is adapted to the social structures by previous acquisition and inculcation. The manner in which the habitus places emphasis on the strong influence of history accounts for the sturdiness of the dispositions and may be seen as a weakness of Bourdieu's approach, as it seems difficult to find space to explain the processes of individual and social change using this concept by, for example, rupturing the cycle of symbolic violence in Figure 3.1b.

Layder (1994) offers an approach whereby agency and structure are closely knitted together through habitus and function through practice, creating difficulty in exposing and examining the 'impact of structure on action and action on structures in different empirical and historical circumstances' (Layder 1994: 157). He goes on to propose that this could flatten out diverse experiences and influences of class and gender. I believe Layder makes a sweeping generalisation that reduces Bourdieu's concepts to an over simplistic level. Indeed, rather than being implicitly a 'flattened' stereotype, I address this by placing the learners' narratives in the context of the personal and public domains through which they travel, and through which they aim to travel. Their narratives are grounded in a social and cultural context, rather than being flattened and one dimensional. Working with Bourdieu's concept gives rise to individual learners' personal journeys, exposing the inequalities that stereo-typing[1] and symbolic violence (see McRobbie 2004) have on their notion of self and respectability (see Skeggs 1997) and their learning journey.

For Lawler (2004) the habitus is not determining but generative and presented in a more dynamic way. Habitus is 'a kind of transforming machine that leads us to "reproduce" the social condition of our own production, but in a relatively unpredictable way' (Bourdieu 1993: 87). This is driven by the expectations and choices people encounter on their day-to-day journey through life, gender, class and ethnicity, all of which are vital in giving rise to habitus. This offers me a useful extension to Bourdieu's concept, as it allows for change in the habitus and a break in the cycle (for example, deeper exploration of possible ruptures to cycles 3.1a and b). The notion of this change being 'unpredictable', however, is something that will require further exploration. It supposes chaos, as opposed to how, for example, critical education can transform learners' habitus in perhaps more predictable ways.

Reay et al. (1998b) have included Bourdieu's notion of habitus within narratives which highlight the tension between schools and family life. Reay et al. (2005) discusses how 'habitus can be transformed through a process that either raises or lowers an individual's expectations. Implicit in the concept is the possibility of a social trajectory that enables conditions of living that are very different from initial ones' (ibid: 435). This is exciting when considering the Basic Skills learners in this study and the possibilities of a critical pedagogical perspective in education to offer them opportunities of what Freire (2004: 102) describes as 'hope' to improve their life – for example, their dreams, family life, job prospects and so on. Reay et al. (2005: 28) also links agency and structure, recognising that sometimes the unpredictability of the habitus when encountering a field with which it is not familiar can result in disjunctures which generate change and transformation but also disquiet, ambivalence, insecurity and uncertainty. For example, when a learner's habitus is not in sync with the middle class discourse of schooling (see Figure 3.1b), they can become discouraged by the fact that they are labelled and pathologised by teachers as early as primary school for lacking the qualities deemed necessary to succeed (see Steedman 1988). As Oakley (1994: 25) puts it, 'there are . . . so many categories of children who pose problems that we are forced to conclude that it is children themselves who are seen as the problem'.

The notion that the labelling and pathologising of working class children is a conscious activity is problematic. Bourdieu believes that to 'speak of strategies of reproduction is not to say that the strategies through which dominants manifest their tendency to maintain the status quo are the result of rational calculation or even strategic intent' (Bourdieu 1996: 272). According to Bourdieu (Bourdieu

1986; 1991; Bourdieu and Wacquant 1992), it is the inculcated, durable, structured, generative, and transposable dispositions that constitute the habitus that are to a large degree accountable for the reproduction of culture and subsequently the reproduction of the inequalities in society.

The study will consider how the habitus can become a type of capital exchanged for goods (Bourdieu 1986). Those who have more of the dispositions valued by the structuring process in the field (site it takes place) are likely to be positioned more positively than those who do not have the dispositions. For example I will consider how learners who exhibit what is esteemed in the field are more likely to be successful, for example in the fields of school, employment, adult education, the home and the streets where they live.

When considering the learners' position in the field and the impact of the flow of capitals it is worth considering how they engage in and navigate across these fields (see Figure 3.2).

I have elaborated on Bourdieu's analytical framework by proposing a model (see Figure 3.2) which views the habitus as a mediating construct, not one which determines (Harker et al. 190: 13). It illustrates how the flow (or lack of flow) of capitals, carried over time by the learners in the study across the domains of their lives, is linked through the habitus. It shows the impact these capitals can have on the learners' lives and how this can lead to struggle, resistance and conformity

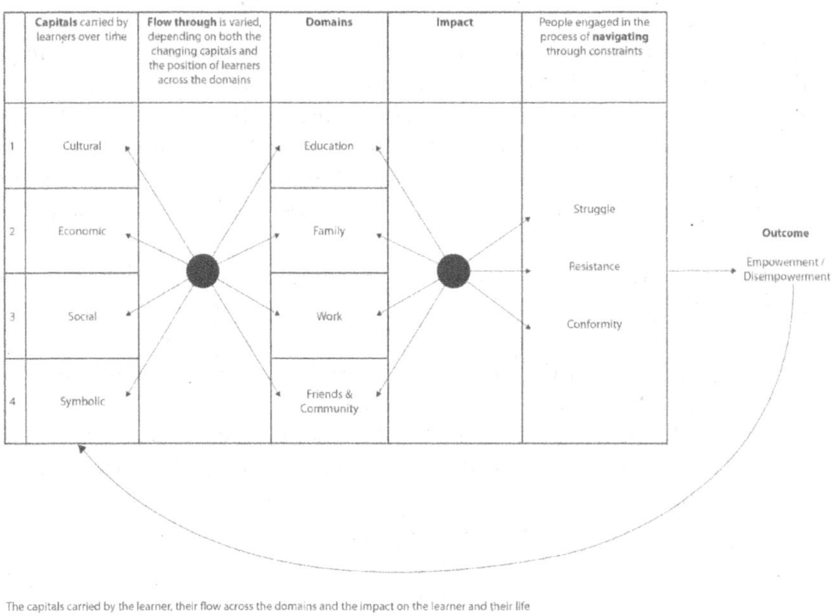

Figure 3.2 Capitals carried by the learner, their flow across the domains and the impact on the learners and their lives

of the habitus. Within this cycle, the process of inculcation is not complete and habitus is capable of transformation through the flow of capitals. Modifications to Figure 3.2 will be used to illustrate the findings of the research.

In showing the cycle and capital exchange the model also recognises Bourdieu's recognition that history and theory are linked. Rather than the weight of history being determinist however, for example, not being able to break the cycle of poverty, the awareness of historical constraints, such as the structural inequalities of class and gender can in itself become a tool for consciousness raising (Freire 1996). This allows for the production of knowledge by people reflecting on their positioning in the field and in turn shaping their habitus. Indeed, one strength of Bourdieu's concept is that, like Foucault, he positions himself in a place where analysis does not divide history and theory. They are wrapped round each other as skin to bone, functioning to support and feed the other. For Bourdieu (2004) historical reflexivity is a quintessential mechanism in the continuing production of knowledge. This is because any historical critique, which is a component of reflexivity, can counter pre-suppositions of the social world about what is taken for granted or indeed perceived as 'natural'. Historical reflexivity is essential for building and producing meaningful knowledge about the world we live in. It is addressed in this research, as it helps account for the grounds on which interpretations (which include my own and those of the learners) are constructed.

Reay also developed Bourdieu's theory by introducing useful new concepts like 'emotional capital'. For example Reay (2000, 2004c) used the concept of 'emotional capital' to investigate the affective role of mothers' emotional involvement in their children's education in an attempt to operationalise the concept of 'emotional capital'. She argues that working class women are being viewed by those in positions of power as lacking the right attributes for promoting either emotional or cultural capital. I build on Reay's concept of 'emotional capital' to explore, for example, how the learners in the study are located as mothers by those in power positions, such as social workers.

Tracy, a mother of three, described her experience of being visited by social workers:

Tracy: It's the way they look down on us, me and the kids. Nothing I do is never enough. Yer can see them weighing everythin' up. They think they have it all sussed when they start tellin' me what I should and shouldn't do with me own kids. I'm not perfect, who is. But I don't need them puttin' me down, not when I'm tryin.

Interviewer: How do they make you feel?

Tracy: Like a nobody, worthless

Reay (2000) identifies how working class women often lack the right conditions for promoting either emotional or cultural capital (ibid. 2000: 575). The proposition that their habitus is out of sync with the dominant legitimate emotion is an area which I will explore. Emotional capital is something Tracy is finding difficult to conjure up as are 'many of the mothers on benefit and income support'. She is 'emotionally preoccupied with surviving from day to day on inadequate resources' (Reay 2004c: 70).

Cultural capital, language and literacy

Together with other forms of capital, this study will investigate the impact of social conditions on linguistic capital as an embodied cultural capital in its recognition that:

> language is not simply an instrument of communication: it also provides, together with a richer or poorer vocabulary, a more or less complex system of categories, so the capacity to decipher and manipulate complex structures, whether logical or aesthetic, descends partly on the language transmitted in the family.
>
> (Bourdieu and Passeron 1977: 73)

In developing his approach to language and linguistic exchange, Bourdieu applies and elaborates the ideas that make up the theory of practice (Bourdieu 1994: 17). He applies this to the relationship of linguistic habitus and the linguistic market. The agent's positioning within the linguistic exchange is in the context of family, school, peers, college, work and so on. Bourdieu et al. (1994), Bourdieu (1994; 1999) and Goffman (1981) argue that when considering 'talk' and its function, more than a linguistic analysis is required. The position of the speaker in relation to class, gender and ethnicity and so on needs to be located. Indeed, speech is a signifier of positioning in the field and, in recognition of this, accents and dialect are recognised as working to scribe an agent's linguistic identity on their body. Lawler (2004) draws on *distinction* as a 'significant way class operates'; the dominant classes in society are in the power position to define their 'cultural arbitrary' as superior to that of the working classes, and thereby to naturalise their superiority. Symbolic power is present in the legitimate authority of the middle and upper class dispositions, which includes ways of speaking.

Bernstein (1971a) asserts that there are two language codes, restricted and elaborated. Elaborated is aligned with the middle and upper classes and is defined as a richer use of language that, for example, uses more adjectives. Restricted, by comparison, is viewed as more clipped and monosyllabic and aligned to the working classes. Bernstein believed that working class has access to one code, while the middle-class has access to both as a result of them having the opportunity to be more socially, culturally and geographically mobile throughout their life. Bourdieu argues that Bernstein fails to relate language and its codes 'to the social product to its social conditions of its production, or even as one might expect from the sociology of education, to its academic conditions', (Bourdieu 1994: 53).

Bourdieu's work on education and its impact in the reproduction of social inequality (Bourdieu and Passeron 1977) provides a framework to explore literacy as a cultural capital, as well as examining literacy education as a site of the production and reproduction of power positions, where certain literacy practices are considered more legitimate than others. When considering literacy as a site for *distinction* and *legitimate* cultural capital, it is useful to draw on Street's (1984) distinction between 'autonomous'[2] and 'ideological'[3] concepts of literacy, and Barton and Hamilton's (1998) later work on New Literacy studies which includes *privileged institutional* versus *vernacular literacies.* Bourdieu and New Literacy Studies (NLS) enables me to explore what counts as literacy in the lives of the learners and how this relates to instrumental models based on political and economic drivers, for example increasing the skills of the workforce[4] and meeting government targets. Drawing on literacy as a cultural capital, literacy education and symbolic power will also be explored. The study will identify the value of the literacies the learners bring into the classroom and how social inequality – which includes being poor – serves to position the learners as 'other' and thus lacking the legitimate language skills (vernacular) which are valued in schools and, in many cases, further education. Without this symbolic capital, which is in this case *institutional literacies*, Bourdieu (1994: 72) identifies:

> The question of performative utterances becomes clearer if one sees it as a particular case of the effects of symbolic domination, which occurs in linguistic exchanges. The linguistic exchange of power is never defined solely by the relation between the linguistic competencies present and the weight difference depends on their symbolic capital – that is, on the *recognition*, institutionalised or not, that they receive from the group. Symbolic imposition – that kind of magical efficacy which not only the command and the password, but also ritual discourse or a simple injunction, or even threats and insults, purport to exercise – can function only if there is a convergence of social conditions which are altogether distinct from the strictly linguistic logic of discourse. For the philosopher's language to be granted the importance of its claims there has to be a convergence of the social conditions which enable it to secure from others a recognition of the importance which it attributes to itself.

This study seeks to contest the symbolic domination of institutionalised literacies and open up a frame of reference which draws on literacy practices in the context of the learners' histories and lives. For example, it seeks to highlight how different learners are positioned differently depending on the value of the literacy practices they bring with them from home. These literacy practices also include addressing the different discourses (Gee 1999) and narratives the learners bring into the classroom. Hymes (1996: 115) describing how:

> —the narrative use of language is not a property of subordinate cultures, whether folk, or working class, or the like, but a universal function. The great restriction on its use in a society such as ours has to do with when it is considered appropriate and legitimate. Generally speaking, it is considered legitimate, a valid use of language in the service of knowledge, when it is used *among co-members of a group*. If the narrative function is excluded in an institutional setting, such as a college or school, the implication is that the students are defined as *not co-members* of a group with those who teach them.

NLS offers a space for transformation where learners can explore their narratives and the society around them. The study sheds light on literacy as being historically located and socially embedded in relations of power which challenges traditional models of symbolic domination which serves to both legitimise and reproduce structural inequalities.

In the context of narratives and discourses, the study also explores the use of creative writing in the learners' lives as a means to share their words with other members of the group, make meanings out of their life and circumstances and shape their identity, while also developing literacy skills (see O'Rourke 2005).

For Bourdieu, cultural acts are a form of cultural capital. Bourdieu sought to 'historicise' culture as a field, with the aim of deconstructing the ideologies interpolated within it, which may be deemed to align culture with 'nature' and so naturalise the difference. This again directly impacts on the reproduction and reinforcement of the class structure, in that it functions in linked fields of aesthetics. As identified by Bourdieu 'it must never be forgotten that the working class aesthetic is a dominated aesthetic which is constantly obliged to define itself in terms of dominated aesthetics' (Bourdieu 1984). The research explores how, in breaking with the dominant ideology – which positions creative writing and poetry in the realm of *distinction* – bringing it into the field of a basic skills class has had an impact on the learners' identity and lives.

Symbolic violence and the habitus

Symbolic power includes various modes of social/cultural/economic domination in which dominant values of those in positions of power are imposed on others as norms, for example notions of 'different cultural tastes'. These are themselves a product of a specific class habitus. How the habitus is valued in the field varies. For example, consider the classed habitus of the children in Figures 3.1a and 3.1b. In Skeggs' (1997) study, the working class women were very aware that they did not have the 'right' habitus and so they dis-identified themselves with being working class. This awareness is an area I will explore, in relation to how feelings of being judged and labelled give rise to feelings of shame. The power of symbolic capital and what is valued and why in different fields offers an insightful avenue of enquiry into the experience of the learners in this study, and how they are viewed by those in a position of power across the domains of their life. It allows for a further understanding of the dominant process and its impact on the learners' lives (see Figure 3.2). Drawing on their narratives, I aim to identify features of symbolic capital – or the lack of it – across the domains of their lives and to consider the impact of this. Uncovering and understanding what are often invisible forms of symbolic capital and trying to understand how this has an impact on the learners' lives, and on their communities, offers valuable knowledge. Indeed, by drawing on the learners' narratives, I can identify features of symbolic violence that are embedded in everyday life. This allows me to explore the different forms of violence that can co-exist and indeed support one another, each affecting the other in a cycle of violence (for example, see Figure 3.3).

The force to acquire and defend symbolic capital derives from the dispositions generated by the habitus, inherited at birth and then inculcated by family and school; the arbitrary value of whatever symbolic capital is at stake not being recognised. Misrecognition allows symbolic violence to go unexposed. 'Misrecognition' (a Bourdieuian phrase taken from Marx's idea of 'false consciousness') occurs when those in more disadvantaged contexts 'play the game without questioning the rules'. This amounts to what Bourdieu terms 'symbolic violence'. This concept of misrecognition is a central part of Bourdieu's analysis. Symbolic violence is characterised as:

> the coercion which is set up only through the consent that the dominated cannot fail to give to the dominator . . . when their understanding of the situation and relation can only use instruments of knowledge that they have in common with the dominator, which, being merely an incorporated form of the structure of the relation of domination, make this relationship appear as natural.
>
> (Bourdieu 2000: 170)

As identified previously, it is often carried out not by the use of physical force but by non-physical and very often unnoticed actions, for example, everyday societal rules that control lives and movement. This lack of recognition is how symbolic violence maintains its effect; however it is important to note that symbolic violence is as real and harmful as any other form of violence (see Figure 3.1 b). For example, when learners see some groups punished or rewarded more than others and some receive fewer resources, less praise and encouragement, they learn that some students deserve more than others. Thus, inequitable outcomes seem natural rather than the result of inequitable inputs. The dominant class asserts its culture and lifestyle as the benchmark of 'norm' to which others must aspire, and in so doing legitimises class differences under the guise of individual high merit or ability.

Figure 3.3 highlights the symbolic and physical, which can result from unequal distribution of capitals such as being poor. This cycle is vital both in trying to understand how and why violence continues, and in addressing issues of injustice.

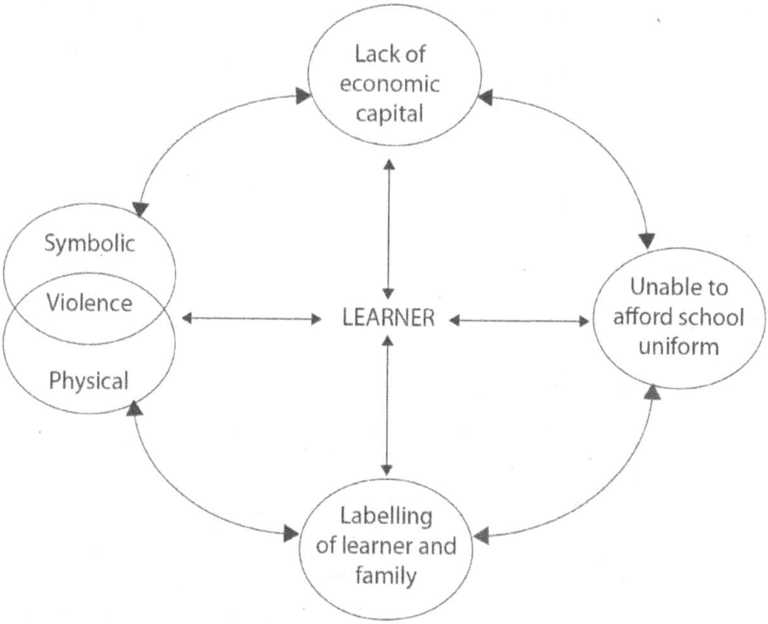

Figure 3.3 Cycle of being poor

As such it is worth exploring notions of labelling and stigma that may result from a lack of capitals and lead to experiences of violence and trauma.

Labelling

Bourdieu's concept of symbolic violence has limitations, in that it does not fully engage with the nature of labelling as a symbolic act of violence. In this study I expand on Bourdieu's notion of symbolic capital to include Becker and Goffman's work on labelling and its impact. Howard Becker's (1963: 9) study of deviance highlighted that:

> Social groups create deviance by making rules whose infraction constitutes deviance and by applying those rules to particular people and labelling them as outsiders. From this point of view deviance is not a quality of the act a person commits, but rather a consequence of the application by others of rules and sanctions to an offender. The deviant is one to whom that label has been successfully applied; deviant behaviour is behaviour that people so label.

As an Interactionist,[5] for Becker it is not the individuals' actions but the social reaction to those actions that creates deviance. His ideas are important to this study since they can be used to highlight how membership of the working and underclass is defined by those in a position of power as deviant and thus label the individual (see Figure 3.3). This demonstrates how identity can result from the views of others rather than personal views of the self. This study uncovers who does the labelling and in whose interest it is, and the impact of labelling on marginalization and exclusion will be explored.

Joanne was labelled because she came from a 'big family' the antithesis to a *respectable* 'nuclear family'. The idea of a big family, I would suggest, is linked to poverty, lack of restraint, sexuality and savagery, and as such is pathologised.

Every day interactions

Erving Goffman (1959), whose work focuses on the analysis of everyday interactions, compared social life to the theatre and as such his perspective of the self is dramaturgical, much like a performance. Dependent on the context different roles are acted out. The roles which we can choose from are based on patterns of behaviour, responses and routines like parts in a play. Much like habitus, not all our actions are conscious. Goffman offers a frame to explore the links between the society, the learner's life and the limitations offered by the roles they play. Like the habitus there is room for agency in that while 'playing the parts' – like 'playing the field' – people can become familiar with the performance, deriving agency from the fact that they have given their own interpretation to the role they are playing.

Stigma

Goffman's (1963) work on stigma facilitates the exploration of the relationship between the learners' interactions, individual attributes and labelling. Stigma is socially situated and may occur when an individual is identified as deviant and linked with negative stereotypes, such as being labelled 'thick' or 'poor'. This can engender prejudiced attitudes, which can thus lead to discriminatory behaviour towards the person. In turn, this can have an impact on the person thus labelled, who might therefore (for example) experience low self-esteem. The stigmatising process is dependent on the social, economic, and political power necessary to impose discriminatory experiences on the labelled individual or group. Advantaged groups can stigmatise less advantaged groups, such as the poor, in order to justify why they have more. According to Goffman, stigma can be classed under three categories: 1. Tribal identities, 2. Abominations of the body, 3. Blemish of individual Character (Goffman 1963). These are not mutually exclusive.

Childhood labels such as 'daft', 'thick', 'a scruff' manifest as 'visible' tags worn on the body. Lawler (2004) draws on *distinction* as a 'significant way class operates'; the dominant classes in society are in the power position to define their 'cultural arbitrary' as superior to that of the working classes, and thereby to naturalise their superiority. This is clearly demonstrated in McRobbie's (2004) study of the media, whereby the bodies of women who are on the television programme 'What Not To Wear' for a makeover, are viewed as symbolic representations and labelled as either a 'shabby failure' or when conforming to the dominant habitus 'respectable professionals'. The school may also be seen as a site where wearing the *right* clothes is important. The mandatory uniform does not stop designer labels being displayed as markers of respectability, while the children who do not have the economic means to buy them wear what are deemed 'rags'. Habitus, as the learners have experienced it, is clearly a place for symbolic violence.

This process of ascribing symbolic value to forms of capital is referred to as 'legitimation', and is embedded in many social and cultural interactions at many levels. In particular, teachers are in a position to legitimate the cultural and social capital exhibited by their pupils through their acceptance of certain forms of behaviour. For example, the insistence on tight adherence to rules of uniform can work against those who lack the wherewithal (or social knowledge) to conform. The way that teachers (and indeed fellow pupils, as we shall see) communicate acceptance or rejection of symbolic capital with their pupils can have a profound effect on outcomes. The use of the word 'uniform' is apposite – it does not simply refer to the regulated clothing that many schools require pupils to wear, but also to the uniformity of expression which pupils impose within their own friendship groups.

Legitimation is a process which can often lead to acts of symbolic violence because of the (often unintended) consequences of the action. The violence lies in the large and unwanted shift in the life of the victim. The body is a symbolic representation that acts as a process of social production.

Stella, in the research group, opened up about how at junior school, the teachers labelled her and the other 'scruffy' kids who struggled with their school work:

> The teacher tied me left hand to a chair and tried to get me to write with me right hand . . . distressed I went home heartbroken.

From then on she would go in school for her mark then 'wag it'.

> The teachers didn't care about us scruffy kids . . . kids from poor families were left to do whatever they liked.

Stella clearly identifies how as a member of the working class and being poor, her tribal identity was seen as a blemish on her individual character. Moreover, struggling to read and write, her body was used for abomination.

Steedman (1988) shows how children are labelled as early as primary school. 'The semi-skilled and unskilled working class that she and her colleagues taught was not how children ought to be, not "real" children – though they represented most of the children in society.' She points out the urgency to outline the history that has made working class childhood into a kind of pathology in this way (Steedman 1988: 82).

It is this very pathology which I will address when seeking to explore schooling as a site of institutionalised capital (see Reay 2005) where people define themselves and their social worth (Luttrell 1997). I hope to uncover the impact of experiences of social exclusion and labelling, and lay bare how the educational system is not a meritocratic system; rather it is a place where intergenerational marginalization and exclusion is encountered. Labelling theory can be linked to teacher expectation and self-fulfilling prophesy (see Ball 1981). Activities by the teacher may lead to learners being labelled as 'intelligent', slow', 'average'. This study will uncover the links between the amount and type of cultural capital the learners bring to the field of school and college, and how this affects the expectations and behaviour they experience from those with symbolic power, for example, teachers.

Rather than being limited by a focus purely on the social interaction of the group and how, for example, they interact with models of literacies in the classroom, this study also explores how the learners have lived with identities tainted by stigma of being labelled poor and illiterate (for example) and the limitations of compulsory and post-compulsory education in meeting their needs.

As identified by Hanley (2007) in her personal memoir and social history of estates, children who live on estates and attend the local school receive a 'council estate education'. Where 'you can't ever hope to reach your potential; it's just that very idea of having lots of potential to fulfil that isn't presented'. The idea of having potential is indeed something many of the learners hadn't even been told. Many had been labelled as 'no hopers', and they didn't have the confidence to think further than the next lesson.

Subversion of labels

The study also explores how negative labels are subverted by the learners and re-worked to gain respectability. For example the negative label of a meat head[6] is turned on its head when it is substituted with 'muscle capital' which is accrued for distinction and recognition on the streets the learners live. Wearing emblems of sovereign rings, snide[1] designer gear and having awareness of a drug culture that revolves around spliffs[7] and coke[8] marks out the kids as having 'street capital'. I have coined the concept 'street capital' to represent meaningful symbols that accrue into a form of currency, in relation to belonging and being represented in the sub-culture of what the media has termed the 'underclass'. This form of capital may be deemed a powerful one, as it a threat to the dominant class in terms of the media's hype about being attacked by a 'hoody'[9] – or 'youth'.

In the bigger scheme of things, however, this doesn't shift the balance of power away from the dominant classes. It is still the dominant classes who obtain the qualifications that perpetuate the class system, and thus the dominant classes retain the privilege, power and domination which come with it. Bourdieu (1973: 72) notes that:

> among all the solutions put forward throughout history to the problem of the transmission of power and privilege, there surely does not exist one that is better concealed, and therefore better adapted to societies which tend to refuse the most patent forms of hereditary transmission of power and privileges, than that solution which the educational system provides by contributing to the reproduction of the structure of class relations and by concealing, by an apparently neutral attitude, the fact that it fills this function.

Bourdieu's concept of cultural capital provides a meaningful tool for understanding how the learners' past, present and future have been influenced by the habitus; this concept therefore provides shape and meaning to their narratives.

Together with the dominant value system, there are different value systems which are positioned outside of the dominant symbolic ideologies. For example, this study explores how dominant notions of masculinity and respectability are subverted by the males in the study. Middle class perspectives equate 'male' to logic and mind; qualifications, 'brain capital' and having a good job are replaced by males who adopt the roles of 'the street' where 'masculinity' is equated to muscle and power: visits to the gym and having street credibility replace work and qualifications. The notions of what it means to be a man differing depending on the field, and these fields are related to class. On the estates (field of street) the learners' 'muscle capital' may be deemed as a more valued capital than brain capital. The streets, like any other field, have their own rules, which feed into the habitus giving symbolic power whereby 'respect is given to those who can look after themselves'.[10]

Research questions

To summarise, in this study I will elaborate on Bourdieu's concept of the habitus. I would argue that Bourdieu underestimates the power of agency and reflexivity which people have. I explore the ways the habitus involves resistance as well as compliance. I recognise the potential of the habitus for change. I will explore this change by drawing on the learners' changing experiences across the domains of their lives.

The overall aim of my research seeks to explore the work of Bourdieu's capitals across the learners' lives in the domains or fields of education, work, family and friends. The theory has enabled me to elaborate on this and the main questions posed which have emerged from the theoretical framework are:

1 How are learners positioned in each of the domains/fields? And how does this change with the varied flow of capitals?
2 How do people navigate through the flows and domains?
3 What impact does this flow (or lack of flow) have on the constraints, possibilities and empowerment of the learners?
4 How does the development of a critical curriculum empower people across the domains of their lives?

Conclusion

Cultural capital (for example achieving a qualification, owning pieces of art) is not the only capital accruing to individuals. It is primarily a relational concept and exists in conjunction with other forms of capital (see Figure 3.2). Therefore, it cannot be understood in isolation from the other forms of capital that, alongside cultural capital, constitute advantage and disadvantage in society. As well as cultural capital, these include economic, social and symbolic capital. Social capital is generated through social processes in the private domain, for example family, and the public domain, for example at work and in wider society, and is made up of social networks. Economic capital is wealth either inherited or generated from interactions between the individual and the economy, while symbolic capital is manifested in individual prestige and personal qualities, such as influence, authority and charisma. In addition to their interconnection, Bourdieu envisages a process in which one form of capital can be transformed into another. For example, economic capital can be converted into cultural capital, while cultural capital can be readily translated into social capital. In applying Figure 3.2 to the learners' trajectories we have a powerful model to explore how learners navigate across the domains of their lives, which include the fields of education, work, and family. In these privileged spaces, identities are conferred on learners by those in a position of power, including teachers, peers and social workers, who use what is deemed 'legitimate' to carry out symbolic violence on those positioned as not having what Bourdieu characterised as the right 'habitus' or 'capital'. For example, those who teach or are in a position of power have the power to transmit their values, their world visions, their ideologies and prejudices; this makes, for example, the teaching–learning process a non-neutral one. It is positioned by the subjectivities of those who are involved in it and by the symbolic-cultural determinations that are representative of the educational system, constructed from a privileged logic where those in a position of power (having the valued forms of capital) can determine whether the capital the learners possess are legitimate or illegitimate. I seek to highlight how symbolic violence and the relations between groups and class at school continue into the 'choices' the learners make during adulthood and also into the learner's working life.

The study will also explore learners' hopes and experiences of transitioning from the field of further education to higher education. For example, the habitus is used by Bourdieu to refer to the norms and practices of particular social classes or groups (Bourdieu and Passeron 1977). The habitus 'provid[es] a conduit or medium through which information and resources are transmitted to the activities that they inform' (Layder 1994: 156). The habitus of many of the learners was not geared to even consider the field of higher education. I shall explore how symbolic violence was oppressive and stopped the learners reaching their potential and in a number of cases realising their dreams.

Summary of chapter

In this chapter I have explored Bourdieu's concepts of economic, social, cultural and symbolic capital and habitus to offer a useful framework for analysing the learners' narratives and their encounters across fields in the private (for example, in the family sphere) and public domains (for example, education) of their lives. I have also identified other researchers who have applied Bourdieu's concepts to their investigations, for example, Reay (2004a) and Skeggs (1997), and explored the limitations of Bourdieu's concepts. As such I have extended the concept of symbolic capital to include labelling theory and extended his concept of the habitus to allow for the power of agency and reflexivity. I have drawn on notions of literacy as a cultural capital; literacy education and its symbolic power and potential for agency. This agency has been supported by the exploration of New Literacy Studies and critical approaches to education, offering a potential space for transformation where learners can explore their narratives and society around them.

Notes

1 I would suggest that stereotypes provide a vehicle for ideologies. As such they can support and reinforce ideas of legitimate and powerful vested interests in society. For example, the social advantages accrued by the middle and upper classes in education.
2 Based on an instrumental model, literacy is viewed as objective and technologically bound for the development of cognitive skills.
3 Based on historically located body of social practices.
4 See, for example, DfES (2002) *Success for All: Reforming Further Education and Training – Our Vision for the Future which set out* to produce a qualified workforce by 2010 and DfES (2006) paper *FE Reform: Raising Skills, Improving Life Chances* DfES, available at www.dfes.gov.uk.
5 Interactionists aim to understand what the labelling means to the individual. Every individual's understanding and interpretation is different, for example, on being labelled as 'stupid' at school one learner may aim to prove the label wrong and work harder to achieve marks which contradict the label; while for another learner it may be a self-fulfilling prophesy
6 'Meat head' is a term used to refer to a male who instead of having brains has muscle.
7 Cigarette paper filled with tobacco and marihuana.
8 Cocaine.
9 A sweat shirt with a hood on the back, which 'youths' wear with the hood up. Perceived as a means to hide their identity when committing crimes such as street theft and assault.
10 'Looking after oneself' being equated with being able to fight and win.

Chapter 4

Method

Research design methodologies

My research approach is based on strategies which include participatory action research and feminist standpoint theory, whilst also drawing on life history, literacy studies and ethnographic approaches to exploring social practices. I am politically driven in my initiation of this study and in the choices I make regarding research methods. To offer an overview of why I have chosen them it is worth presenting a brief discussion about wider approaches and how they sit in relation to claims of knowledge.

Participatory action research (PAR)

PAR has emerged in recent years as an approach which strives to be liberating and not controlling (see Habermas 1974) for social transformation, and 'consciousness raising' (see Freire 1996) among the underprivileged and minorities, where an ever-growing underclass is accepted as the norm. This 'underclass' refers to those parts of society which are cut off from the mainstream working class and left behind (see Clarke 2002); the word is a label of stigma given by society and amplified by the media (see Beresford et al. 2002). This approach was particularly important as the research group identify themselves as 'underclass', 'stigmatised', 'left behind' and 'caught in a stinkin' trap of despair'. PAR, with its alignment to social action, enlightenment (see Habermas 1974: 113) emancipation (see Kemmis and Wilkinson, 1998), adult education intervention, development and change within communities and groups (see Carr and Kemmis 1986; Kemmis 2001) therefore fitted my purpose.

A drive to address the above is to provide the environment and tools to facilitate learners to celebrate *their* ways of knowing, rather than the dominant models of what is considered 'legitimate' knowledge (Barton and Hamilton 1998). There is recognition of the vernacular literacies and other embodied knowledge that learners (and the teacher) bring into the classroom. In engaging in collaborative research, researchers may help participants acquire the critical tools to transform their own lives. Indeed, praxis involves a dedication to challenging the status quo and helping people from marginalised communities understand their oppression, for example by recognising the structural inequalities of class, gender and ethnicity. My study is therefore strongly linked to praxis and adopts a critical perspective (see Carr and Kemmis 1986; Mezirow 2000; Duckworth and Taylor 2008).

PAR challenges the positivistic form of enquiry in its political approach and establishes a relationship between researcher and participant (Reason and Bradbury 2001). It does this by facilitating the research group taking 'ownership' of the whole process from commencement to conclusion and sustaining an effective dialogue between researcher and respondent.

Although I developed strong relationships with the respondents, I still initially had concerns relating to the power of participatory research and its deemed lack of impact on the community it studies. I sometimes felt at a loss listening to their words. They wanted solutions, answers from me that I couldn't offer. Tracy describing how:

> I want to help me kids, make 'em go to school and get me self right but it's like as soon as I think I'm moving forward something knocks me back, a probation worker at the door, a bill, just summat that makes me think what's the point. It's like me feet can't move but talking to you my mind's moving and I can see where I want to go, but the trick is getting there, Maybe I'll wake up and it'll be clearer that's what I think anyway. What do you think?
>
> (Tracy, speaking in 2004)

Kelly et al. (1994) argue that the power of small scale participatory research is minimal (Kelly et al. 1994: 37), and I believe that she has a point. My six-year longitudinal study allowed me, however, to follow the learners' changing positioning across the fields of their lives and explore how literacy classes can influence their habitus and positions in the field. For example, Tracy began to use writing and painting as a means to make sense of the confusion in her life. She also became involved in community writing to inspire and motivate others who had experienced bullying (Dolan 2008).

> It's been good for me this writing and sharing it. It's like before I thought that no one really bothered about what I'd been through. Now I can share what's happened and also perhaps help someone else who's going through the same. Knowing this and getting involved in the community groups is a good feeling, it makes me feel better about myself – makes life less complicated somehow. It's like I'm part of summat that has meaning so I do to.
>
> (Tracy, speaking in 2005)

Kelly fails to recognise that 'empowering people in communities is integral to the process of mobilisation' (see Dominelli 2006: 45). In adopting an egalitarian epistemology (see Coare and Johnston 2004; Dillabough and Arnot 2001), the research aimed at providing a critical space where the learners and the researcher could reflect and move towards a deepened consciousness in which they recognise that they are products of history. As such they can challenge the conditions of oppression (see Freire 2004), changing the way they interpret their own experience (McGee 2002). This in turn may lead to transformation, specifically in the realm of learning as transformation (see Mezirow 2000).

As such, the study drew on the tradition of community education[1] and a feminist dimension. It sought to provide the participants with the tools to raise their awareness of how their experiences were shaped by structural inequality and through realisation, reflection and change they were able to shift the accountability of their traumatised narratives away from the pathologised self (for example, see Figures 3.1a and b).

PAR and Freire

PAR builds on critical pedagogy put forward by Freire as a response to traditional, formal models of education in which the teacher takes the power and imparts information to the students, who are passive, empty vessels, waiting to be filled. This model fails to recognise the powerful knowledge learners bring into the classroom with them, such as socially situated knowledge (see Barton and Hamilton 2008). In this vein the main goal of PAR, as identified previously, is for both researcher/practitioner and participant to work in egalitarian ways and develop effective dialogue and critical consciousness and, in the case of this study, a critical curriculum which facilitates this. It is very important that the participants (learners) are involved in the research (and curriculum design) process, the goal of PAR being democratic, participatory, giving a voice to the oppressed.

It is worth drawing on Weiler's (1991) feminist critique of Freire, which recognises the strengths of his work whilst also addressing areas which would benefit from being developed. One such area is to suggest a move away from his universal claims, instead placing each study in its own political, economic and historical context. I have attempted to do this by providing an overview of Oldham's historical landscape (Duckworth 2012). In an age of neo-liberalism and globalisation, the Freirian concept, based on the premise that by overcoming oppression people will move towards true humanity, is problematic. Indeed, transformation and empowerment of the learners/teacher may be individually focused rather than community bound, leading to the oppressed becoming the oppressors and a failure to engage in social justice and liberation.

Whilst realising areas of Freirian concepts may need developing for this study, I was also very much aware that education was a setting where people acquire an awareness of the structural inequality and their struggle under a dominant ideological system (Freire 2004). This awareness provided the opportunity to challenge hegemony and engage in an 'approach to social change which puts knowledge back into the hands of the people' (Heaney cited in Byrne 2005: 179).

The PAR facilitated the development and delivery of a critical curriculum. Critical educators/researchers reflect a critical pedagogy, providing a curriculum which is culturally relevant, learner driven and socially empowering (Freire 1993;

Barton et al. 2007). Dialogic communication between teachers and learners was the key to actively involving learners in their own education; this active participation included the co-creation of the curriculum whereby learners' needs, motivations and interests were the driving factors (see McNamara 2007; Duckworth 2008a; Thomas et al. 2012). Assessment was measured by each learner's own goals and aspirations, and the distance they have travelled in relation to their learning journey. Offering an egalitarian model takes into consideration the cultural, psychological and educational factors related to the learner. This values their history, present and future narrative, rather than fitting all learners into one learning narrative and prescriptive framework.

Insider and outsider position

Being positioned as an 'insider' is the lynchpin of action research as is its democratic ethos (see Kemmis 1993; Cohen et al. 2007) and emancipatory nature (Zuber-Skerritt 1996). At the beginning of the study, I was situated as an outsider in relation to my workplace and the college's institutional ethos of a more remedial take on staff development, which contrasted with carrying out PAR (staff are seen as the receivers of knowledge rather than the generators). In relation to the participants, however, I was positioned as an 'insider' in the sense of my working class history, my role as research practitioner and the participatory and collaborative nature of the ethnographic

This position challenged positivistic approaches to knowledge which suppose that those with distanced and 'objective' views of practice (for example, researchers from the academy) can best understand and steer practitioners who are seen as too close to practice to embrace an accurate perception of it (Harding 1991). I would argue that this moves to a hegemonic understanding of knowledge where as a practitioner, I cannot begin to take ownership of and understand my own practice. Therefore, I must seek 'experts' to make it clear it to me and create knowledge. This is very much a position where the institution takes control and I am positioned as passive and disempowered – not a maker of knowledge, but as latter identified a receiver. Becoming a researcher practitioner and the impact of this, in strengthening me as a critical educator, has helped me to challenge this barrier. Indeed, I would argue that unless I can critically engage in examining my own practice, I cannot critically examine others' claims to knowledge.

Zuber-Skerritt (1982) claims action research as 'critical collaborative inquiry by reflective practitioners who are accountable in making the results of their inquiry public, self-evaluative in their practice, and engaged in participative problem solving and continuing professional development.' In relation to this account, action research is critical because practitioners not only seek the means to develop their practice within the limitations of the context they are addressing, but are also change agents of those limitations, and importantly of themselves. Indeed, there is recognition of the value of the research practitioner and the emancipatory nature of action research (Zuber-Skerritt, 1996).

As such the dialogical relationships between my teaching, research and learners led to continual changes in all three. This change and praxis flowed between the researcher/practitioner and learner as identified and described in Figure 4.1.

For many empiricist researchers, despite being removed from the classroom setting, defining the 'best practices' for teachers has been a priority. I was able to take ownership of this alongside the learners and, working together in an egalitarian way, to engage in negotiations and develop solutions (see McNiff and Whitehead 2007). Developing my classroom practice was an integral part of my research. Moreover, participatory research and action offers an ideal model for me as a literacy practitioner to look for ways to develop my practice as a literacy teacher and work towards effective, collaborative ways to build a curriculum which meets the needs of the learners rather than my own assumptions of what a curriculum should be. The acquisition of literacy skills is strongly bonded to the creation of knowledge, and by developing a pedagogy which develops these skills, learners can reveal stories of their lives, and offer knowledge of marginalised groups that have historically been silenced.

Feminist standpoint theory

In seeking to break the ties of masculine domination perpetuated within androcentric epistemologies, there was a conscious move away from the positivist approach (see Carr and Kemmis 1986: 158) that was deemed by feminists as offering a distorted world picture; this study instead looks towards building and sustaining alternative frameworks which challenge the focus on the public domain which

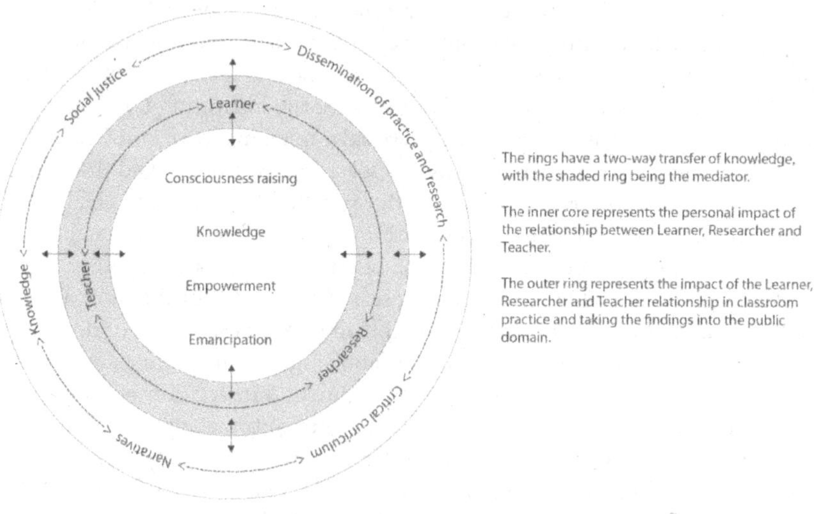

Figure 4.1 Personal and public impact of PAR

causes many women's voices to be unheard and the male perspective viewed as 'universal' (Cohen et al. 2007). Feminist methods therefore fit my purpose.

Standpoint Feminism's strength lies in the recognition that the 'feminist struggle can begin wherever an individual woman is; we create a movement that focuses on our collective experience, a movement that is continually mass-based' (see Hooks 1994: 29). Inequality is addressed at a collective structural level, the struggle challenging what is considered the normative culture grounded in ontological assumptions that pathologise gender and class (see Skeggs 1997/2002). Seeking to explore and challenge these negative stereotypes of women's and working class experiences (see Walkerdine et al. 2001; Skeggs 2002), it is feminism as a praxis not simply about women sharing a 'gender in common, but on a common agenda – the liberation of women' (see Kelly et al. 1994: 28).

Juxtaposed to the collective experience, there is a deep awareness that 'women's oppressions are complexly varied and need equally complex means of analysing and understanding them' (see Stanley and Wise 1993: 2). As such, the research group's individual experience and narratives are a vital place to commence; their experiences are placed in context of their lives. As pointed out by Maguire (2001: 65):

> Feminist action research seeks to connect the articulated, contextualized personal with the often hidden or invisible structural and social institutions that define and shape our lives. How do things work? How do we contribute to the workings? How can we collectively change them?

Ethnography

I chose ethnography as the method by which to explore learners' life experiences because it offered me the opportunity to provide 'thick descriptions' (see Lincoln and Guba 1985; Denzin 1989) and has the potential to provide a 'space for the articulations and experiences of the marginalised' (Schostak 2006: 23). Barton and Hamilton (1998) also show how ethnography has the power to address itself to real people's lives, taking a holistic approach, aiming at whole phenomena. A multiplicity of research techniques can be used to collect rich data which reflects the multidimensionality of the interviewees' experiences.

Its strength also lies in allowing the researcher to position themselves as an 'insider', a position that Walkerdine et al. (2001) with her working class history so clearly identifies in theory but is unable to fully explore within the limitation of her approach. One almost feels that the theoretical make-up in Walkerdine et al.'s study outweighs the women's lives. The result is that it lacks deep layers which lend themselves to greater validity of the women's stories.

The strength of ethnography lies in the close proximity between researcher and respondents. It offers an approach at the micro level providing insights into the impact of poverty on the learners' lives in a way macro analyses cannot. It enables researchers to observe, document and monitor their own impact on the situation they are researching. As a female researcher, this allows for the inclusion of women's perspectives (see Smith 1974) as well as men's. This is crucial strategy for illumination and validation of data (Mercer 1995: 65).

Reflexivity and the position of the researcher

To gain these insights, access was vital. As I was already a member of the community this was not a barrier. 'When researchers are already members of the settings they choose to study, entrée is unproblematic, they are already there. What may become problematic is not entrée and finding a place but rather 'keeping' their place or negotiating a new one' (see Warren and Hackney 2000: 12).

There was and remains an awareness of a dichotomy between feeling simultaneously both the 'same' and 'different'. As identified by Back (1993) in his choice of doctoral research which closely related to his experience (see Warren and Hackney 2000: 13) his ethnographic study took place in the area where he grew up and he used his working class origins 'as a way of gaining credit for this research and thus fastidiously dissolving the division between self and other' (Warren and Hackney 2000: 13). The fact remained however that Back was no longer the adolescent or a participant in the commentaries in the study. This recognition of one's changing position is vital to positioning oneself in relation to the study and offering validity to the research process. The recognition of my changing position and how this was managed within my own research was fully followed up in the study.

The retelling of the participants' narratives wasn't without difficulties. I was shifted from the position of privileged arbiter to being a socialised mediator. To offer validity to the narratives, it was important to include my own life history and writing self into the knowledge (Stanley and Wise 1993). The difficulty for me was feeling at times impotent as I watched respondents live lives of deprivation, poverty and struggle. This was set uneasily against the respondents who, like myself, had shifted their position; they moved through the education system and were offered new jobs and opportunities. I was left with feelings of guilt and hurt for those participants who called themselves 'stuck in the muck'.

In writing up the narratives of the respondents there is an awareness of the narratives' reconstruction through the lens of my enquiry where 'a moment comes after the talk has been inscribed as text and become data, when it must be worked up as sociology' (Smith 1989: 35). It was therefore vital that I was reflexive and kept myself in the text, which also included my inner dialogue about my changing positioning. Indeed, the inclusion of my own changing position in the research juxtaposed with that of the other respondents, allows the reader an insight into how the narratives were formed and a recognition that the stories told, sometimes of pain, are separate stories, even if they are linked and allow us to make connections (see Ahmed 2000, 2004).

Sharing life stories gives rise to ethical consideration. Although all the learners had informed consent and collaborated in making sense of the findings at every stage, I was aware that I did not want to misinterpret, do a disservice or take ownership of their narratives. Therefore, throughout the research, although the stories have been shared and I include their voices in this study with my name as the author of the study, they have authored their stories for populist audiences (For example, McNamara 2008) and the academy. A number of the learners chose not to be anonymised for the activities which have resulted from the research (for example, see McNamara 2007), demonstrating that – as British Educational Research Association (2004) revised ethical guidelines concede – 'researchers must also recognize participants' rights to be identified with any publication of their original work or other inputs, if they so wish'.

Informal interviews also took place on social nights out. The group shared their experiences and celebrated success. Although, it wasn't always so straightforward, as one learner expressed how she felt a failure as she watched others progress onto university. However, when the learner expressed the obstacles they had faced on entering Higher Education, and the obstacles they continue to fight against, the learners grew closer in acknowledgement of the barriers they all faced in post-compulsory education and really spurred each other on. This was particularly evident in the stories the women told each other, many involving the physical and psychological abuse they had regularly encountered from fathers, brothers, uncles, partners, sons and strangers. As identified by (Dominelli 2006: 109) this was a key concern and one which had been an obstacle in their progress.

Over the course of the study, the interviewees drew my attention to mutually recognised geographical locations. I was able to refer to these places from my own history and this bound us in a sense of place, not just related to the here and now, but the historical. This connection in time and place allowed me a real insider's position.

A number of the learners decided that they preferred meeting in more informal settings and so these areas became the meeting ground for our interviews. I never tape recorded these meetings, but would bring along a brief questionnaire, my journal and camera. Surrounded by woodlands or in a shopping area, the meeting felt very relaxed and learners always stressed to me how they had enjoyed them.

I was aware that there may be discrepancies between interviewing male and female learners (Finch 1984). Women tend to be more enthusiastic about talking to a female researcher, under the impression they share social experience with them related to gender, whilst men may hold back (Finch 1984). In this study, however, the men were also enthusiastic. This may have been because, as educator and teacher – outside the sphere of domesticity – I was not viewed in a gendered way. I was viewed as a teacher, not a mother, wife, girlfriend, sister or wife.

The male learners made no request to meet me alone outside college, however, apart from on the informal research nights out and at their workplace where there were others around. I would have felt more uncomfortable meeting a man in a location that had sentimental meaning for him and I'm sure the feeling would have been mutual. A number of the women had voiced how they were single and sometimes felt lonely; I was able to empathise, and meeting them on a one-to-one resulted in a greater unity. Although approachable, I did not want to be over friendly with the single and lonely men as this could have sent out the wrong signals. The men did, however, open up to me and a rapport developed. Whether this rapport would have been stronger with a male researcher remains to be seen.

As an 'insider' in many ways, the impact of my positioning on data analysis will be a major consideration (Miles and Huberman 1984). By virtue of the transparency of my changing role and positioning, I hope to increase the validity of the findings. Importantly all the data findings were shared with the group. Their own thoughts and analysis were incorporated into the findings and writing up of all aspects of the research.

Documents as sources of data

I accessed and used, by consent, creative writing, art work, greeting cards, family trees and so on. History archives, statistical and economic records and media reports were also incorporated into the collection framework. A quantity of the information was collected from visits to the library and local history centre. Where possible I collected the learners' screening and diagnostic results, individual learning plans, Educational Support Unit reports showing mental health issues, learning difficulties (for example, dyslexia) and course work. As a result of the undertaking of this research, papers, articles and presentations at conference have been produced. This production has also been utilised.

Incidental data

As expected, incidental data has been encountered in everyday situations, such as shopping, and also when it was least expected and in compromising situations. The situation occurred when visiting Oldham Hospital's psychiatric unit to visit a family member who had recently been sectioned with a severe schizophrenic attack; I walked through the lounge door but instead of being greeted by my family member, the familiar face of one of the research group met me. Meeting Melanie in a context that I would have otherwise avoided has strengthened our relationship and allowed me a deeper insight into how bi-polar disorder has an impact on her life and her learning. She asked me to come and see her again, which I did. She also telephoned me to say how bored she was in hospital. It was evident that visits were really important to her. One visit found she was over-medicated to the point of sleeping the day away. It was very sad to see someone normally so vibrant and full of life dosed up to the extent that she could hardly move. On leaving hospital, she contacted me about returning to college. I passed her details onto a tutor and she progressed to a Level One end test in literacy. Extremely creative and a lover of nature, when I meet with her now, it's always in aesthetic surroundings that inspire rather than depress. Together with studying Reiki she is also involved in networks to support other adults with mental health issues. As for my relative, on that first visit I said goodbye to the learner and discreetly made my way to my relative's room minus a bar of chocolate which was given to Melanie.

On the way home from work I occasionally saw some of the other learners. After not seeing her for over 12 months, I saw Stella. She told me she was back working in a care home and gave me her new telephone number. We met subsequently and it gave me the opportunity to record her progress as well as give her the number of Adult Community Services, where she would like to continue literacy classes as well as her NVQ in Care. She has consequently passed her Level Two and Level Three and is working as a care assistant.

Conclusion

By using PAR and moving towards a form of research that is grassroots oriented, the aim has been to use research tools which can, together with the research group, enable us to explore our lives and the issues perceived by them (and me) that have and continue to directly affect our lives.

The appeal of PAR is that in claiming to 'empower', it has the potential to address the profound inequalities in power between the participants and the researcher. Indeed, as well as the knowledge gained in the form of outcomes and findings that we will explore next, there are additional benefits gained from the process of the research, such as the relationships formed. This has been so much so that I consider myself to be a friend of the research group and, for a few, a good friend. These friendships have enriched our lives, enriched me as person and are an important impact of the research.

Note

1 Community Education is based on the Freirian principles of *conscientisation* and *praxis* (for further elaboration, read Freire 1996, 2004).

Chapter 5

School as a site for violence and trauma

Section I

Introduction

This chapter addresses the question of how the learners are positioned in the field of schooling, and looks at how this is influenced by and changes in relation to the flow – or lack of flow – of capitals. Further to this, it will explore how the learners navigate through these flows and the impact this has on their constraints, conformity, resistance, potential for disempowerment and empowerment. For example, for some learners, there was resistance to the dominant expectations of being at school (that is, attendance) and instead they fell into the habit of 'wagging school' to escape being pathologised. I will explore how schooling can act as a constraint that prevents learners from achieving their potential because they do not have those capitals that are deemed legitimate or valuable by those – that is, teachers and peers – with symbolic power (for example, see Figures 3.1b and 5.1). I will explore how schooling is a site for symbolic, embodied and physical violence and how the learners struggle against this by resisting or conforming. The learners' stories demonstrate the impact of the unequal distribution of cultural, economic and linguistic capital and the impact of this on their schooling and subsequent trajectories.

This chapter answers the research questions premised on how the learners are positioned in the field of education.

When the respondents were asked about their experience of school, a recurrent theme and struggle for them was fighting against feelings of worthlessness and a lack of respectability (Skeggs 1997) due to being labelled (see Goffman 1970) and bullied by teachers and peers for being poor (for example see Figures 3.1, 3.3), having undiagnosed dyslexia and struggling at school with school work. I will show the symbolic and physical violence carried out by teachers and peers. Examples of this are the link between symbolic violence and the symbolic capital of clothing; symbolic violence enacted by teachers ignoring the respondents; physical violence and dyslexia; and school and identities. Further to this, I will explore how the respondents resisted and conformed to symbolic violence.

Most noteworthy aspects of the narratives

What was striking to me was that although the learners' experiences of school span from a few years since they left school to over five decades back, each of their narratives was recounted with a vivid emotional engagement. Small details, such as the weather, what they were wearing, the words used against them by teachers and peers, and how they felt were remembered with clarity. Their experiences of schooling had clearly left a deep footprint on the learners' lives. The participatory nature of the research aimed to empower the learners by the sharing and validating of their narratives. As the respondents and I read our words together, it provided us with a pathway to try and make sense of what had happened to us and why.

Symbolic violence by the teachers

The participants experienced the constraining factor of being labelled negatively by their school teachers for being poor; struggling with their school work and their habitus being out of sync with the school (see Figure 3.1b). Respect (especially for teachers) is tied into public legitimacy, which demands authority for those in a position as legitimate holders of power. Teachers are deemed to have 'legitimate knowledge' to pass on to the children (who do not in many cases have the 'right' knowledge, for example, vernacular literacies rather than dominant literacies). This legitimacy is strongly linked to what and whose knowledge is important and is thus tied to symbolic power. The exploitation of this symbolic power is explored in the labelling carried out on the learners in the study by school teachers. Fourteen out of the 16 participants in this study described how they were labelled (see Goffman 1969, 1970, 1971; Becker 1973) and pathologised (see Steedman 1988) by the teachers. Labels such as 'thick' 'stupid', 'rough', 'scruffy' and 'no-hopers' were used. Only one female participant Sally described a different experience. Her experience of school was not constraining, but empowering:

> I came from a nice house and got along well with the teachers.
>
> (Sally, speaking in 2004)

Across the fields of education and family she did not experience bullying. She was also the only participant who said she could relate to school and left school with GCSEs, progressing into college to train as a nursery nurse. At the time of the initial interviews she was also one of the youngest participants and apart from one other female, Stella, in her 50s, was the only other female to be married. She was also the only student living in private property, again apart from Stella who was buying the council house she had lived in for many years. It may be considered that Sally was empowered by having legitimate capital; she came from a stable home and both her parents worked, thus bringing home economic capital, as well as giving Sally emotional support (emotional capital). Sally's habitus was in sync with the institution of schooling and she instinctively knew how to play the game (see Figure 3.1 a). She was aware of the 'field' and, although she described herself as working class, unlike 13 of the other participants her parents attended the parents' evenings and participated in her learning journey. In her use of language when describing her learning journey, initially she was the only participant to voice how she was 'empowered', which was a term not used by any of the others until the third year of this study when it became part of the dialogue of Joanne, Tracy and Stella when describing the impact of education on their lives. Stella describes how:

> getting an education and doin' my NVQ in health has given me other options, not just cleaning, I can care for the elderly. 'avin' these choices is empowering, it makes me feel good.

Sally also described how she felt 'valued' at school and 'fitted in':

> I was always in a smart uniform, me mam and dad made sure it was the best. I didn't want to be a no-mark in say scruffy shoes. What I wore was important; it made me stand out as being from a family who cared.

Using economic capital Sally's parents bought in the cultural capital (the means to facilitate her to gain qualifications) to support her through her schooling. They paid a tutor to help her with school work. Sally describes how 'this helped me to keep up, even though I really struggled. Without it I'd have fallen behind and probably felt like one of the thickies.'

For Sally, school was a place of empowerment, where she was equipped with the cultural capital to progress to college and train to be a nursery nurse. She also had high self esteem and confidence in her ability. Interestingly though, she only considered going to university when she had her vocational qualification and had worked in the caring industry. Clearly, even with the support mechanisms in place, going to university was not a transition that could be taken for granted (Metcalfe 1997). Sally offers an insight into how having the right economic capital to wear the right clothes and have a home tutor can be empowering and make schooling a happier and more fulfilling place to attend. Sally's parents did not, however, have the cultural capital in the form of qualifications, above Level Three, to guide Sally towards higher education or have aspirations for her to attend university. None of her family had been to university and this was never considered. Here, we can see that although Sally had aspirations to be a nursery nurse, these aspirations were limited to further education courses rather than higher education. Clearly, Sally experiences symbolic violence in that the idea of 'choice' and going to university was not an option, or importantly ever even considered.

The constraints of lacking economic capital

The narratives of the other participants were similar to Sally's in that the idea of going to university was not considered as an option. Indeed, the notion of 'choice', or 'lack of choice' as identified by Reay et al. (2005) is far removed from these learners, where higher education does not enter their psyche. They differed from Sally in that 14 of the other families were poor and lacked the economic capital to buy in extra tuition or the cultural capital to help the learners with their school work. This meant that they struggled without getting any outside help or support. This was a real constraint as six of the learners' parents were illiterate and unable to help them with any form of school work. Lacking economic capital, which is the main principle of domination in a capitalist society, had an impact on their needs being met. As such, the other learners did not feel a part of the the field of education as they were unable to keep up with the school work; due to the fear of being further pathologised a number of learners did not ask for help. It was not as simple as that, however, as others who did want help were ignored when they asked for it. For them, rather than continuing to resist the label of being 'thick' by asking for help to improve, their resistance shifted to conforming in class, by being silent and thus being further sidelined and ignored by teachers. They became compliant in the teachers symbolic violence of ignoring them, by adopting the same behavior as the teacher and not engaging with the teacher or the lessons. The learners refused to become part of more humiliation when they reached the point of realisation that their progress/or lack of it did not matter.

Being poor and not being able to get the help they needed to move forward in their school work can be equated with symbolic and physical violence (for example see Figures 3.3 and 5.2). Teachers are positioned to legitimate the cultural and social capital exhibited by their learners through their acceptance of certain forms of appearances and behaviour. The impact of class inequalities and the insurmountable obstacles which being poor represent had a profound effect on the learners' commitment to and achievement at school. Class disdain, indeed sometimes hatred, in regard to the learners' appearance was marked out by the clothes they wore. These clothes carried markers of being poor and lacking symbolic capital and thus became symbolic of their perceived lack of worth and of their being considered to be academic failures. The learners were forced to leave behind ideas of academic success and face the inevitability of not achieving. The landscape of their lives was shaped by their families' lack of economic capital and how this was viewed by those with the legitimate capital to judge and pathologise them.

The symbolic capital of housing and symbolic violence

As discussed in Chapter 1 the study took place in Oldham. This is an area of deprivation and large housing estates. Apart from two learners, the rest lived on the council estates around the borough of Oldham. The areas participants live in are not neutral: they hold or lack symbolic power, and the streets hold capitals which may be deemed as legitimate or illegitimate depending on how one is positioned in the field. Like the locations where people live, names, including family names, which arise from estates, are also not neutral. Names have or lack symbolic power. It should be noted that the symbolic power that areas and names have depend on the field and the lens (whether legitimate or illegitimate) from which they are viewed, see Figure 5.1 below.

Joanne and Stella were labelled by the teachers because of the connotations related to their family name and the area in which they lived. Within the field of school, the teachers had the symbolic power to pathologise and carry out symbolic violence. For Joanne, coming from a big family and not ''aving nowt to buy new clothes', meant she was viewed as a 'scruff' and 'pushed to one side.'

> If you come from big families you were just pushed to the side. I remember being really good at badminton, but 'cos I was a McNamara, come from a big family I couldn't go on the team. Anyhow – we could do what we want

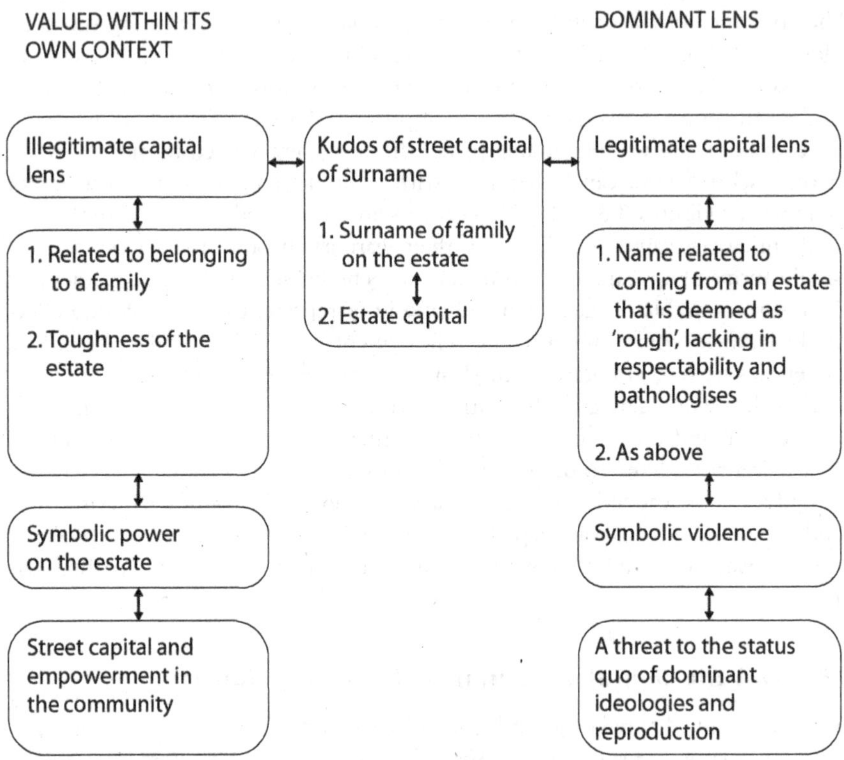

Figure 5.1 Illegitimate and legitimate lens of capitals

> the teachers weren't interested in the end . . . It was 'cos we were the ones who stood out 'cos of our clothes. Yer know they're looking down on yer 'cos yer wearin' hand-me-downs. Yer feel dirty somehow, daft really 'cos all our clothes has been washed, they were old that's all. Yer can't wash the tattiness out I suppose.
>
> (Joanne, speaking in 2004)

Stella also spoke of feeling like an outsider because of where she lived, and remembers the teachers having no time for kids from the estate:

> They'd 'ave yer address in the mark book, sometimes they'd call out yer name and where yer lived. From Holts Estate, I'll 'ave to keep me eye on you the teacher'd say. Yer knew then that you were being told yer were bad, the estate had, still has a rotten reputation. I wished they just had me name in that register book and not me address, perhaps then they'd 'ave just thought it's a nice girl, like.
>
> At the end I got to the stage in seniors where I was that unhappy with being bullied and if I reacted bad because I wasn't a well dressed child at school because I was brought up in a big family I used to be looked down on. Obviously I wasn't taking on board what was happening in the class. I was a scruffy child they used to think I was a bother causer which I never was if people hit me I hit them back.
>
> (Stella, speaking in 2004)

The impact of being devalued and being labelled negatively because of where they lived left learners resisting this symbolic violence. Emily spoke of how she hid her true emotions and pretended she did not care. Her last four words ''cos I could yer know' seem to indicate that she is fighting back at the system where she feels excluded.

> We didn't have much and everyone knew it. You felt like you were singled out, you'd be the one the teachers set about; it was like you shouldn't 'ave been there. I guess that's why I messed around trying to pretend I couldn't care less, 'cos I could yer know.
>
> (Emily, speaking in 2004)

Symbolic violence and the symbolic capital of clothing

The clothes the learners wore had high symbolic capital in the study (for example, see Figures 3.3 and 5.3). The learners were very aware of how their appearance was viewed by others. The way they reacted to the close scrutiny of their appearance by those in a position of symbolic power (such as teachers and peers who could afford to buy designer clothes, which are associated with taste and distinction) may have differed, but for the respondents it contributed to shaping their experience of school. A form of symbolic violence is that schools have compulsory uniform policies. School uniform may be thought of as giving learners equal symbolic capital, as it aims to clone learners in one identity, that of the institution. Rather than uniforms being a means to place everyone on a similar footing, however, designer badges and labels created a divide. The term 'uniform' is apposite, in that it does not simply refer to the regulated clothing that many schools require pupils to wear, but also to the uniformity of expression which pupils impose within their own friendship groups. This can have an impact on learners who do not have a uniform that's 'smart' and 'trendy'. In order to wear the correct uniform, economic capital is needed to buy it. Therefore being poor and not being able to do this was evident in the way the uniform was worn. The uniform had symbolic power to reflect the economic capital of the wearer's family, and their history. Further to this, the uniform may also symbolise the value the learner's family place on schooling; those with a smart uniform reflect a value placed on learning, those who do not, reflect this lack of valuing. Again, the learner becomes the recipient of symbolic violence which is not only aimed at them but at their family, and what they represent is a lack of economic and cultural capital and respect for education. Clearly, capitals and the influence they have on symbolic power do not stand alone; they accumulate in deprivations as well as power, each having an impact on the other. Below, Figure 5.2 illustrates the impact of the cycle of dominance: the individual is positioned as virtuous and held in esteem because they have the legitimate capitals to buy and wear the *right* clothes – these symbolise respectability and are held in esteem; counter to this is the cycle of symbolic and physical violence, whereby the

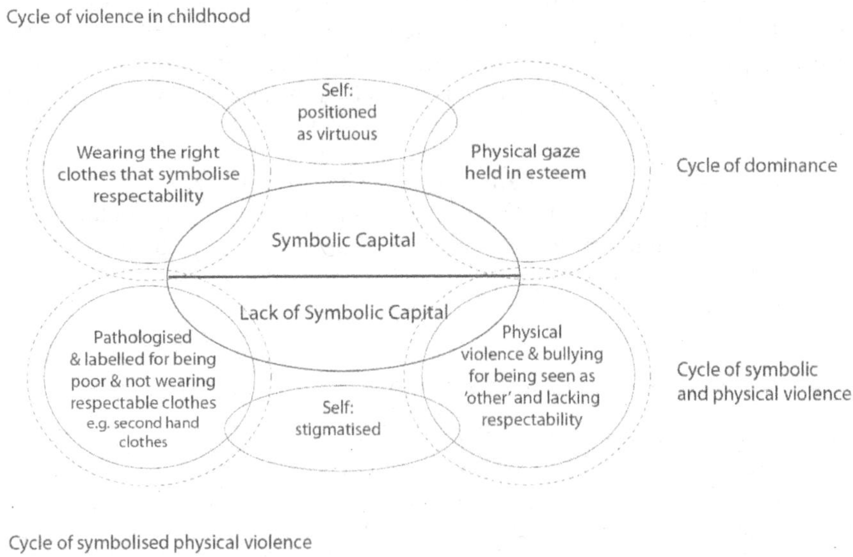

Figure 5.2 **The accumulation of symbolic domination and symbolic and physical violence**

person does not have the right capitals and is stigmatised because they are deemed not to be wearing clothes that are considered *respectable.*

Learners who did not have the 'right' uniform struggled because of the symbolic violence conferred on them by those in a position to exercise the process of legitimation. They were stigmatised (see Goffman 1969, 1970, 1971) and not deemed to have respectability. This process of legitimation is typically carried out by teachers but was also carried by peers. Rachel was very aware she was being judged on her appearance, though she resisted the labelling and the symbolic violence of this. Her way of hiding being poor was to keep her head up and walk straight. It was behind closed doors that the emotional energy put into presenting this image made her angry and hit out at the situation.

> I'd keep my eyes in front and yer know keep me head up. I didn't want the snobs to think they had one up on me because they wore new clothes. 'Course when I got home I'd fling me clothes on the floor and shout at them, really shout wishing like by magic when I stopped telling them off they'd be new and not the mess they were. 'Course they stayed the same and after a while I stopped shouting and I suppose me head stopped being held so high. Even now I feel self conscious like people are looking and pointing 'cos I'm a scruff. Course I'm not I keep all me clothes nice, look after 'em I do.
>
> (Rachel, speaking in 2005)

The symbolic violence crossed cultural fields. Shammy, a British Asian, raised issues of wearing traditional clothes that didn't fit in with what the teachers expected. He described how these seemed to mark him as being poor; however, he was keen to emphasise that they were far from cheap and in fact they were more expensive than Western outfits.

> At juniors we'd wear our clothes from 'ome. Mine were traditional like, what all the boys in our family wore, but not like the white kids. My trousers were white and baggy and my tops long. You'd get some teachers eyeing yer up like yer were in fancy dress, made me feel really uncomfortable. I'd tell 'em at home, ask if I could get clothes like the white kids, but me mum would tell me how mine were better, more expensive, more respectable. It didn't feel like that though. One teacher told me that there's catalogues to buy proper clothes and I should tell me mum about them, yer don't even 'ave to pay it all at once she said. When I went home and told me mum, she made sure that I took the receipt in from the material shop me mum went to, course I never shown it to the teacher. I didn't want to look stupid or anything.
>
> (Shammy, speaking in 2004)

The label of being poor was not neutral. Poor was equated with being deviant; this led to being an outcast and marginalised by the dominant group (see Becker 1963). This had an impact on how the learners viewed themselves:

Sheila:	I used to get so frustrated.
Interviewer:	Yeah.
Sheila:	Because I couldn't help the way I were . . . I couldn't help that my mother couldn't buy the fashionable clothes . . . I couldn't help being dyslexic, but I didn't know that I was dyslexic at the time.
Interviewer:	Yeah.
Sheila:	I just knew that I were thick, and that's how I put myself down as and even being embarrassed in front of your children, not being able to help them, but I always made them stand up for themselves at school, because I wouldn't let anyone put me down at school . . .

Symbolic violence and being ignored by teachers

Another constraint hindering achievement, success and enjoyment at school was the symbolic violence the learners experienced when they were ignored by the teachers. Stella describes how being poor and struggling with her work lead to the teachers ignoring her.

> I'm a person who has always stood up for myself so I used to rebel back and I used to end up getting myself in more trouble because I'd hit them (peers) back you see.

Later at secondary school she describes how:

> It got to the stage in the seniors where I just stopped going to school 'cos I were that unhappy with school, and not one teacher took me to one side and tried to help me, I think what happened were they were that they had to get the rest of the pupils in the class through to the next year that you were sat in on the outskirts of the classroom you might as well have not been there. And that's how I were made to feel at school. Not one teacher thought oh that girl there must be something wrong with that girl well do we'll sort a test. The only time I got attention at school off a teacher I think was to have me arm tied down, to see if I could write better with me right hand, 'cos years ago they used to think if you were left handed there was something wrong with you.

Joanne also recalls:

> When I knew they'd be no help, just a tellin' off I stopped asking. Yer just mess about don't yer, hoping someone will say pack it in and get yer back working, sort yer out. They couldn't be arsed yer. If I could go back now I'd make them teachers come and teach me, rather than just leavin' us to do what we liked.

Melanie described how:

> I was shoved to the back of the class and sort of ignored. Yeah well because I was sort of not clever at school I used to get called names like thick, stupid and they would shove against the wall those who weren't clever –
>
> I was looking forward to science in the senior school but the class that I was in was really disruptive and they nearly set fire to the science labs so we were barred from doing science experiments. So we were just copying out of books. We never learnt nothing in science, so that pee'd me off really. Because I didn't learn anythin' I lost interest. We weren't given time.

Being ignored by teachers did not only relate to the activities of teaching and learning in class. It was also present when the teachers were complicit in the bullying carried out by peers, failing to intervene and stop the bullying. The peers became instruments for the teachers to further pathologise the learners. Below, Rachel describes how the teachers ignored the peer bullying that was aimed at her. Rather than teachers taking action and protecting Rachel from the abuse, it was a prefect who took action.

> Nothing, nothing was done about it. She had her hands round me neck. Teachers were in the playground. But it was the prefects who came and pulled her off me. I always remember that. I hated it.
>
> (Rachel, speaking in 2004)

Physical violence and dyslexia

The symbolic violence was also significant in learners with dyslexia. Labelling by teachers at school was particularly significant in the case of six of the learners – Melanie, Joanne, Stella, Rachel, Martin and Shammy – who all arrived at college with undiagnosed dyslexia. Craig arrived with dyslexia that had been diagnosed in adulthood rather than at school. The violence the learners experienced was not isolated to symbolic or physical violence. Each fed into the other, in a cycle of violence which was fuelled by lack of legitimate capitals (for example see Figures 5.2 and 5.3). In this case the lack of capital was cultural/linguistic capital.

Below, Figure 5.3 illustrates the impact of a lack of linguistic capital and elaborates on the learners' struggling and falling behind at school and their experiences of separate and mutual symbolic and physical violence by the teachers and peers.

Struggling to read and write led to the learners being labelled as thick and experiencing symbolic violence. Stella describes her experience:

> I was quite happy as a child I think until I got to the juniors where spelling and writing everything like, the teachers would look on – err – and spelling I was never good at, me hand writing was terrible I was left handed and one teacher actually tied my left hand to the chair and tried to make me write with

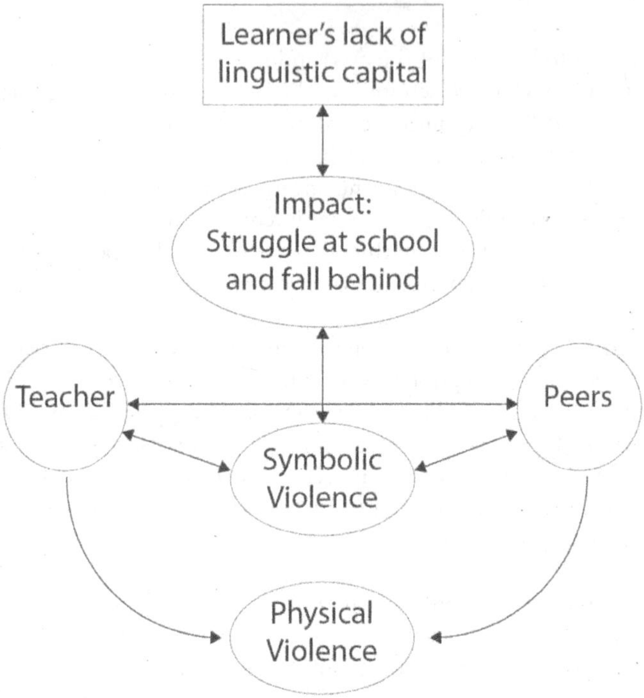

Figure 5.3 Linguistic capital and the cycle of symbolic and physical violence by peers and teachers

> me right hand thinking that he was doing good and but I got that distressed I went home and I was heartbroken, my mother came into school and I won't say what happened because my mother was a big lady and she wasn't impressed and he honestly thought he was doing me good by trying to make me write with me right hand. And – err – I always knew there was something wrong with me because I could never take on board proper what was going on in the class room but I never knew what until I got older I realised that I was dyslexic 'cos I used to think I was thick and I think as you got further up the years into the seniors if you weren't coming on with the rest of the classroom you were sort of shoved to the back of the classroom and oh well they say she doesn't know what she's doing so we'll leave her there. That's what, that's how I think I was labelled as a child because I wasn't taking on board what was coming across in the class room . . .

It was on returning to college that Stella took the screening test for dyslexia. The result which confirmed she was dyslexic was initially received with confusion and anxiety. Stella voiced how she was angry about how she had been treated at school:

> that I was shoved to the back of the classroom and sort of ignored, where I didn't realise that I was dyslexic so I came to college last year and you did them tests for me . . .

My field notes describe how Stella reacted to the results of the screening test:

> Stella caught me before class today. She was very worked up. She had the letter which had been sent to her home confirming she had dyslexia. She explained that she had not showed it to anyone. Is it catching she said, like it was a disease. She seemed really ashamed of having dyslexia and told me she was too embarrassed to say anything to her husband or her family. I spent time with her, explaining it wasn't an illness and going through the many people who had been diagnosed with it, such as Richard Branson, and how now that she had been diagnosed strategies could be put in place to offer her one to one support from the support centre. Stella seemed relieved that something could be done to help her. She starts her one to one classes next week. I'll need to work with the dyslexic tutor to support Stella's development.
>
> (Journal Extract 2004)

The label that had at first confused her was soon transformed into an empowering one. Being diagnosed with dyslexia provided Stella with the knowledge she needed to understand the reasons why she had struggled to read and write at school. Her label became a positive factor:

> Stella seems to be progressing well and is a lot happier doing her work independently. She told me that now she knows she has dyslexia, she doesn't feel thick, it's something she has, rather than that she is lacking in intelligence. She explained how she just wishes that it was discovered earlier then perhaps she could have done something about it, rather than keep brushing it away.
>
> (Journal Extract 2004)

Melanie also felt she was unable to progress at school and spoke of struggling at school and being in the remedial group. She experienced difficulty 'picking up' things like time-tables and spellings. Rather than support and encouragement there was the threat of physical violence and intimidation:

> And there was this like a teacher there that had us reciting timetables and I used to dread that because that because I wasn't very good at remembering what was coming next so I used to dread doing that. I could never finish it off. I never did anything at school that was wrong as such . . . the one time I did get punished was like not being able to spell. I got strapped; she used to slap my legs you know 'cos I couldn't spell. She had you up in a line in class and you had to spell the word out to the class, if you couldn't spell they used to slap your legs.

Rachel also explains how she was shouted at as she struggled with the lessons:

> Being shouted at made it worse, I think if I would have been helped I'd have got on and done it.

Martin's defence against the symbolic violence was to switch off from learning due to the threat of the teachers getting mad with him.

> I'd panic when the teachers got mad at me 'cos I couldn't understand summat. That's when me mind would go into nothing. I'd switch off, try and not hear their shouts. I learnt nowt.

Melanie also experienced the threats of violence:

> In the seniors there used to be quite a strict teacher and erm he used to pass, he wasn't taking us in our classes but every time he passed us on the corridor if we were standing on the wrong side of the corridor he'd threaten to strap us or and once he did strap nearly the whole class for standing on the wrong side of the corridor.

School was clearly a place where fear and intimidation were used as a means of controlling the students in order to make them conform, even if that conforming had nothing to do to learning, and was more to do with being passive. Rather than being unaware of these labels, in a similar vein to the learners in Skeggs' (1997) study they were aware they were being viewed in a negative way. While Skeggs' learners dis-identified with being working class to avoid shame, the learners in this study resisted the labels in other ways. For example, they ignored teachers, wagged school, and pretended they did not care how they were viewed or treated (even if they did). In hiding their true emotions of pain and despair, the habitus presented to the public gaze was different to that of their internal habitus. They resisted being viewed as showing emotions that might have been seen as weak (for example pain or despair) and instead wanted to present a public image that had not been traumatised by the stigma of labeling (see Goffman 1970). This arena of violence, fear and control was also played out among peers as explored in the next section.

Section 2: Peer violence

Violence and trauma from peers

A further constraint for the learners was the sense of shame that resulted from the symbolic and physical violence they experienced from their peers. The impact of being bullied was significant in the accounts of the participants in this the study. Twelve of the 16 participants experienced symbolic, verbal and physical violence from their peers, which resulted in six of the learners feeling isolated and alone. They did not have the social capital or peer networks to support them at these difficult times at school, and there would appear to have been negligence and lack of continuity within the family. Tracy describes how she felt:

> I'd 'ave really liked someone to talk to about the bullying. Who can you talk to it about though when there's no one but bullies about yer. They'd be in gangs. They had each other I was owt on me own.
>
> (Tracy, speaking in 2004)

Rachel describes how she felt:

> It got to the stage where I was happier on me todd. I'd stay in my house, not bothering to go to school or owt. No one can hurt yer then, but yerself.
>
> (Rachel, speaking in 2004)

The symbolic capital of school uniform and bullying by peers

As well as being judged by the teachers for not having the symbolic capital of a new and smart school uniform, the respondents were also judged by their peers (see Figures 3.3 and 5.2). Below, Martin tells of his experience:

Martin: You could tell them that had a bit of money, they has a top make jumper and the rest of the gear. That's what made yer popular at school. If yer didn't wear the right things they'd look down at yer. I hated being called a div.
Interviewer: What's a div?
Martin: Someone who wears old fashioned crap gear that no one else'd wear.

Tracy tells us about her experience of wearing 'education shoes'.

Tracy: I used to love Maths and English, Maths I used to ask for extra homework so people used to call me a swot but I loved learning, but I did let the bullies push me out of school so I just stayed away it made me ill going . . .
Interviewer: Yeah.
Tracy: 'erm I think that's why I'm the way I am now because I just I feel like I've totally missed out because I allowed because I let them bully me so . . .
Interviewer: Why do you feel as though you let them bully you?
Tracy: Because I could have fought back and now I think about the things they used to bully me about they were silly little things but they really hurt at the time you know education shoes and . . .
Interviwer: Education shoes?

Tracy: They used to be brown leather lace-ups, horrible things I used to cry when my mum got them me, but fashion never really bothered me because I used to make my own kind of style up, I used to be a punk so it didn't really bother me at school except for the fact everyone said I looked like a boy, so I think because I didn't have that many friends as well I think I just like reading and, I was in bed for 8 o'clock even at 15 year old, when everyone else was out playing I was in bed. But yeah I would say I did like it at school it was just, I mean it would be different now because there's all that anti bullying campaign and everything, I mean teachers used to just stand there and ignore you what were going on.

Interviwer: Did you experience being ignored by the teachers?

Tracy: Oh yeah a lot yeah.

The'education shoes' were issued free to those who had uniform vouchers from the welfare service. The shoes and what they signified (poor and needing welfare) equated to Tracy being a 'shabby failure'. She failed to conform to the dominant habitus of respectability (for example, see Figures 3.1a and 5.2), because her shoes were not bought by earned economic capital. Even when Tracy returned to school after being ill, she could not shake off the label of being poor. Her body was now marked with a lack of respectability, and the illness compounded it rather than stopping the bullying. On returning to school Tracy was subjected to threats and physical abuse.

Interviewer: Do you want to tell me about one of those experiences?

Tracy: Yeah, erm when I was 13 I got Yellow Jaundice, right, and it left me with a really bad kidneys and I was off for six weeks holiday and when I went back this girl called Jodie she was supposed to be my best friend, we were all sat in the registration room and erm this girl called Jodie came up and said Tracy you can bang me I said if you hit me I'd hit you back, do you know I'm not just going to sit there and let you hit me, and she was like oh really and she jabbed this umbrella and it was like one of those telescopic ones but it had a point on the end and she jabbed it right in the kidney and I think it was just was pain that made me jump up and I was going to hit her and all her mates all stood up and crowded round and said go on then and I went oh yeah then you'll all hit me, you won't always have your friends Jodie I said and I'll get you back and I ran out of the room but the teacher was sat at the top of the room watching. I ran all the way home and said I was never going back to that school again. It took me a good few weeks because I was just vomiting all the time you know when I was going, I was being sick all the way to school it was awful but that's what it was like.

Clearly Tracy was aware that the umbrella was being used as a weapon, that the threats were very real. Her escape from the classroom was an escape from physical and emotional injury. Both the teacher and the schoolgirls were exerting joint power to humiliate, frighten and force Tracy out of the classroom. She describes how:

Interviewer: Anybody ever confront the teacher? Did anybody ever . . .

Tracy: Well my mum went mad and phoned and said I'm not having it, she's being bullied and there's no adult present, she said it shouldn't happen but she were a soft teacher that everyone used to take the mickey out of her and just messed about in class and they wouldn't, and I thinks that's one of the reasons, the main reason that I wouldn't go to school because I weren't learning anything because half the lessons was spent listening to the disrupt the lesson, you couldn't hear properly . . .

Interviewer: Right.

Tracy: so I mean I think they'd just started that were you don't get dis– like disciplined, like, get the strap or whatever . . .

Interviewer: Yeah.

Tracy: they'd just; I think they'd just stopped doing that when we went to senior school . . .

Interviewer: Right.

Tracy: . . . so it was I think it was a lot of running riot in class. But it was just a horrible atmosphere and like nowadays they do a lot of fun things like hand on experience like whereas then it was just learning and you'd be falling asleep in the lesson bored.

Interviewer: Yeah.

Tracy: So I know now if I was to learn it would be a lot better because there's a lot more visual and hands on experience, I'd probably learn.

Not having the right appearance seems to be a cause for bullying. Below in an extract taken from Tracy's story (Dolan 2008) she describes her experience:

> I started to get bullied the minute I stepped into secondary school. It started off with name-calling, but soon I was being physically pushed about. Once, I tried to stand up to the girl, but her friends said, "Hit her and we'll hit you!" I knew it was pointless, so I got up and ran out of the classroom and continued all the way home.
>
> I started to pretend I was ill so I wouldn't have to go to school, but my mum got wise to it and made me go in. I threw myself down the steps at home, hoping to sprain my ankle so I could have a few days off. I ended up fracturing two bones in my spine and had to spend six weeks laid flat with a board under my mattress, on my bed downstairs.

I remember once standing outside the dinner hall and one of the girls who regularly bullied me, pushed in front of me and said, "Bastards to the back of the line!" I was so humiliated. I spent most of the next four years pegging off, even though I loved learning and school; I just hated the daily taunts about my looks, my hair and my clothes. The experience left me with little confidence, very low self-esteem and self-hatred.

I've seen the bullies since leaving schools and I pity them. They haven't achieved any more than I have – maybe they let their bullying affect their future like I allowed it to affect my past. My life was made a misery not because of anything I did, but because I was skinny and made to have short hair; because my shoes or sweaters didn't have brand names; because I had freckles and didn't have a dad.

One positive thing to come from being bullied is that I don't care what people think of me. The only opinions that matter are those of true friends and loved ones.

Nobody has a right to put someone down because they don't agree with their lifestyle or views, but definitely not because they don't like the way someone looks. If you don't like the way I look, then don't look at me! I'm not bothered. I would never judge someone on their looks or their clothes, or on what they have or haven't got.

(Tracy, speaking in 2008)

Being an outsider

Tracy is able to reflect on her experience and describe how the pedagogy of school failed to engage her. She described how school was boring and held no interest for her, compared with a more hands-on approach which she may have found more relatable. Here we can see how when Tracy's habitus encountered the field of schooling it created ambivalence, insecurity and uncertainty (see Reay et al. 2005). Tracy is deemed to lack the right qualities. She was unable to focus on the lessons and found that the didactic approach left her feeling dislocated from the experience of schooling as it did not recognise her practical skills, but recognised instead both her lack of economic capital (in that she did not wear the right clothes) and lack of health capital. Further to this her habitus was not in sync with the middle class discourse of schooling, nor in sync with her peers' habitus and what they perceived as the intrinsic cultural value of fashionable, new and clean uniform and shoes. She was discouraged by the fact she was labelled and pathologised by her teachers and peers for lacking the qualities deemed necessary to succeed in school and be popular with her peers (see Figures 3.1 b, 5.2).

Martin also felt like an outsider and was bullied by his peers:

Martin: At school I was quiet . . . I didn't get on with anyone; I used to get a bit bullied . . . Err, I failed all my exams and all that . . . messed up really . . . so . . .

Interviewer: When was this?
Martin: Well in secondary school, I got bullied there
Interviewer: What sort of experience did you have?
Martin: It was like verbal at first, then it like turned to fighting like, and that happening every day, I used to always miss school but my parents didn't know about it, I just got behind with everything.
Interviewer: Did the teachers, were they aware this was going on?
Martin: No
Interviewer: Did you feel as though you could tell the teachers?
Martin: No.
Interviewer: Why?
Martin: I don't know.
Interviewer: How did it make you feel about yourself?
Martin: Upset
Interviewer: Did it continue right through to . . .
Martin: Yes, it even come up to like when I getting attacked with knives at one time
Interviewer: And you still didn't tell anyone
Martin: No
Interviewer: How did you deal with it?
Martin: I just tried to block it out. That was all I thought about at school nothing else.
Interviewer: How did you feel when you had to go to school?
Martin: I just didn't want to go.
Interviewer: Do you think that's affected you?
Martin: A bit yeah
Interviewer: How do you think it's done that?
Martin: I think it's got something to do with that's why I'm quiet I think.

The peers demonstrated the process of legitimation on the learners in the study. They identified their displays of economic and social capital (hair style, dress sense, dispositions, clothes, demeanour) and decided that they did not want them in their social circle, that the learners were not 'good enough' for them. The profound effect a rejection like this can have is clearly seen in the learners' responses. Moore (2004: 451) identifies how:

> The return to cultural capital includes not only access to high cultural resources, but qualities of the self – reflected in aspects such as speech, demeanour and dress that privilege individuals in the micro-politics of everyday life – as parents dealing with their children's schools, for instance. It is at this latter end of the spectrum that much of the work of cultural capital is accomplished.

Martin, Tracy and Rachel did not want to go to school because of the fear of what they might face from the bullies. The symbolic violence they experienced occurred because those in a dominant position applied rules and judgements according to their own value system (their own habitus), and those learners subjected to the violence are in a weak position (in this case a lack of economic and cultural capital) to challenge the dominance, even though the rules and judgments are applied in an arbitrary fashion that does not relate to or take account of the victim's habitus. The victim accepts and internalises the status quo as if it were the natural order (Mills 2008).

For Tracy, empowerment came when she was able to share and validate her story of dealing with childhood bullying. Tracy wrote a story about her experience to help support others who might be being bullied (Dolan 2008).

Physical peculiarities and bullying by peers

Damage was done to learners' self esteem by the way they looked in relation to being 'ugly' or 'pretty'. Learners had to deal with being bullied because of their physical peculiarities. Melanie describes how a lazy eye led to her experiencing name calling:

> Yeah, yeah . . . it wasn't just me it was a few others. There was one time when I did, I think I'd written a poem I think it was and she actually stuck it on the wall and I felt really good about that [laughs] so that was one good thing [laughs]. Then in senior school, because I was erm, I had a bit of a lazy eye and they used to call me cock-eyed bat in junior school, erm when I was in senior school before I went in the senior school me mam took me to have an operation on my eye to straighten my eye, so when I was in senior school my eye was straight but the same people were in the class [laughs] so I still got called cock-eyed bat [laughs]. It didn't bother me because I used to not bother with the names calling and not let that bother me so much. Me mam was a bit, you know she used to get a bit upset about err.

Appearance was important and, like having the right clothes, having the right physical features also mattered. For example, like Tracy with her 'wrong haircut' as discussed earlier, whilst Melanie was subjected to ridicule because of her lazy eye.

Impact of bullying by peers

The impact of the symbolic and physical violence by teacher and peers was not something that was isolated to emotional responses at school. It left a legacy that strongly influenced the choices the learners made on leaving school. Martin recalls:

Interviewer: Yeah.

Martin: . . . and I were like I couldn't, I mean if you go to school for three year and they haven't noticed that you've got your mark in the register and you haven't gone to the classroom that shows you what the school were like.

Interviewer: Do you think it affected the choices that you made?
Martin: Yeah 'cos when I left school I said I was never going to college, 'cos I thought it's be the same . . . so I got a job worked at Warburtons for a three year contract and did a few other things, er decided to see the education support unit . . . got ill and stuff. It's like I was dead scared or something . . . I'd still erm haven't told you this but I've got schizophrenia.

Rachel also describes how the bullying she received affected her confidence and the choices she made:

Rachel: I didn't tend to make friends that easy, I was you know introverted you know.
Interviewer: Yeah.
Rachel: But when I went to Casten Moor I hated it even more.
Interviewer: Do you want to tell me a little about this bullying? And how it made you feel about yourself.
Rachel: It made me want to stay at home; I didn't want to go to school. I don't know I can't really explain it's just groups of girls bullying you every day, I hated it, I just wanted to get out of school and that's why, I could have done my CSE's at school, you know my exams but I didn't want to stay there any longer so I came home.
Interviewer: How did it make you feel about yourself the bullying?
Rachel: I wasn't confident at all, I had no confidence in myself just picked on, being picked on every single day, I didn't really have any friends apart from one girl she was a coloured girl she was my best friend, right up until leaving school. That was the only real friend I had, I've not kept in touch with her and I think she went back to Jamaica.

Although Rachel struggled emotionally because of peer bullying, peers could be empowering as well as disempowering. Friendship remained important, perhaps even more important, with the memory of childhood friendships remaining strong in the narratives the learners told.

Tracy describes how this had an impact on her choices:

Tracy: It made me have low self esteem, erm no confidence really I mean I went for the first job I got I mean I got the first job I went for, which wasn't, you didn't need any qualifications and it was making suitcases, putting the metal zip part and I stood there all day opening the zip and putting this metal thing on turning it over and doing the same on the other end and then it was just monotonous and boring . . .

There seems to be a recognition that rather than the habitus being at an unconscious level of response, whereby the actions of the learners were pre-reflective[1] (see

Sayer 1984) many of the learners had a well-developed habitus, with heightened awareness that they did not have the 'right' legitimate capitals in the site of the schools. Many of the learners were denied the same status of learner that had been accorded to Sally whose habitus was in sync with the dominant symbolic power. This did not mean that she did not struggle, as she also found it hard to keep up with schoolwork, so private tutoring was brought in to support her. Like Sally, the other participants knew when and how they struggled, but unlike Sally there was no economic support to help them plug any gaps in their schoolwork. The respondents were certainly not blind fools as raised by Bourdieu and Wacquant (2002: 130):

> people are not fools; they are much less bizarre and deluded that we would spontaneously believe precisely because they have internalised, through a protracted and multisided process of conditioning, the objective choices they make.

Their resistance to the dominant symbolic power of schooling and labelling which pathologised them was taking agency in the realm of counter culture.

Counter culture

Although the learners were constrained by and struggled with the labels that were conferred upon them inside – and out of – school, many took agency and found spaces to empower themselves. This seemed to take place in a counter-culture based on the learners escaping from the dominant expectations and aspirations of the middle and upper classes' attitudes towards education, and indeed the heavy weight they place on passing exams and gaining qualifications. Although qualifications are the dominant capital in education, this 'weight' wasn't placed upon them. Instead, the 'weight' of symbolic violence was placed on them and labels related to failure (see Figure 5.2). They found spaces to escape and to 'get out of school' as soon as possible. Part of this struggle included finding empowerment, by wagging school. Shammy describes the bullying at school and truanting because of the bullies:

> Yer see I didn't feel like I fit in, I was goin' in and learnin' nothin' but how to try and get away from the lads who were after me. I hated it. me head full of avoidin' them rather than learning
>
> (Shammy, speaking in 2005)

Rachel describes her experience:

> I didn't go back to school cos the bullying happened every day. I didn't want to go and it held me back. I knew I was bright, I'd always been told that, but the bullying made me feel bad.
>
> (Rachel, speaking in 2005)

The participants resisted being 'hammered down' by the violence that was going on in school and sought to escape the site of violence. Stella describes how:

Stella: With me being dyslexic and them not recognising it, I was just made to feel I was useless, so I didn't go in.

Interviewer: How old were you when you left school, when you decided not to go back?

Stella: I just used to go in and get me mark and then just come out. If I played truant me mam would find out so I used to just go in and get me mark and slip off. And I was that important to the school I did it for three years and nobody realised I wasn't there. That's'cos I was thick and I was on the outskirts like I said, the teachers were more focused on the children who could get on with their work'.

Interviewer: Did you have any support from anyone, any friends at school'?'

Stella: Oh, yeah, there was a girl called Doreen who I still very much like. She used to say if she was asked that I'd gone to the dentist. She knew what I was like and Doreen bless her even helped me to read and she did it and that's why I can read 'cos me best friend taught me to read.

The paradox is that, although some peers would inflict symbolic and physical violence, others promoted learner empowerment by forging strong links with friends who supported them in ways the teachers could or would not. The idea that Doreen knew what Stella 'was like' indicates how she was empowered in the knowledge that her friend valued who she was, while teachers only viewed her by the symbols she wore rather than getting to know who she really was. Indeed, for Stella the importance of friendship as a social capital is highlighted. Peer supports and networks will be further expanded in Chapter Eight.

As highlighted above, the experience of bullying and labelling, and lacking support mechanisms in the private domain of family and public domain of school meant that many learners 'hit out' at the system by 'wagging it' and not 'bothering to go in for exams or 'owt for that matter'. Exams were viewed as a 'waste of space'. On leaving school, they did not have a long-term plan about the following year, let alone their future career. As in Willis' (1977) study, the choice still reflects a distinctive cultural pattern of social reproduction for the learners this study. Aspirations were low and they were expected to go into unskilled jobs, rather than progress through education, gain cultural capital and land a professional job. Their trajectories suggest, however, that the routes they take are a result of the violence they experience. All except Sally wanted to escape a school that to some was more a prison sentence than a place to develop their knowledge and build enthusiasm for a future. They wanted 'fast results', a job and a wage. Most of the group went into unskilled work; Joanne, Tracy, Craig, Carol, Stella, Rachel had children in their teens and early 20s. Only Sally and Sarah, who are in their mid-20s and both in long-term relationships, have decided to wait before having children. Interestingly, these two had economic support for their transition from school into further education; both of their parents, still together, were in full-time jobs. Parental interest and support can be seen as offering valuable capital to the learners' early educational progress.

Rather than the participants being 'anti-education' they were instead 'anti-school' due to the bullying and symbolic violence they were experiencing across the domains. As identified by Hanley (2007) 'you don't know what your potential is because nobody has told you about it.' The idea of having potential is indeed something many of the learners hadn't even been told. Many had been labelled as 'no hopers', and didn't have the confidence to think further than the next lesson.

The learners were constrained because their habitus was incongruent with the field of schooling; they did not have the right clothes, appearance or dispositions. In contrast, Sally, a well-dressed schoolgirl, with economic and cultural support from her family, had the perfect congruence for a 'proper schoolgirl' with a habitus which was in sync with school (see Figure 3.1 a). The poor children were perhaps seen as seeking to get what is not rightfully theirs, that is 'an education'. The women in the study may also be seen as failing to meet gender norms. In their 'scruffy clothes' and with their lack of academic skills they are seen as lacking femininity and thus respectability (Skeggs 1997). Indeed, the aesthetics of their appearance functioned to mark out their body as other and pathologise them (see Figure 5.3). The aesthetic they were judged by is classed and gendered. Old clothes, shoes with holes in, un-brushed hair and the rest were used to signify a form of learner who lacks morality and indeed worth. I would argue that markers of domination can be resignified, for example hoody tops[2] which are equated with thuggery and deviance by the bourgeois, who do not want a challenge to their ideological dominations; this is an essential element of class domination. There is an awareness of the ideology put forward by the bourgeoisie which masks inequalities through notions of meritocracy in order to dominate the outlook of the working class and thus dominate social order. This notion of what is 'dominant' is subverted, whereby dominant symbolism can serve as symbolic capital, or 'street capital', which is accrued when wearing these clothes. Street capital is a valuable capital on the estate many learners live. This is a field where they know the rules and can take agency and challenge dominant ideologies with capital valued within their own context (see Figure 5.1). Here they can get respect for what the hoodies represent – a unity which challenges the bourgeois authority and power exerted over them and the way they live their lives. Rather than resisting the media stereotypes, they play up to them.

School and identities

Clearly, school is a site where identities and futures are formed. Rather than being a site that offers a meritocratic model where everyone is on an equal footing however, school is often experienced as a site of intergenerational marginalisation, social exclusion, and labelling by teachers and peers, as this research has shown.

At a critical time when the participants were becoming aware of themselves and how they fitted into the classroom, self-conscious emotions such as pride, shame and guilt began to emerge. School should be a place where the learners feel comfortable and respected; instead they were anxious, confused and worried for their own wellbeing.

The dominant institutional literacies which were key to being successful in the school curriculum set the participants up to fail. Dominant literacies were inherent within the schools the learners attended and were regarded with high value culturally. These were subject to formal rules and were linked to power and prestige. Not only did they struggle with understanding the lessons, but the barrier to this understanding was not identified. Instead they were labelled as stupid and 'bad' because they 'messed about'. Ignored, ridiculed and labelled by the teachers and peers, the learners experienced symbolic and physical violence. They blamed their 'messing about' on being ignored by the teachers 'fobbed off as nothings' (Stella).

The fact that they did not adhere to the academic norms required for distinction was internalised by the participants and led to negative emotions. This hid the symbolic power schools have in the continual reproduction of social hierarchy. These emotions arose from the negative labels that were attached to them because they struggled at school: '[the teachers] called me thick and stupid' (Stella, speaking in 2005); because they were poor: 'We were left to the side. The teachers knew we had nowt so they put us to one side and carried on with the smarter kids. We were nobody's, the bottom of the barrel' (Joanne, speaking in 2004). They were left with feelings of self consciousness and the belief that there was something wrong with them (McNulty 2003).

Freire (1996) reflects on 'cultural invasion,' in which invaders penetrate the cultural context of another group, in disrespect of the latter's potentialities; they impose their own view of the world upon those they invade and inhibit the creativity of the invaded by curbing their expression (Freire 1996: 133). In this capacity many of the participants have been labelled as lazy, because they struggled with traditional academic tasks. The dyslexia served to lower their confidence and self-esteem and left them with feelings of shame (see Skeggs 1997). Often they did not have the social capital of friends or any kind of social network to share these feelings, which resulted in feelings of isolation. The learners, however, were not passive. They reacted to the trauma and symbolic violence, and as they had no other options they were forced to either resist their situation by not attending school, that is wagging it, or pretending to be ill, or by appearing to conform in the form of being silent and invisible in the class. These reactions demonstrate how the learners struggled to find spaces to challenge the violence that was happening to them. This challenge was something that helped them keep some self respect in the face of such violence and demonstrates the strength of spirit the learners had. This resilience is a capital in itself and one which is needed on an estate where many of the learners had and still have to live on their wits.

Conclusion

The collective and individual histories of the learners' experience of schooling provided me with the means to understand how the concept of habitus and capital (or lack of it) interplays in the field of schooling (see Figures 3.1a and b, 3.3, 5.1 and 5.2). Using the habitus as a conceptual tool provided me with the opportunity to consider agency against the backdrop of larger structural inequalities, and allowed for the recognition of what Bourdieu and Wacquant (1992: 144) describe thus:

> the structure of those worlds is predefined by broader racial, gender and class relations

Their bodies were sites for symbolic violence, which affected their experience of education and had a huge impact on their learning experience, how they define themselves and their subsequent trajectories. The learners' journeys carried an emotional landscape of pain and disillusionment as they attempted to navigate through the educational system (see also Stone et al. 2000; Ball 2003). Their emotional and psychological responses to class inequalities serve to add greatly to the making of class (Reay 2005) and their own positioning within the 'field'.

The 'blame and guilt' the learners carried affected the way they viewed themselves. In a neo-liberalist society, where myths of everyone having equal choice and options permeate through institutions and public life it is hardly surprising they carried the guilt. As Bourdieu (1990b: 131) says:

> It is this lack of awareness that leads even the most disadvantaged to tend to perceive the world as natural and to find it surprisingly acceptable, especially when one looks at the situation of the dominated through the eyes of the dominant.

Education was a privileged space, and identities were conferred on learners by those in a position of power, including teachers and peers, who use what is deemed 'legitimate' capital to carry out symbolic violence on those positioned as not having what Bourdieu characterised as the right 'habitus' or 'capital'. Education is positioned by the subjectivities of those who are involved in it and by the symbolic-cultural determinations that are representative of the educational system, constructed from a privileged logic where those in a position of power (having the valued forms of capital) can determine whether the capital the learners possess are legitimate or illegitimate.

Personal reflections

I connected with the learners' narratives of symbolic and physical violence at school. I attended state schools in the same location; my experiences and background were not unlike theirs. At primary school I first felt the physical and symbolic violence from the teachers. I stood out at school because my mum would put me in coloured socks and my dad would cut my fringe short. I can remember a dinner lady saying 'who's done that to your fringe?' That's how it was; you didn't go to the hairdressers. I felt the pain of physical violence when one of the male teachers threw a board duster at me for speaking, it hit my head hard. That memory is vivid, because I felt humiliated and embarrassed. I also remember feeling confused and not knowing what the teacher wanted from me when she said I needed to 'pull up my socks'. I remember those words so well, because at nine I took them literally. I looked down at my socks and she laughed. I did not have the right habitus and I certainly did not have a feel for the game of schooling.

When I arrived at secondary school I was wearing a pair of shoes two sizes too big because they were in the sale and real leather. With a uniform from the market and Tib Street in town, I fitted in with the kids from the council estate like me. We stood out from those who lived in the private houses, with their leather modern shoes and matching bags. The divide was there for all to see from day one and we all knew it. It was a male teacher who called me to the front of the lesson when I was 13 and hit the back of my legs hard – they bruised. He'd do that to the girls. I was too frightened to tell my mum and dad in case they shouted at me for making him do it. That's the way it was, teachers were to be looked up to and if they hit you there must be a reason. The reason for me was talking to the girl next to me – as simple as that. When you're being hit at home and at school it begins to be the norm. I didn't question it, they had the power and I had none.

How it differed for me from a number of the learners in the study is that I had lots of friends. I was not a loner. I'd have a laugh and liked being around my mates. Friendship meant a lot to me and it still does.

Keeping quiet about the experiences of violence was a common occurrence with the group and me. Not telling is a way to keep your respectability and not be judged. To tell would be to put shame on you. Neither I nor the learners wanted this shame from peers, even though we felt it ourselves. Taking part in the study is the first time we have shared our stories and I have penned my narrative and shared my poems. It's the sharing of our stories which helped stop that dislocation. When you carry it yourself you think you are the only one who is experiencing being hit and called names, but when you share it you realise you are not to blame for the 'hits at school' and the 'hits at home'. Initially, many of the learners blamed themselves and their backgrounds. Stella and Melanie show this when they spoke about the teachers' attitudes towards them.

Stella: I wasn't a bright child so that's why they picked on me.

Melanie: If I'd been prettier then maybe I'd not 'ave stood out.

The telling and sharing of the stories was a way to share what had happened and make the connection with someone who would not judge, but who had come from a similar background. For many of the participants, speaking to me was the first time they had revealed what had happened to them at school. From telling me they then went on to share it with each other on nights out. In sharing their histories the learners began to recognise that what had happened to them at school was not their fault, and they were able to take agency over their lives. This will be explored later in the book.

Notes

1 Pre-reflective suggest that actions are carried out unconsciously rather than being acts of awareness.

2 A tracksuit top with a hood attached. The hood is worn on the head, and viewed by the bourgeois as a means to hide one's appearance so that illegal acts can be carried out in anonymity.

Chapter 6

Home life, identity and learning in childhood

Class war

It's easier for a poor boy
To read in bed, torched
Of a lady debauched;
Than it is for a rich boy
To climb gates to the park
When they're locked and it's dark.

It's easier for a poor boy
To sing sonnet shape
About his team's great escape;
Than it is for a rich boy
To run from a shop,
Without stolen sweets drop.

It's easier for a poor boy
To appreciate appeal,
Of proof a canvassed girl's real;
Than it is for a rich boy
To understand lies,
Many nooses untie.

It's easier for a poor boy
Who's told he's not bright,
To punch out the lights
Of the rich boy in class,
Who laughs like an ass
At his stumbling part in Twelfth Night
(Vicky, 1991)

Introduction

This chapter examines the learners' experience of childhood violence and trauma in the domain of family and home, and the impact this had on their education. On tracing the impact of violence and trauma enacted on the learners by their family, I will show how their experiences are classed and gendered. Bourdieu's theory offers socio-cultural explanations for why under-represented groups remain excluded from the educational process. Savage (2003: 536) argues that 'the unacknowledged normality of the middle-class needs to be carefully unpicked and exposed'. I suggest that within the limited forms of capital available and carried by them, learners struggle in limited movement through social space (Skeggs 1997). They are not, however, passive in their struggle; they resist disempowerment by subverting the violence and trauma they have experienced in the public domain of schooling and the private domain of home into a 'resistance capital'. They take agency by turning the violence and trauma into street credibility, respect, optimism and opportunities for employment. For the males, an outcome of this is 'muscle capital' which flows through the domains of work, friends and community as a means to gain credibility and respect in the field of the 'street' and in employment which values 'muscle' power (see Figure 6.1).

For the females, 'glamour capital' is used for both resistance and empowerment. It offers the learners the possibility of building a home with a partner away from the confines of their childhood home and family, and 'domestic' capital transfers to finding employment which places values on domestic skills such as cleaning (see Figure 6.2).

Violence and trauma

Wykes and Welsh (2009: 66) note that:

> There are two key areas for any violence and justice study: the private sphere where violence is overwhelmingly carried out by men against women and/or children in intimate familial relationships.

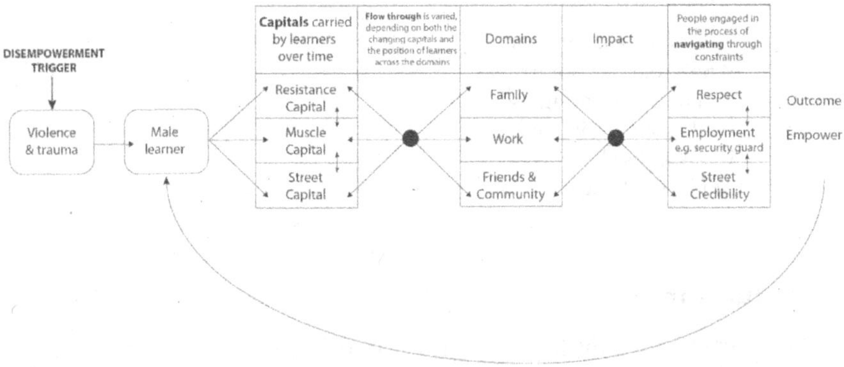

Figure 6.1 Violence and childhood trauma: male

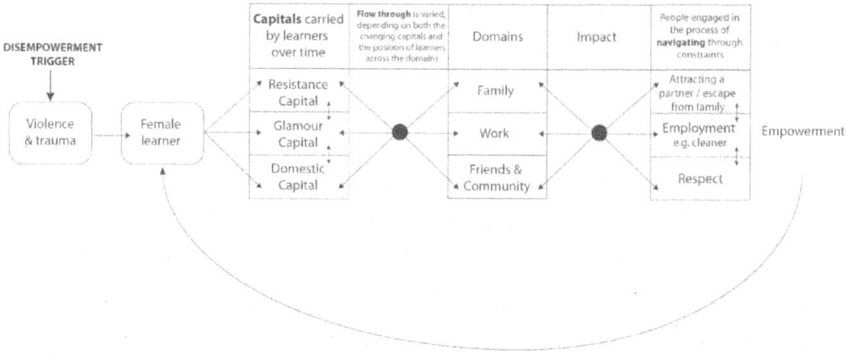

Figure 6.2 Violence and childhood trauma: female

Twelve of the learners in the study spoke of their experience of violence in the home and how this was a barrier to them progressing at school. Gender and gendered and domestic violence worked in conjunction with one another; and gender and gendered violence had an impact on both the males and females in the study. Only the females, however, spoke of being sexually abused. For Joanne, brought up with a step father, she struggled to come to terms with her step dad's abuse within the family.

> He was rotten, scum, he'd get yer when yer was alone. A perv. I couldn't wait to get out of the house, leave home away from it all.

Joanne found that she couldn't focus at school because of the abuse which was happening at home.

> Me head was not with it. How could it be? I'd be bogged down with what was gonna happen when we walked through the door back home. Course it didn't help that the teachers were at their bullying too. It was like you kept it all inside cos you were ashamed that people'd be at yer more if they knew about things at home that were happening. All that keeping it inside, it's hard yer know. Me and me sister who got it worse got out as soon as we could. We got our own flat when we were 15. I could hardly read and write but that was the last thing on me mind what mattered to us was being safe yer know. That freedom of getting out of the house away from the perv was all I wanted. I wish I'd've got me exams though, me head wasn't in it like it is now. All them years to put yer head in the right place, a waste innit but that's it that's how it was.

On reaching 15, along with her twin, Joanne left home and moved into a flat. For her, the home was a place of constant fear and anxiety from which she wanted to escape (Smith 1989).

Melanie, meanwhile, described how when she was looking for a father figure she was 'groomed' by one of her dad's friends and her swimming instructor, when she was 15 and he was 50.

> I saw him as a father figure as we used to do everything together, you know he'd show me sea fish and snorkelling and stuff like that. It wasn't the love, looking back it wasn't the love for a relationship. We went onto a relationship when I was 16. But it didn't last long and trying to end it was really hard work, we were supposed to go living in Scotland together but it was a good job that I didn't really, cos it was getting to the point that he was quite domineering, he wanted me to stand in certain ways, he'd be jealous if I looked at anybody, you know he was quite insecure in that way – with him drinking and all that he was a bit of a Jekyll and Hyde stuff he'd do.

Rather than adult company being a refuge for Melanie's unhappy school and home life, her vulnerability was abused.

The males in the study did not speak of experiencing sexual abuse. This may have been because of its nature. As identified by Wykes and Welsh (2009):

> An area of male violence within families that is significantly under-represented in recent work is familial child sexual abuse. It took twenty years to force a law against incest in 1908 . . . twenty years since the furore following the exposure of high levels of incest in families in Cleveland, the Orkneys and setting up of the Childline phone help centre for abused children in the late 1980s . . . family abuse soon slid towards disbelief and then to blame and then finally to symbolically restoring the credibility of the family.
>
> (Wykes and Welsh 2009: 96)

Hidden violence

For two of the females in the group, the interviews were the first time they had spoken of the abuse to which they had been subjected. On reading the transcripts, they marked out chunks of their transcript which spoke of their experience. They removed this and emphasised that they did not want it in this study. These silences can have an impact. Horsman (2004) states that:

> Silences often continue when youth are long past the age where violence must be reported. The focus on getting children out of violence as the key solution parallels an idea that girls and women are addressing their issues adequately only if they leave abusive partners, and engenders frustration with those who don't leave, or who return. Negative judgement may make it harder for young people to speak about violence they continue to experience.

> It contributes to a sense that the experience of violence is private and shameful, not to be spoken about.
>
> (Horsman: 11)

Further research on sexual abuse and learning would be of benefit in the area of literacy and learning. It remains partially hidden in this research, but was a factor which contributed to two of the learners lacking concentration at school and carrying feelings of shame. This shame led to them having low self-esteem and withdrawing from the company of their peers. They stopped going to school and became loners.

For a number of older learners in the group, Childline was not available. This is a channel which allows silences to be heard. The statistics for calls to the NSPCC show a marked increase over the decade from 1997/98–2007/08.

Recently, Professor Shepherd headed a research project with the Violence and Society Research Group at Cardiff University. They carried out research on the number of violent injuries being treated in hospital wards across the UK. The figures for 2010 showed that, worryingly, violence towards children under ten is increasing: 'while violence following which children aged 0 to 10 years needed emergency hospital treatment increased by 20%' (Sivarajasingam et al. 2010: 1) .

This rise does not account for those aspects of violence which stay hidden in the private domain of the family. Although the nature of the calls to NSPCC are not identified and the full extent of children who have been subjected to violence revealed on hospital wards, these are stark findings when considering that Horsman (1999); Barton et al. (2007) and Feeley (2007) show in their studies how violence affects learners and their learning. As noted by Barton et al. (2007)'Some people bring fear of violence, of threat and intimidation' (Barton et al. 2007: 165).

The physical, psychological and symbolic impact of violence and trauma affected the learners' ability to concentrate in lessons, form relationships with their peers, communicate with their family, learn new skills and progress into employment. The other forms of violence and trauma varied, but whether they had a bruised face or a hungry belly, on arriving in the 'educational field' of schooling they were ill equipped to deal with the demands of schooling.

Table 6.1 Childline calls and letters in the UK (000s)

	Girls	*Boys*
1997/98	91.031	24.115
1999/2000	98.811	28.097
2001/02	86.744	26.081
2003/04	111.188	30.684
2005/06	114.959	44.576
2007/08	117.874	58.311

Source: National Society for the Prevention of Cruelty to Children

Physical violence

Of the 16 learners, in childhood, four of the men and five of the women experienced physical violence. The acts ranged from the occasional hit to being beaten; the incidence varied between once every couple of weeks to occurring on a regular, daily basis. Each of these acts of physical violence was inflicted on the learners by a male. The violent acts were never discussed within or outside the family. They were a secret. The reason for keeping the abuse secret was due to feelings of guilt and shame. Rachel spoke about how she was frightened to tell anyone in case her dad found out and punished her further.

Rachel: He knew everyone on our estate, if I'd 'ave said owt it'd be up for it.
Interviewer: So you kept quiet?
Rachel: Yes. I would have felt daft tellin' anyone anyway, like I was to blame somehow. I started to cut me hair because of how I felt. I had nice long hair, but I cut it off.
Interviewer: Why?
Rachel: Don't know. It just made me feel easier, like better, like I had some control.

Joanne also spoke of the fear of telling about the physical abuse she was experiencing:

> I didn't want to upset anyone, that's why I kept quiet. The house would 'ave gone up if I'd mentioned it. What if no one believed me?
>
> I didn't want to be looked down on, yer would 'ave been where I lived if word had got out. Besides I didn't want to 'ave to explain it. By not telling I could put it to the back of me mind and pretend it didn't happen. I didn't want be thought of as a slag.

For Joanne, she did not want to be labelled as deviant and a 'slag', while Melanie did not want to cause concern to anyone. She also questioned whether she would be believed. As identified by Wykes and Welsh:

> Male violence is secure in the family, in the home, behind closed doors, because it is invisible and so symbolically and physically protected and kept secret. If it is exposed and made manifest in ways that make it newsworthy then the familial masculinity at its core is disguised. Blame is regularly shifted from home, husbandry and paternity to attributes of deviant femininity, psychopathic, beastliness, evil and stranger danger.
>
> (Wykes and Welsh: 2009: 98)

For Shammy the violence that he experienced at home stopped him concentrating in class.

Shammy: Vicky, I just didn't want to go in because I was thinking I'm getting it at home and I'm going to be getting it at school as well and I just got fed up and I just went loopy after a bit.

Interviewer: What did you do?

Shammy: Many a time I could have got arrested as well by the police because they got called as well, I'm not going to lie to you, I'm going to be honest with you.

Inteviewer: Who was you fighting with?

Shamy: I wasn't actually fighting I just used to smash things up, when I used to get fit and the police, the neighbours used to phone the police, so it wasn't very good. I don't think about it because it's gonna hurt me when I think about it but.

Craig, who lived with his parents and siblings, described how his father regularly beat him after a 'skinful of booze':

> You had to be tough and take it or you'd go under. He'd think nothing of whacking me with a belt or his fist, that's the way it was, you took it, what choice was there.

When it came to schooling, he describes how the idea of being tough and having 'muscle capital' had more credibility with his family and friends than being successful in exams or schooling:

Craig: It was being able to look after yourself, being handy on the street. Not letting someone say treat yer like shit cos you were a pushover. That's how you got yer badges having a bit of respect because people knew yer could handle yerself like.

Interviewer: What about the credibility of getting school qualifications?

Craig: They were way down. The swots got a kickin' cos they couldn't handle themselves. Even if you were good at summat you'd play it down like cos being handy meant not caring about getting it right at school. As I've said you got yer cred' on the street without a piece of paper or owt. Me dad wanted me out of school as soon as to bring money into house. Exams meant crap to him.

For Shammy the 'muscle capital' was something that his uncle tried to instil in him with brute force.

Interviewer: Can you tell me about your home life when you were growing up?

Shammy: It wasn't very good, because I was picked on from home off my uncle and stuff when I was younger, and he used to beat me up all the time. One of my uncles used to pick on me all the time a bit like that, but they just used to bully me all the time. Like, petty things.

I just don't go to my mum's side cos they used to beat me up all the time, over just petty things.

Interviewer: How old were you when they did this?

Shammy: All my life, since I was nine, ten years old,

Interviewer: And did it stop?

Shammy: It just stopped at 13, I went off me head after 13, you know, being I was beat up I lost the plot. He'd give me a kickin' sayin it'd stop me being mard but I'm as soft as owt. I just hit out at myself.

For Shammy there was a feeling that it wasn't taken seriously by Shammy's parents

> They thought I was kidding, they really didn't take me seriously. He used to beat me up in front of people, but not me ma and dad but you know in a full room, he used to just beat me over little things even if I'd gone and picked a drink up or something out of the fridge you know if like I know this sounds silly but if I used to like open up a can of coke out of the fridge he used to say why you picking that up are you greedy or something don't you get things like that at home? I used to get embarrassed and I never used to drink it and then I used to go quiet on my own, you know sit within myself and he used to start when he would pull me hair and drag me and punch me, I used to have bruises on me face and I didn't want to go to school you know, do anything, bullying at school, bullying at the family, I didn't want, I've not had a pleasant – pleasant life really.

Shammy is still affected by his uncle's abuse, and recalls how scared he was to tell anyone. Shammy learnt at an early age how to protect himself and his dignity.

Shammy: Yeah, because he told me if you say anything to anybody you'll get punished for it I'll beat you, and I was weak I was scared so I didn't say anything. Sometimes I used to get nightmares about the way I used to get beat up off him. It still haunts me sometimes but I've never told this to anybody and you're the first person I've ever told this too. Why I wasn't one of them naughty kids I was a quiet lad. I've always been quiet,

Interviewer: Was there anyone in your family that was positive, that you could look up to? Someone who would help you at all?

Shammy: Well you know the guy who used to beat me he [my uncle] used to say to my parents why don't you throw him into a home something and I just started smashing things up and I just lost it big time and he used to say to my parents get rid of him, throw him in care or in a home. I remember a time I came home from school and I don't know what happened but he came to our house and I was sitting in the living room and I don't know what the argument was about, but he just picked up a table and rammed it right in me in the back of me and he was he was kicking me in the head and everything and it was just awful. After that that was the last time he ever hit me and after that day I didn't want to go to their house. I didn't want to go their house and didn't want him to come to ours at all. I told my mum and dad I don't want him in the house again.

Interviewer: How old were you?

Shammy: Well I was 12 or 13. I've not been to their house since, to my mum's family's house.

Interviewer: Does he ever come to the house?

Shammy: No, none of the family come to the house now, because I've told them if you want to see them go but don't bring them here. I've got scars in me hands because I used to punch walls. At the time I felt rough, like there was something wrong with me. Maybe he's right and I'm wrong. I piled on a load of weight cos I was eating and I got depression. I didn't bother with studying at school or owt like that.

Muscle capital, empowerment and work

Shammy described how the muscle capital he had gained as a child helped him to secure a job as a security guard (see Figure 6.1).

> I suppose being beat up does makes you harder. Like look at me I've got to be tough to be a security guard, not that I'd ever hit out at anyone but I'm not afraid of some of the brick heads that try to cause trouble when I'm on the job. When you've been beat up as a kid you sort of get immune to the kicks, know what I mean?

Indeed, as described, it appears that '[the idea of] masculinity is one of the last refuges of the identity of the dominated classes . . . it's characteristic of people who have little to fall back on except their labour-power and sometimes their fighting strength' (Bourdieu 4: 1993). Habitus is about social training. Bourdieu refers to habitus as 'a societal imperative which has become second nature and has been developed into motor schemata and physical automatism' (Bourdieu 1993: 239). The working-class practice of toughening boys up was held up as training them to be tough; this carried with it more capital – 'muscle capital' – than the legitimate capital of acquiring qualifications. Muscle capital equated to street capital. This capital was 'symbolic capital' of masculinity and was perceived and recognised as legitimate on the streets and indeed in employment needing muscle capital (Skeggs 1997: 8).

Verbal abuse and symbolic violence

For the men and women in the group, the capital they acquired from home life seldom aligned itself with the legitimate capital of schooling. In this study, 12 of the learners experienced symbolic violence and other forms of verbal abuse from their family. As they described how they were called names and sworn at they said that this was natural. Mike recalled that the swearing used at home was as natural as using everyday words. Words were used to hurt and humiliate. Mike spoke of his experience.

Mike: It was the way it was if you done somethin' wrong you would be called an f---in' idiot or a shit. They were like saying yer dickhead. You got used it. I swore back in the end, but louder, let 'em know I was no soft touch.

Interviewer: How did that make you feel?

Mike: What?

Interviewer: Being sworn at

Mike: Tried to shrug it off. When someone you look up to slags you off it's crap. Makes you feel bad about yourself. I fucked up at school so the respect came in my being like him, my dad and givin' the slagging off back.

For the both the men and the women in the group patriarchal relationships were in place where the man of the house wanted to control those he could dominate. Bourdieu (2001b: 33) says:

> the dominated apply categories constructed from the point of view of the dominant to the relations of domination, thus making it appear as natural. This can lead to a systematic self-depreciation, even self-denigration.

This patriarchal violence was normalised and invisible to the outside world.

Joanne spoke of how her stepdad put all the family down with his verbal attacks:

Joanne: He was always on at us. What he said we did otherwise he'd have a screamin' match. It was easier to keep the peace

Interviewer: How did it make you feel listening to his screamin?

Joanne: I hated it. When I was younger I'd stay in me bedroom and put me radio on just so I couldn't hear him bangin' on at me mam. It made me feel sick. I'd pinch meself 'til I bled cos the pain felt better than what I was hearing. He'd pick on owt to get an argument. He had to let us all know he was the big man. As if. It was a joke he wasn't even our dad.

Interviewer: Did you tell anyone?

Joanne: No chance, you kept it to yourself.

Violence that was going on in the house stayed behind the walls. These unrecorded silences hide the pain and suffering inflicted on families by domineering men. The asymbolic violence inflicted on Joanne led to her hurting herself. As identified by Barton et al. (2007: 43) violence is 'part of everyday experience'. For the learners in the study it shaped the way they viewed themselves and thus shaped their identity. Their identity was linked to silences they could not share, secrets of shame. This shame was manifested in the self harm carried out by two of the learners in the group.

Domestic capital

Within the patriarchal mode of production 'domestic capital' was a key aspect for Melanie and Carol's childhoods. Carol, whose mother put her into the care of an Irish convent at two and half, spoke about how her schooling revolved around cleaning and caring for the younger children:

Carol: It was hard work but at least I was fed and watered. Just felt like I couldn't do anything right, if they took a dislike to you, or if you did something wrong they were always picking on you then so you couldn't do anything right. Just I used to suffer from chill blains and my hands used to be damaged from them and I couldn't write properly and I always got a battering because I couldn't write properly.

Interviewer: What did you do out of lessons

Carol: We'd all have to pull our weight with the cleaning. That's what I was good at I suppose. All that cleaning gave yer summat to think about. At least I knew I'd be able to put me hand to cleaning jobs when I left the convent, no problem.

Carol describes how her experiences in the convent also involved using 'caring capital'. The transference of caring capital has been explored in the realm of adulthood, but rarely in the realm of childhood. The use of Carol's caring capital is particularly poignant as without a family, she lacked caring herself.

> I got on well with the girls alright, because I was as daft as the younger ones but I knew if you were older than someone you looked after them, just sort of a mother figure you took over.

The transference of the domestic capital Carol acquired at the convent was empowering for her: it enabled her to gain a job and become independent when she found got various cleaning jobs. Carol travelled to Dublin, working as a cleaner, and then moved to London. From London she travelled to Oldham where she settled and brought up her three daughters as a single mother.

For Melanie, who lived with her mother, father and sister, life at home meant that toys were relegated to certain rooms. Childhood was about listening to her mother's instructions and making sure all the chores were carried out in the house. Bourdieu recognised the pivotal role of the mother in the family:

> It is because the cultural capital that is effectively transmitted within the family itself depends not only on the quantity of cultural capital, itself accumulated by spending time, that the group possess, but also usable time (particularly in the form of mother's free time) available to it.
>
> (Bourdieu 1986: 253)

Melanie's mother had no free time as her days were spent cleaning. Her mum's energies were focused on domestic tasks rather than play and interaction with the children. Melanie speaks about how she wanted to play but this was not allowed.

Melanie: I'd want to play and the like but me mum 'ld be mad keen on cleaning the house. That's how it was then, the cleaner the house the happier she was. She'd get all agitated if we made a mess or didn't help. I'd be washing the pots at five.

Interviewer: Did you find time to play?

Melanie: We weren't allowed in the inside with our toys and things, we weren't allowed in the kitchen or in the bedroom with our toys . . . My mum was quite proud of the furniture and things. We used to have to sit on the couch while the hoover and dusting was an everyday ritual. Still is actually. As long as everything is in its place in the living room the world's alright according to me mum. Her world is there yer see. There might be a riot outside but she'd not notice if the rooms clean and tidy.

Melanie would also become very nervous when arguments erupted between her parents. It got to the point where she did not want to come home from school.

Melanie: Sometimes I weren't so sure about going home really, I wasn't sure what'd be happening. They were at each other's neck all the time. I think trying to keep on top of the cleaning an' that made me mum irritable especially when she got a job.

Interviewer: Did your dad help in the house

Melanie: No, he was old fashioned. Men didn't do that sort of stuff. He'd sometimes wash up, every blue moon like, but that was it.

Melanie felt anxious about what was happening at home. She recalls how she felt at school:

> I hadn't much concentration I was always one to be away with fairies.

Death also played a part in unsettling the childhoods of the learners in this study. For Sarah the death of her dad's mum, when she was 14, left the house shattered.

> He [dad] was depressed. He was at home a lot, so he was getting on me mum's nerves, under me mum's feet and stuff. So like he used to go out drinking and he'd come in drunk and shout and throw things around and stuff. He changed he used to sit me on his knee, we were really close and then he was like you alright, hiya, not that close. And then I seen him hit mum and I've never forgiven him for that.' It was really horrible. I've never really forgiven myself that I just couldn't do anything.

Seeing her parents arguing and losing the stability that she had felt comfortable with had a knock-on effect on her education.

Sarah: It affected me quite a lot really. I was really good in my first, second and third year. Then I got to the fourth and fifth year and just messed around, that's why like I'm still studying now. It was horrible I couldn't do anything. I was just sat in. Me dad was always going on to me mum about me attitude to him. Mum pulled me up once and I said do you think I'm deaf. You know I told her I can hear what you say to each other and I reminded her of that night when he hit out at her.

Interviewer: Were you hurt?

Sarah: Oh god yeah. Really really hurt because it was wrong All the things went wrong they just went out of the window everything that I just like expected, like I'd been brought up in this close family and when dad got depressed everything stopped and changed. Me sister left home and never came back staying in the North East. Me relationship with me mum changed too cos I was annoyed at her for letting it happen. Not standing up to him and being a victim.

Poverty

For Stella, being poor meant her parents did not have enough money to heat the house. This led to their burning the furniture for fuel. Stella felt different to the others when she went to school and thought that being poor left her open and vulnerable

> You felt ashamed somehow, that people were looking down at you like if you was hungry it was your fault and had nowt to do with not having enough money. You kept everythin' in so no one singled you out. Me husband says that I still worry rather than sharing it with him. I try to make out all's well even if sometimes it's not. At least now you can knock up a decent meal for under three quid.

Being poor did not stop Stella from describing her childhood as happy; however, as she was going to school hungry she found it hard to concentrate. And seeing her mum and dad struggle over money made her sad.

Stella: Yeah. That's where your energy went on surviving not school work. It's like you were expected just to get on with at school no matter what was happening at home or in your belly for that matter. Try concentrating when you're mad hungry – no chance. The teacher would be speaking and you'd be imagining some lovely meal – it's odd now people have too much to eat, then there wasn't enough, no cheap frozen food. It must be a nice feeling to be a child and have nowt to think about but learning. A luxury really, don't you think? Still I've got a bit of a chance to that now more than me mum had, eh? Me mum and dad they did struggle but there were a lot of love with me mum and my dad . . . I've seen me mum and dad go without food to feed us, and I always saw me mam . . . doing a bit of cleaning here and there to get us clothes. In the summer I can remember her paying off a couple of bob a week at a shop to get me and me sister these white patent shoes for Whitsuntime and then she paid money at another shop at the top of the street on Ashton road to get Whitsuntide outfits. Me mum really did struggle but she were a good mother she used to – we used to have a bath every night and . . . she used to iron all the clothes they used to be on the back of the settee lined up on the morning for us to get them on. No she, me mum, had a hard life, then me dad had an accident at British Rail he was in hospital for a long time – he crushed his ribs and he was on sickness benefit and I can always remember we'd moved to Oil Avenue at the time, at Primrose Bank, and they hadn't sent his sick pay and it were February and it were really really bad weather and the icicles run on the inside of the window . . . It was absolutely freezing and she'd no coal left, and me dad went all round the house and got all the old shoes and burnt them on the coal fire. She made a pan of hash on the fire because there weren't gas for the gas cooker. And, by the end of the weekend he'd burnt everything he could burn and me mum had this beautiful – I mean it must have been worth a fortune today – highly polished sideboard left off by grandma, and he had to chop it up. I mean I can remember me mum going in the kitchen absolutely heartbroken, but he had to keep us warm and we had to bring all the mattresses down stairs. We thought it were brilliant and then the electric went and they had candles and me dad was making us shadows on the wall and he played the mouth organ to keep us occupied because there were no telly. We'd be singing Christmas carols in February. [Laughs]

Interviewer: And how many children were they?

Stella: There were seven of us. But you know and them are my memories. They're good memories – my mum and dad could have just put us in care and I can always remember that we couldn't go to school on the Monday morning because there was no hot water for a bath and the house was too cold to go upstairs for a bath. So she went into school and told the headmaster what had gone on and the headmaster phoned the social services, they came down and they'd been paying me dad £14 a week short in his benefits and that's why me mum was struggling. In fact if it weren't for . . . this lady called Vera and John her husband . . . they had the off licence and they ticked me mum potatoes and bread and things to get us over the weekend and corned beef, she made this big pan of corned beef hash. And she never ticked cigarettes and me dad smoked woodbines and John Slater come round to the house and give me dad forty woodbine and said 'here Danny don't be telling our Vera them are off me'. I always have that memory because he really realised my dad always worked up till this accident, me mum and dad were never on benefits you see and they never knew and . . . we survived that weekend but we thought it were brilliant . . . Downstairs sleeping on mattresses . . . and me dad was on the mouth organ . . . Playing the Christmas carols and we were all singing them. And when I look back now and I always say, when I'm having a laugh with me mum, you know when my dad chopped that side board up you should have told him to burn one of the kids – there were seven kids and only one side board (laughs). And we laugh about it now, but at the time me mum . . . was so heartbroken because it was such a beautiful side board . . . It was all you know velvet, green velvet in the drawers, and she really looked after it . . . It was her pride and joy but it had to go on the fire (laughs). Anyway I can remember them sorting me dad a book out then he didn't have to wait for a giro . . . but they were paying me dad £14 a week short, which were a lot of money. That's how me dad's benefits got sorted out until he went back to work at British Rail when he was fully recovered.

The influence of a child's background is significant to their experience of schooling. Fourteen of the learners spoke of the poverty they faced in childhood. Poverty is very stressful and can result in negative symbolic capitals (see Figures 3.1a, 3.3, 5.2, 5.3) which may cause stigma and shame, and had an impact on the learners' experience of school and how they viewed themselves.

Glamour capital

Rachel was taunted at primary and secondary school, but found that as she reached her teens she was gaining attention from boys

Rachel: I'd 'ave a few boys ask me out when I left school. I didn't 'ave much of a job but I always made sure I looked my best.
Interviewer: How did that make you feel?
Rachel: Good
Interviewer: Why?
Rachel: Cos it did. I suppose I knew it was a way out of their house.

Joanne also tried to look her best:

Joanne: My hair always was styled. I had a Purdey cut when that was out, I always kept it modern.
Interviewer: Who did you keep modern for?
Joanne: I wanted everyone to know I looked after myself.

The learners were aware that their bodies and their dispositions form the 'physical sites where the relations of class, gender, race, sexuality and age come together and are embodied and practised' (Skeggs 1997: 82). They were aware that glamour was a capital that offered them power to attract the opposite sex (see figure 6.2) and to gain respectability (Skeggs 1997).

Conclusion

Schooling was something that came second to surviving and dealing with what was happening at home. When the learners entered the field of schooling, they did not have the right capitals – which included support from home and a stable home life – in order to progress, navigate through the field of schooling and reach their potential. For many of the families this instability was exacerbated by poverty. Both at home and at school there was 'misrecognition' as the learners did not question what was happening to them. The symbolic violence they experienced by those in a more powerful position, particularly at home, left them bruised and silent. Their silence may be viewed as conforming to the constraints placed upon them; however, I would argue that their silence was a weapon of empowerment whereby they could protect their identity from being soiled by the public gaze (see Figure 5.2), rather than leaving it open to shame. They were very aware of how they might have been viewed and made determined efforts to prevent this by keeping their silence.

The middle class enter the educational field possessing a set of dispositions that are deemed the 'norm'; this allows them to take to the school system like 'a fish to water' (Bourdieu and Waquant, 1992: 121). The value of different capitals are linked to the context in which they are found; for example something that is greatly valued in an academic field may not be so highly revered in the world of 'street capital'. While 15 of the working-class learners in this study did not possess the right dispositions to succeed at school, they transferred the pain of trauma and violence into what I have coined 'resistance capital', 'muscle capital' (see Figure 6.1), 'domestic capital' and 'glamour capital' (see Figure 6.2). These were deemed as important for them to survive on the streets and for them to gain the 'look' (in the case of glamour capital) to find a man who'd give them a decent life, or a job which could utilise their skills in the case of 'domestic capital'. They are not passive victims: they gain the capitals needed to survive at the time and in getting work, albeit in unskilled jobs.

If sociologists and educationalists are to understand how social class and gender impact on education it is vital to examine the links between schools and families of different social classes. Standards of the field are always shifting and changing and this includes the educational field (Bourdieu 1994; Bourdieu and Wacquant 1992). Bourdieu's theoretical model allows us to explore the diverse cultural practices in these changing fields and society. As such it allows us to expose how some practices have pathologised the working class as 'other'. This allows us to avoid a deficit model where the families of the middle class are idealised.

The concepts of capital are very good at overcoming these problems. Without entry level basic skills in literacy many of the learners in this study were pushed towards unskilled and low paid jobs from school. Schools were seen as privileging the middle and upper classes and exploiting the working class through preparation for unemployment or unskilled employment.

Personal reflections

Hearing the learners' narratives of their abuse cut me to the quick. Joanne's childhood emotional abuse from her family and at school, Tracy and Martin's experience of continual bullying, Shammy who was beaten by his uncle; all of them, their pain bled into the tape recorder, it was tragic to hear and even more tragic to see the impact it had and continues to have on their lives. I felt so impotent. I did not want to be a voyeur and I had to process the information and really think about its consequences. I wanted the findings of my study to create change and social justice; but also I wanted to be the best teacher I could in order to facilitate them believing in and reaching their potential. I felt a responsibility to ease their pain and mend the past: but this wasn't a movie with a crisis and – an hour later – a happy ever after. These interviewees are flesh and blood, they cried and their pain and sadness doesn't switch off.

They made me think about how I perceived all this information. I felt angry, very angry at the people who had hurt them. I also felt very sad at a child's innocence lost and their vulnerability in the face of emotional and physical violence that – for some – has been hidden in pain for many years. While listening to and reading again and again the learners' narratives, and thinking about my own,

I've realised that trying to make sense of someone hurting you psychologically or physically is the hardest thing in the world. Perhaps, I felt, if I delved deeper into how I coped with my own pain I could understand their choices and also find support strategies for them; so I had to travel deep inside myself (to a place I really did not want to go, with a young family to take care of, and my home life so different to that of my childhood) to where my roots were formed, motivations driven, my narrative merging into a stream of emotions with the learners.

The need to be deeply reflective (which was a constant part of the research) remains the most draining and difficult thing to do. Living in your head is intense, especially when what you're trying to make sense of hurts. I was unravelling memories and emotions I'd sooner put to bed, but instead I needed to go back and make sense of my life and the choices I made to understand why I made those decisions. I felt almost guilty for putting my experiences and feelings onto paper, exposing my inner self to another's eye. School life is out there in the public domain, the world can dip into it and it won't hurt me half as much as people dipping into life behind my childhood front door. This is a field that only the family cross; a personal field that never was an easy field to navigate through. I struggled to accept the violence in my childhood and kept it secret. At home, my habitus always seemed out of sync with those around me. Like watching a film of my life, as it unfolded, I stood outside the violence and felt like an outsider looking in, a spectator. I suppose this distance kept me sane. Privacy is power, and letting go of this means handing over the power, which is not easy. Everything I have kept hidden suddenly exposed everything that I felt; shame being put in black and white on pages of paper. These words and the emotions embedded in them provided me and the learners with a shared dialogue and wider context to turn this shame into shared liberation.

Chapter 7

The public field of work

Overview

In this chapter, I will explore the learners' experiences of violence and trauma as adults in the public field of the workplace. Further to this, I will follow the resistance, conformity and struggle they make when faced with these experiences and how this shapes their further trajectories. I have taken the view that adulthood is not distinct from childhood, but an extension whereby the habitus shaped in childhood is taken into the field of adulthood. The experience of violence and trauma on the learners' lives both in childhood and adulthood can influence the way they view themselves and the choices they make, whether these be about the form of employment or no employment they enter into and reasons they make for these choices. I would suggest that these reasons are very much linked to the childhood experiences the learners have had in the public and private domains (Walkerdine and Lucey 1989; Luttrell 1997; Skeggs 1997).

Introduction

In Willis (1977) and Bourdieu and Passeron (1977) the purpose of schooling was seen as the means to 'reproduce the means of production'. The hidden curriculum (see Bowles and Gintis 1976) can be seen to play a part in this social reproduction in that school works to differentiate the status of workers into what may be considered factory floor workers, and the leaders and managers who offer surveillance of the factory floor. Similar to Willis's findings, a number of the learners in this study took agency to think and act for themselves against the structures of inequality embedded in both their schooling and the wider society which created barriers to their success. As seen in the previous chapter, knowing they were being labelled for being poor and struggling to read and write, the learners took agency by wagging school, not engaging and in a number of cases leaving school before the compulsory leaving age.

The agency the learners took at school often left them without cultural capital and did not equip them with the qualifications and references needed to progress into any work other than unskilled labour. In many cases this was 'labour' intensive and lead to precarious working conditions.

On entering employment, out of the 16 learners, only one learner, Sally, went into a job from school which required qualifications; this was nursery nursing. She was also the only learner who left school with any qualifications. It is worth referring to the chapter on schooling which highlights the support she had received from her parents, which included paying for a private tutor to support her studies. For the other women (and men) in the study, however, this was not an option. Many struggled but were unable to get extra support and being thus unmotivated, gave up putting any effort into schoolwork. Parsons and Bynner's study highlighted how:

> For women, poor educational achievement underpins poor employment prospects, especially in the non-manual office jobs that young women tend to favour. In contrast to men in this situation, the outcome for low-skilled women is frequently early partnership and parenthood, offering the alternative career path of mother and carer.
>
> (Parsons and Bynner 2008: 29)

Six out of the nine women in the study had their first child when they were teenagers. Out of the six, five were unmarried and one married during the pregnancy. Three of the mothers were intermittently in relationships as their children were growing up. At the time of the interviews, however, they were single parents and remained single mothers throughout the study. Joanne described her experience of early motherhood as:

> It's what everyone did round near where I lived and I was no different.

While Tracy recalls:

> It just sort of happened – it wasn't planned. But I was happy when it did.

Combining motherhood and work

In the study, only Rachel did not work when motherhood came along. She married in her teens and had her first child shortly after. Her husband was able to support her so she took on the traditional role of homemaker. For the other women with children, rather than motherhood being an alternative route, as described by Parsons and Bynner (2008), it was combined with work. The jobs they took were often unskilled and meant they had to put in many hours of labour to take get a wage that was decent enough to make ends meet and pay bills. For Stella and Emily, they could work fewer hours as they had a partner's wage contributing to the household, while for Tracy and Carol, theirs was the only wage coming into the home, so they worked full-time time. Soon after the birth of her first child at 17, Joanne returned to work as a sewing machinist. Below she describes the work:

Joanne: Machining is all about piecework, the more you do the more you get paid.
Interviewer: Does that put pressure on you?
Joanne: I suppose so, but you know you'll get a decent enough wage so it's worth it.

This type of work also leaves insecurity and anxiety related to the prospect of being laid off or becoming ill. Joanne describes the insecurity of piecework:

> You can make good money machining; it's piecework. You'd push out as many as you could and know it'd be going in your wage. But it was hard work. If you were ill or owt you were paid nowt. And if the business went slack you'd be laid off. It paid off when the orders were coming in but when they weren't you'd had it and had to go spongin' for a borrow to pay the rent.

Joanne's wage and economic security was directly linked to the prosperity of the business. She worked under these precarious conditions with the threat of being laid off hanging over her working week and the prospect of having to sponge off someone if a wage did not materialise. She took this for granted and worked hard to keep her job.

Joanne: I was just glad of a job, so I worked really hard yer know. The girls who didn't put the effort in got their cards soon enough
Interviewer: How did that make you feel?
Joanne: What?
Interviewer: Girls around you losing their jobs.
Joanne: I felt shitty but that's the way it goes. You had to be able to cut it to keep your job.

For Joanne, keeping her job and receiving a wage was earned by 'labour power'. This labour power only offered job security, while it was needed and while it was working to maximum output. Joanne did not question this mode of production and her part in it. Labour capital was clearly linked to symbolic violence, which occurred because Joanne was being denied the rights of job security, denied a voice to contest the workload and treated as inferior by the management. This caused her anxiety and stress. The symbolic violence of domination was misrecognised as natural rather than recognised as being a result of structural inequalities. These structural inequalities included her poverty and lack of cultural capital, such as qualifications from school, which would have offered her the possibility of working in an environment which valued her skills and led to job security. Competition was also set among the girls in order to get the maximum output from them. The competition was linked to neo-liberalism where each worker was competing to keep their own job. There was no union to support them. Survival was based on understanding the rules of the game and aiming to win. For Joanne, with a child to care for and bills to pay, not participating in the competition was not an option. Removal from the field would have led to further poverty. Figure 7.1 demonstrates the cycle of labour power and competition for Joanne and how she struggled as she navigated across the constraints.

For both Joanne and Tracy, work was also not viewed as a stimulating alternative to home and unemployment. Tracy described her job

> Well at work all I do is look for part numbers and I put them on the table. Swing a machine on. I start puttin' one part in and it's like a number on top. Pullin' a handle, flickin' a button, getting it out and puttin' another number in. And I do that all day. It's repetitive and it's boring. So it doesn't take brains. You don't need any degree as long as you just turn a knob on and off, that's it.

For both Tracy and Joanne, however, working in the factory was something they enjoyed because they met friends and accrued social capital. Tracy describes how:

Tracy: The jobs I've done have been boring, no brainers.
Interviewer: What do you mean no brainers?
Tracy: You know, you don't have to think. Any idiot could do it.
Interviewer: How do you feel doing the jobs?
Tracy: Okay because it gets me out of the house and come break time I have a gab with the girls there.

Figure 7.2 illustrates the cycle of survival using labour capital for Tracy. She is both empowered and disempowered by work. She is disempowered by the constraints, but empowered by the social and economic capital the job offers.

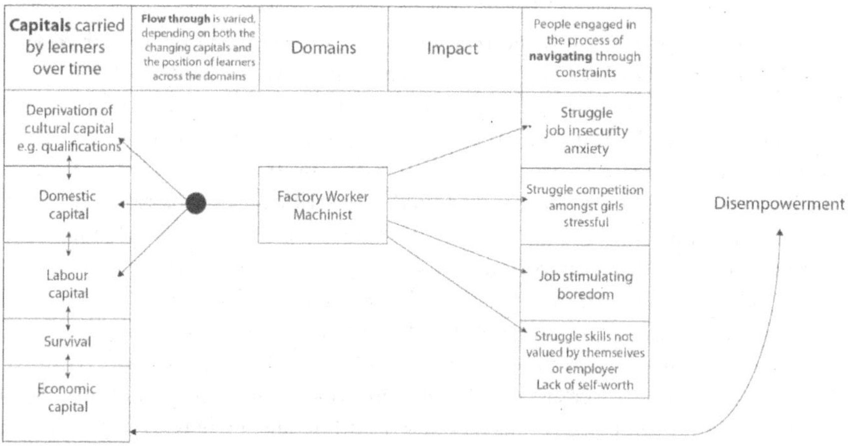

Figure 7.1 Cycle of labour power and competition for Joanne

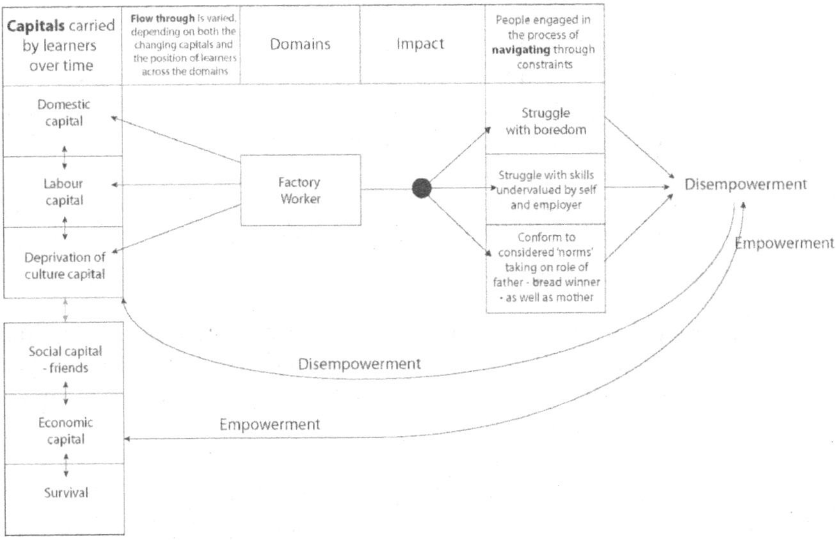

Figure 7.2 Cycle of survival using labour capital for Tracy

Joanne also talks about the social side of work:

> At the cig break you get to have a gab. I like that, it sort of breaks the day up even if it's only for five minutes.

As identified by Luttrell (1997), the women's work was not considered to need any intelligence even though both jobs required skills: Joanne in her sewing job and Tracy to work machinery. Tracy describes her job as a 'no brainer', while Joanne describes how:

> It's what you do if you've no exams. For the ones who are not that bright I suppose.

With low level cultural capital (qualifications) the women utilised their labour power. They undervalued their skills and knowledge as did their employers, even though it was these which earned them the wage to care for and look after their family. As the sole bread winners, they were bridging the gap between what was traditionally the male role (worker in the public domain) and female role (home-maker and care giver). This push to care for themselves and their children, when they were only teenagers themselves, caused them great anxiety. They had to grow up quickly. For Tracy, her children were the third generation without a father figure. She felt she needed to give them what a man could give. She believed that this something was her capacity to earn a wage. Tracy says:

Tracy:	It's like by bringing in a wage in I'm giving them the best of both, you know what I mean?
Interviewer:	Tell me a little bit more about that.
Tracy:	Well, it's the man who normally brings in the wage and I've done it. I've also done the rest of the stuff, like cooking and putting them to bed, yer know just being mum like.
Interviewer:	Is it difficult doing both?
Tracy:	Don't know. Suppose it's hard 'cos it's tiring having no one to help or just to gab to at night about the kids. You end up talking to the telly [laughs].

The reality was that Tracy was the sole breadwinner, but she did not interpret this as the norm. The division of labour – women in the domestic sphere (home) and male in the public (work) – and the symbolic violence of the gendered habitus helps to explain the deeply embodied nature of emotional labour:

> Gendered habitus includes a set of complex, diverse predispositions. It involves understandings of identity premised on familial legacy and early childhood socialization. As such it is primarily a dynamic concept, a rich interfacing of past and present, interiorised and permeating both body and psyche.
>
> (Reay in Grenfell and James 1998: 141)

Tracy felt guilty that these traditional roles were not being carried out. Indeed, part of the drive for her to work was the need to fulfil the role of 'father' while also acknowledging her other role as 'mother'. Tracy expended both emotional and physical labour in carrying out these two roles. Clearly, traditional gender divisions were permeating Tracy's psyche, which surprised me as she was the second generation in her family without a father figure. It is important to draw on the previous chapter and the gendered 'glamour capital' which was used to attract a partner and was a means to build 'a family'. However, 'glamour capital' (see Figure 6.2) was swapped for 'caring' and 'labour capital' once Tracy became a single mum.

The value of the notion of 'the family' is a major one as it makes up essential ground in preserving patriarchy and gender roles. 'The family' reflects examples of structural and symbolic violence (Bourdieu 2001b). The symbolic power and violence describe how culture controls Tracy in a hierarchal domination with symbolic exploitation and taken-for-granted 'norms'. Bourdieu clarified, through this concept, that the dominated accepts and legitimates domination. It is a two way agreement process between the dominant and the dominated. This happens when the dominated, like Tracy, misrecognise the symbolic power and consider it to be the natural order of things. Patriarchy and the gender roles Tracy carried in her psyche are an example of this. For Tracy, family patterns exist in her psyche, even though the impression is that they have changed. Even though Tracy took on the dual role, her psyche was kept in line with patriarchy.

Indeed patriarchal norms continue to be impregnated in the future formation of gender.

Transferring caring and domestic capital into work

For the women in the study there was a need to transfer and utilise 'caring' and 'domestic' capital from childhood and adulthood in order to secure work (see Figure 6.2). Without cultural capital they drew on their everyday skills. Carol and Stella's stories illustrate this.

Carol's story

Carol, who was in her 50s when she started the basic skills class, described how the experience of growing up in a convent involved using caring and domestic capital. The transference of caring capital has been explored in the realm of adulthood (for example, see, Luttrell 1997; Reay 2000; O'Brien 2005; Feeley 2007; Lynch et al. 2008), but rarely in the realm of childhood. The use of Carol's caring capital is particularly poignant as, without a family, she lacked caring models herself.

> I got on well with the girls alright, because I was as daft as the younger ones but I knew if you were older than someone you looked after them, just sort of a mother figure you took over.

Carol also describes her domestic role in the convent:

> We all mucked into the cleaning. I took real pride in it, made sure I did it well.

Below is an extract written by Carol for our journal:

> I was brought up in a convent in Southern Ireland from the age of two-and-a-half years old to 16. I was looked after by my grandmother up until going into the convent. Lots of my memories of that time in the convent are of lots of rules and hard work, some I didn't find too hard . . . One of the jobs I had to do before going to school in the morning was to clean a lot of outside toilets and yard. I had to use cold water even in winter and was late for school if I did not get it finished in time. I got punished for being late a lot . . . I had to help out in the kitchen and cook for the nuns. I enjoyed cooking as I was learning how to cook a lot of different things which come in handy as I got older.

The transference of the domestic and caring capital Carol acquired at the convent was used when she went working in cleaning jobs. The cleaning work enabled

Carol to save the money to travel and make a new life for herself over the Irish Sea. She travelled from Dublin, Ireland, to London. From London she travelled to Oldham where she settled and brought up her three daughters as a single mother.

Stella's story

Stella, who had helped her mum care for the family, used these skills in both caring for her own family and in doing cleaning jobs outside the home. On leaving school with no qualifications and having no confidence, employment meant low paid jobs as a cleaner.

> There's nowt much you can do if you struggle with your writing. Everything's about writing these days.

The domestic capital was directly linked with the heavy labour capital of using heavy industrial machinery. Below is an extract from our journal:

> Met Stella. I picked her up and we went to the garden centre. We chatted about how she wants to go back into care work now she feels more confident to do her NVQ in health. She told me about the vacuum cleaners that she has been using to clean the school where she is employed as a cleaner. She has developed arthritis in her back and is finding it really difficult to manoeuvre the heavy Hoover she has to use. She seemed really determined that she wants to get out of cleaning and get what she described as a better job caring for people. It was really good to see her enthused about it. The sad part is that she still needs to work as a cleaner until a caring job comes up. But now's she has the confidence to go for it – it's a real step forward.

Stella's aim was to once again utilise her domestic and caring skills, but this time in the field of health – to become a care assistant, where she perceived the work as not being as heavy or soul destroying.

Joanne's story

Joanne's story illustrates the difficulty of securing work without the skills and knowledge required. It demonstrates how, even though she had been labelled as not having the practical know-how to sew at school, Joanne used this domestic capital in her role as a machinist. The idea that it is something she picked up at school or at home is problematic, however. Joanne picked it up out of necessity and the need to earn a wage.

> Machining is summat I picked up really easy. It's not like you need exams. It's summat most women can do.

The irony of this was that the needlework teacher wouldn't let Joanne use the sewing machine at school.

> This was in juniors and infants and by the time you got to senior school you just accepted it and so in senior school I can never remember 'avin' many lessons 'cept in history 'cos the teacher was dead strict and 'cos of that I really like history . . . but I remember the needlework teacher wouldn't let me on a sewing machine and I'm a machinist now. But . . . it was awful – the teachers didn't bother turning up. I never remember 'avin' a maths lesson or an English lesson. That's how it were, we were just left in a room to play – basically – that's the truth as well.

Transitions from one field of work to another

Drawing on Bourdieu and Wacquant (1992) and Puwar (2004) the capability of an individual to 'play the game' is dependent on habitus, which affects how people interact within a new social field they have entered. It is worth considering the impact of changing fields on the learners' emotions and trajectories.

For Joanne, college was the mediating site for her transition from working as a sewing machinist to nursing. Joanne describes how she viewed the student nurses:

Joanne: They all seem cleverer than me somehow. Sometimes I wonder if it's worth putting myself through the stress.
Interview: What keeps you going?
Joanne: I suppose it's having you and the others in the research group to talk to. It's daft I know having this self doubt but sometimes I can't help it. I can't believe I actually got here – sometimes I just get a nagging that I'll lose it.

For Joanne, together with the anxiety that she would lose everything (her opportunity to train to be become a nurse), there was also the feeling that she did not fit in:

Joanne: I felt like a fraud on the ward, like someone like me shouldn't be there.
Interviewer: Why?
Joanne: Always thought nurses and doctors were different than me somehow, smarter, so I feel like a bit of a fraud.
Interviewer: Fraud. Why?
Joanne: Like they'll find out about where I've come from and tell me I'm not good enough.

The above dialogue demonstrates the difficulty of moving from the field of casual piecework to that of the professional world. The notion of re-invention and individualisation (Giddens 1991a; Beck 1992; Beck and Beck-Gernsheim 1995) totally ignores the impact of the lack of capitals in the field and their impact on how the learner engages with the field. Indeed what is striking in the elaboration of Joanne's experience above is the importance of social capital in challenging the symbolic violence whereby Joanne felt her habitus was not right and incongruent to the field of health. Without support, the constraints she felt could clearly have determined her chance of success in a new field.

In the conditions of training to be a nurse in the university, and the effort needed on a personal level to develop a habitus where Joanne felt she was not an imposter and develop the meta-language acquisition of nursing, there was certainly a factor of what Bourdieu (1994) described as symbolic violence. Indeed, entering the nursing profession had moved the goal posts, both in the 'elaborated code' that people in the new field she had moved into (Higher Education and nursing) used, and in the further linguistic barrier of having to learn the meta-language of medicine. Reay (2004b) makes a relevant point when highlighting how Bourdieu 'points out that the operation on the habitus regularly excludes certain practices, that are unfamiliar to the cultural groupings to which the individual belongs' (Reay 2004b: 433). Many practices Joanne encountered were out of her world picture; language was one that manifested itself on a moment-to-moment, day-to-day basis. The obstacle of encountering and incorporating new language acquisition into her daily practice proved to be huge for Joanne and listening to new words that 'flew at her from all directions', she described how, 'I couldn't even say 'em let alone spell 'em.' Joanne was clearly in need of what Bourdieu (1986) describes as social capital. In a position to help her develop a network of support, together with myself, one of my friends – a senior practice nurse – met up with Joanne at the local beauty spot Daisy Nook. There, we all walked through the reserve and chatted about the worries and concerns Joanne was experiencing. Further support continued with telephone conversations to the practice nurse, whom Joanne befriended. Joanne revealed how she felt supported in expressing difficulties and learning from someone who had a grasp on meta-language as an 'insider' and someone who could offer advice about working on a ward. Having also been a nurse, I supported Joanne in her acquisition of language with a number of key words used on the ward (for example, hypo means low while hyper means high; therefore hypotension refers to low blood pressure, and hypertension equals high). Joanne voiced how this support mechanism had been extremely beneficial. Study aids of personal dictionaries were also demonstrated to develop Joanne's skills and, importantly, her confidence. My role as a teacher was being utilised in the strategies that I advised Joanne to put in place to develop her skills. This was an ongoing process.

Joanne found the support from the research group, which included myself, a former nurse, and the links I have with other nurses, a way of developing social cultural capital. Joanne described how being part of the research group was supportive. She highlighted how:

> I really don't think I could have carried on with my nurse training if I hadn't been part of the research group. I knew that if I had something I was stuck on or that was worrying me I only needed to pick up a phone. Many a time I felt like packin' it in cos I felt like I just wasn't good enough. It was having someone who believed in me that made the difference.

Drawing on the bonds made at college and subsequently university, Joanne began to feel more confident in the field. For Joanne the social capital converted into cultural capital (qualified nurse status), and the cultural capital was converted to economic capital when Joanne received her first pay packet. Figure 7.3 illustrates the cycle of transitional empowerment, whereby Joanne moved from disempowerment in the field of factory work (see Figure 7.1), to the accruing of capitals and empowerment in the profession of nursing. Although she initially struggled to believe she fit in to the field of health, over time she felt a sense of belonging and

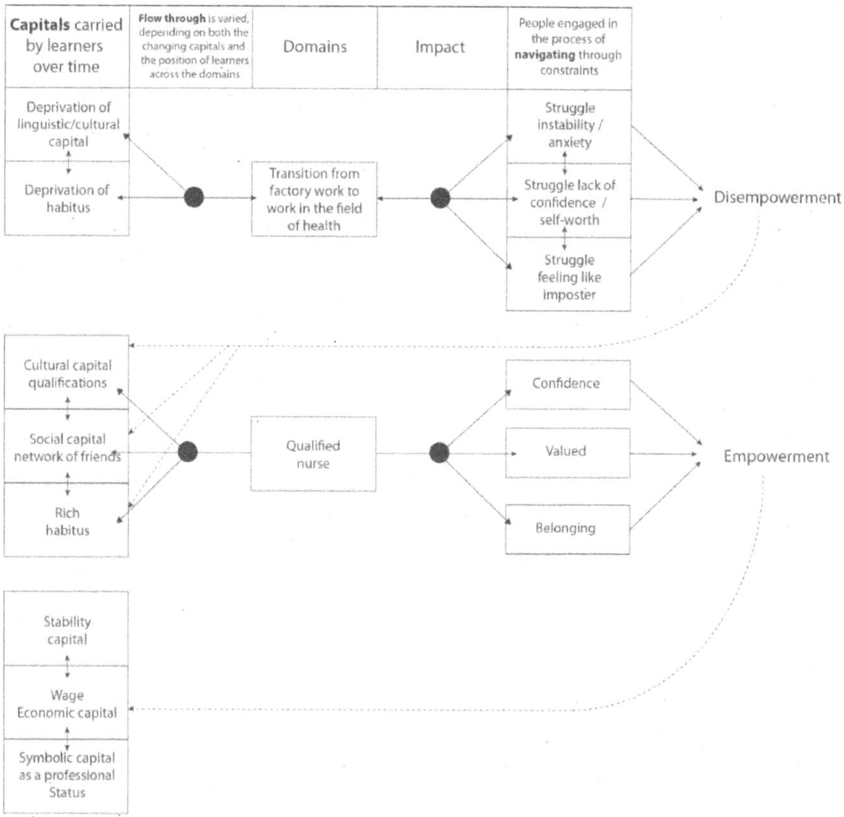

Figure 7.3 Cycle of transitional empowerment

being valued. Having a regular income and a career offered stability and financial security for herself and her family.

In the research journal, I recorded an incident below, involving Joanne, which helps illustrate the above. It also offers an insight into the possibility and uncertainties of change in habitus, allowing me to extend on Bourdieu's concept of habitus.

Joanne contacted me from her local pub very upset and needing reassurance. She explained how 'she didn't fit in anymore'. The picture she created was that people who she knew, didn't understand when she tried to tell them about her nursing. 'They looked at me blank faced,' she said, 'like I was really stupid'. When all this was going on she found out her ex was in a nearby pub with a 'young blonde' when he should have been looking after the children. Joanne was furious and went in to see him and 'give him a piece of me mind'. 'I've got to get out of 'ere,' she told me. Evidently there is now a dichotomy between the behaviour of the people around Joanne and what she now expects from them. As discussed by Reay (2004a) 'Habitus can be transformed through a process that either raises or lowers an individual's expectations. Implicit in the concept is the possibility of a social trajectory that enables conditions of living that are very different from initial ones' (Reay 2004a: 435). Although Joanne's expectations are rising, she remains in the environment that has 'dragged me down for long enough'. What is clearly distressing for Joanne is the need to fit in and belong as she used to, but with her description of how, 'I've changed, moved on from this place. I want more than gettin' pissed and sitting on me arse,' leaves her dislocated from how she describes the people on the estate. If anything, the chasm between Joanne's expectations and what is delivered may tear further apart as she progresses to a staff nurse; however, as a qualified nurse, she may then be in a position to make 'better' moves, like 'getting off the estate.' On the other hand, she may remain there and reconcile the 'difference' in her changing views and expectations compared to the people around her, accepting what 'is' rather than facing being disillusioned with unreal and at times unfair expectations of those around her.

Interestingly, later in the study, although Joanne still felt like an outsider on her estate, she voices how her position in the field of the workplace changed. 'I always felt I wasn't like the other nurses an' that, like an imposter. Maybe I was kiddin' meself, me a nurse? No way.' On having lunch with a group of the staff at the health centre, however, she described how after two years of nurse training, everything 'clicked into place'. She went onto to expand that while eating and chatting with the staff, she suddenly realised 'I knew none of 'em was better than me, we're all doin' a job and I was one of the team.' Working among medical professionals, Joanne had certainly developed her confidence and skills and positioned herself as an insider in the field of health. An empowered and professional woman she says 'I can't believe where I was five years back and where I am now.'

Exposing struggles in literacy in the public domain and symbolic violence

Craig's story

> Men with Entry 2 literacy spent more time unemployed or sick than those with higher skills. They were thrice as likely to have experienced three or more spells of unemployment by age 34. Men with Entry 3 or higher skills who left school at 16 had spent 14 of the following 18 years in full-time employment, while those with Entry 2 literacy had, on average, spent just 12 years in full-time employment.
>
> (Parsons and Bynner 2008: 21)

The statistics above seemed to be contradicted by Craig's story; however, when the reality of his literacy level (Entry 2/3) was exposed in the field of work, his position in the field of work and home radically changed. Each impacting on the other, his world was shot apart.

Aged 16, Craig had begun to work his way up from the shop floor of the factory, having gained no qualifications from school; here, he was using his muscle capital (see figure 6.1). He was then promoted to management in his 30s and the use of muscle capital was swapped for cultural/linguistic capital. He was married with a family, and the wage he earned enabled him to buy a detached house in a residential area. It was a long way from the home of his childhood. Then he was made redundant for what he called 'finding out I was no good at writing'. This 'finding out' came about when the company brought in computers for the managers to use in their working practices. Prior to this, Craig would take the reports and memos home for his wife to help him write and check his spelling for accuracy. Another example of women's hidden labour, she would ensure they were of a high enough quality for him to return them to work the following day and give them to the senior manager. With the advent of the ICT in the offices, however, they wanted the memos and reports produced on the computer at a faster pace, often on the same day. Thus, Craig did not have the opportunity to take them home for his wife to check. Craig speaks of his experience below.

> It's not just that I struggled to write the reports and to spell, using the computers was also new to me. I panicked half the time. Even when I got to grips with typing I couldn't tell if the spell check was checking the right words 'cos my spelling was up the shoot. I'd try to put it off so I could take whatever writing I needed to do home for me missus to check, but it got so the boss wanted it within the day. That's when I was caught out. They'd come and collar me telling me that I was being lazy, not trying. It was as though they thought I was just throwing the stuff I sent them together. Course I wasn't – Sometimes it'd take hours. Their attitude towards me changed. It felt like I was back at school, you know being judged. That's when I was given the

> push, made redundant. I know it's because they caught me, you might get away with not being able to write properly on the shop floor but as manager I was supposed to get it right. Told them I'd go to night school, they didn't care really, they'd made their mind up – what could I do?

He described how he had kept his dyslexia a secret from his work colleagues and managers at work because he did not want to be stigmatised. He struggled with being dyslexic but conformed to the ideals of what he thought was expected of him by utilising his wife's literacy skills and masking them as his own to his employers. He experienced feelings of embarrassment, great anxiety and stress at hiding his struggles in literacy. Unable to meet the traditional ideals of manhood, which include being literate and being able to transfer 'literacy capital' into the world of work, he was subjected to symbolic violence. When made redundant, this was strengthened by the construction of his unemployment being positioned as an individual deficit.

Craig: I know it's because they found out about my dyslexia. Before that and them computers being brought in there was no problem. I was the only one made redundant. Cutting down was just an excuse. I heard off one of the fellas I used to work with they employed someone else when I left and gave him another title. That tells me in no uncertain terms it's about me isn't it.

Interviewer: How did you feel?

Craig: I felt like such a failure, what letting myself, me wife and the kids down it was the worst feeling ever.

Craig did not have the linguistic capital needed for the field he was working in. His habitus was revealed as lacking (Bourdieu 1984) and he was subjected to symbolic violence by his employees. Subsequently he went on to lose his job, wage, house, marriage and economic power. Below, Figure 7.4 illustrates how the deprivation of capitals across the domains of Craig's life led to both struggle and challenge. He struggled with depression and a lack of self-esteem, but challenged his employers.

Craig tried to fight unfair dismissal through the courts; however, he lost the case and ended up in debt. This resulted in further struggles and disempowerment for Craig.

When he lost his job and when he started the New Deal course he was living in a council flat in Oldham. He was very depressed and was put on the programme by the unemployment agency.

New Deal programmes and routes into employment

Together with Craig, five of the learners were put on the New Deal Programme by the job agency. The course seemed to be pushing compliance with the classes

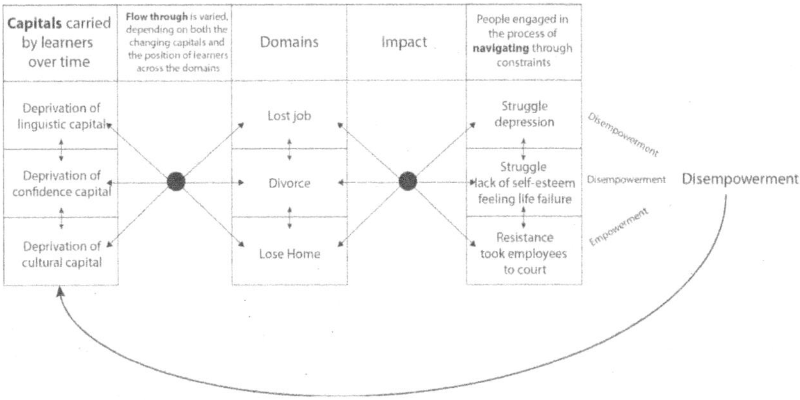

Figure 7.4 Cycle of deprivation of linguistic/cultural capital, confidence and struggle and resistance

very much in line with a clocking in and clocking out system. Even though they were adults, many with a high number of years of work under their belt, they were treated with a lack of trust, as if they needed constant supervision to ensure they toed the line. The instructions were to take the register at regular intervals throughout the day (these registers were audited by management) and the threat that their social security payments could be stopped if they were regularly late or failed to attend. Although Craig was keen to learn, he did not complete the programme. I would suggest that it was because it was not tailored to help him develop the skills he needed to re-enter the field of management. He said:

> If I can look at my English and get that right I'll be able to pick up a job similar as I lost. I can do the rest of the job with my eyes closed, it's just the writing I'm dire at.

Instead of tailoring the course to Craig's (and other individual's needs) it was a generic programme where there was a focus on progressing the learners into the local supermarket to do unskilled work. The programme included the practice applications that they had to complete, no matter what their trajectory, hopes or aspirations. The job centre also worked with the college to ensure that they were all pushing the learners in the same direction. Craig described how:

> The job centre keep telling me to apply for work in Asda's warehouse. Then when I go to see the New Deal adviser in college they shove job applications under me nose for dead end jobs. It's as though all them years I put into working myself up to manager don't count for a thing.

Informal economy

Three of the learners on the new deal programme worked to accrue capital from the informal economy. Raz worked, cash in hand, as a waiter in Indian restaurants. This resulted in low pay for long hours. He described how he needed the money in order to attend the New Deal course at college which did not pay enough to support his extended family.

> Without working at night I couldn't come to college. I still need to bring money into the house.

Working as a waiter in Indian restaurants, Raz worked long and unsociable hours for below the minimum wage. He was unable to choose the courses he wanted to do until he had finished the New Deal programme. He found this frustrating because he felt like this was killing time.

> It's jumping through hoops all the time. It's hard not to just throw it in especially when I'm not getting to bed till well into the morning then I'm back at college at nine. I'm knackered most of the time.

The jumping through hoops was costing Raz time and money. The field of college, with its own structured timeline for commencing courses, which students have to fit in with, rather than having timelines that fit to learners' needs, left time zones where the learners felt they were drifting. Raz had to wait to complete the New Deal course before he could access any college courses he wanted to do. Raz progressed onto book-keeping and accountancy programmes, but due to the needs of the family he was unable to discontinue his informal economy work. He progressed to university but was unable to complete his course owing to the commitment needed to study at university level and the need to continue working to support his extended family. Raz now works full-time in the restaurant and hopes to return to university one day.

Craig found that he could empower himself and earn money in the informal economy by doing DJ'ing. Music is something that he was always interested in, a capital he could trade in to earn money. He describes how:

Craig: With music and DJ'ing I can be my own boss. It gives me something back.
Interviewer: Gives you what back?
Craig: Don't know – suppose I'm doing something I enjoy and want to do, it's not like the New Deal course.

DJ'ing, I would suggest, allowed Craig to take agency in his life. He was doing something he enjoyed and something he felt he was good at. This helped him to gain confidence and earn money. Craig continued to work as a DJ in Oldham and the North West after quitting the New Deal Programme.

Building on from Figure 7.4, Craig's cycle continued. Figure 7.5 illustrates how he took agency and, challenging the dominant economy and expectations to take an un-skilled and un-stimulating job, found confidence and feelings of being valued by pulling on his everyday practices and working as a DJ in the informal economy.

Mike earned money on the informal economy by selling marijuana. As well as getting money for the amount he sold he was also paid in marijuana, which is a drug he says he wouldn't have been able to afford unless he sold it as well.

Mike: Everyone does it. It's easy money. I couldn't live in that mad flat without having weed, fucking keeps me sane.
Interviewer: What, smoking it?
Mike: Both. I sell it to smoke it and get money to get by.

In the field of informal economy the learners could earn money and take agency in their life. However, it was a field where they were also exploited and exploitative. Raz was paid a low wage and worked long hours' work. Mike was being exploitative, by selling drugs to other people like him, but he was being exploited because the profit he made was shared with a bigger dealer who gave Mike the drug to sell. I would suggest that the informal economy contributes to the earnings of a number of people, but the legality of exposing it leaves it silent. This silence allows exploitation, but it also allows a space where people can earn the money for survival and use their skills to enjoy their life.

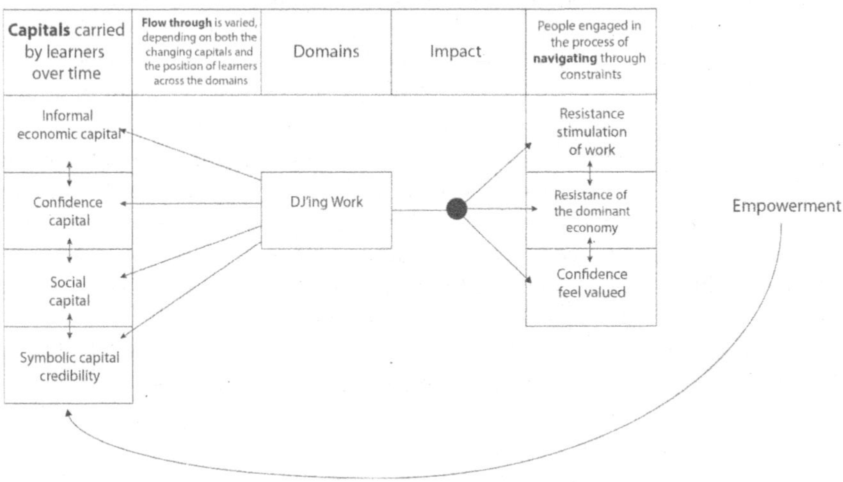

Figure 7.5 Cycle of resistance and empowerment in the informal economy

'Muscle' and 'macho' capital

Shammy: muscle capital

Shammy, in his early 20s, described how the 'macho' capital he had gained as a child helped him to secure a job as a security guard (see Figure 6.1).

> I suppose being beat up does makes you harder. Like look at me I've got to be tough to be a security guard, not that I'd ever hit out at anyone but I'm not afraid of some of the brick heads that try to cause trouble when I'm on the job. When you've been beat up as a kid you sort of get immune to the kicks, know what I mean.

This capital was also valued on the streets:

Shammy: I run and go to the gym a lot. People look at you different when you're built.
Interviewer: What do you mean?
Shammy: They look twice, they know you're not a pushover, you're summat.

Muscle capital was recognised by Shammy as giving him street credentials. It was also an area for him to earn a wage

> They're not going to give a skinny arse a security job, no way. Your muscles are like badges, look. [Shammy flexes his arm muscles to show me.]

Indeed, as described, it appears that that 'the idea of masculinity is one of the last refuges of the identity of the dominated classes . . . it's characteristic of people who have little to fall back on except their labour-power and sometimes their fighting strength (Bourdieu 1993: 3). Habitus is about social training. Bourdieu refers to habitus as 'a societal imperative which has become a second nature and has been developed into motor schemata and physical automatism' (Bourdieu 1993: 239). The working-class practice of toughening boys up was held up as training them to be tough and carried with it more capital – 'macho capital' – than the legitimate capital of acquiring qualifications. This capital was 'symbolic capital' of masculinity and was 'perceived and recognised as legitimate' (Skeggs 1997: 8). This capital was also valued on the streets.

On losing his job, Craig also began to pull on the muscle capital that had been lost when he was promoted to management by starting to work out at the gym.

Interviewer: Do you do anything outside college?
Craig: Course, I go to the gym three times a week
Interviewer: Do you enjoy it?

Craig: I put on loads of weight when I lost my job, going to the gym's got shut of it. I feel better about myself after a workout
Interviewer: How?
Craig: Getting the weight off and building myself up gives me something to focus on, a goal like. I was really fit when I was younger, I suppose it make me feel young again, like I'm not over the hill and that's it.

For Craig, muscle capital embodied youth and hope for the future.

College and voluntary community work as an alternative to work

For Tracy and Carol, both single mothers, coming to college was not only about gaining confidence with their reading and writing but also a way for them to develop social capital and meet new people after they had lost their jobs.

> Tuesday nights get me out of the house and away from the kids. That sounds awful doesn't it? But having something to look forward to, well, you need that.
>
> (Tracy)

> I tell 'em Tuesdays is my night. No teas cooked when I come to college, they can all have chippy. It's a night for me to get out of the house.
>
> (Carol)

It would be too simple to say that college is only about company. Wrapped in the attendance are hopes and aspirations. With these are hopes for getting a better job and doing what they consider to be 'more' with their lives. These aspirations, however, were not always fixed and were emergent. A motivation for changing aspirations was discussing learning journeys with other learners who had started with the basic skills course, but had progressed into jobs they never believed they could do. We also explored the different skills/qualifications needed for different pathways. This helped learners see personal pathways that were further discussed in tutorial and research nights out. Although Tracy did not paint when she started the literacy course at the end she spoke of:

> I'd like to do something where I can get people to do things they never thought they could, like with art really.

While Carol voiced her desires:

> I'd like to help other people like me in the future.

Both Carol and Tracy became involved in working with groups of learners voluntarily. Carol visited community centres and supported them with literacy while Tracy helped neighbours with literacy. She describes how:

Tracy:	I've kept all me work from the course. I'm using it to help A.
Interviewer:	Who's A?
Tracy:	She's a neighbour. She can't read or write or owt. She's always round at mine asking if I'll do this and that for her. I'm helpin' her to do it herself.

Although Tracy stopped doing voluntary work when she became severely depressed and was sectioned, since being discharged in 2010 she has worked closely with a neighbour on the neighbourhood renewal scheme. Part of this included putting forward a bid to start a community educational group and buy in computers. The voluntary work is a stimulating alternative to childcare and unemployment, unlike the paid work she did in a factory. Tracy is hoping that the voluntary work will eventually lead to paid work in the community.

Voluntary work and its impact on an individual's confidence and self-esteem is an area which would benefit from further research and exploring the links with Bourdieu's theory.

Conclusion

The findings demonstrate how the violence and trauma experienced in the public domain of the learners' lives from childhood to adulthood are reflected in the adult gendered divisions of care in the private domain. For example, girls helped with domestic and caring tasks while boys distanced themselves from this role, and lone mothers are left to care for the children while their former partners abandon fatherhood care. Subsequently, in the public domain the capital from these gendered divisions was utilised in work with the females gravitating to domestic and caring jobs. It should be said also that the females were gravitating towards labour intensive work. The males used muscle and macho capital to work, for example, working in security and the informal market in order to accrue economic capital and in some cases take agency in the field of the street.

The fields were not static and in the world of work there was the need to adapt one's habitus in order to have a congruous relationship with it. For example, when computers were brought into the organisation, Craig was unable to shape his linguistic and technological capital to meet the needs of the field and was subjected to symbolic violence. Also, the fields were a challenge when people newly entered them with a habitus that was deemed lacking in the correct capitals. The gap between the habitus and the needs of the fields created a space for reflection. This reflection led Joanne to try to develop her linguistic capital so she felt more confident and comfortable in the field of health. Being critically reflexive can have a negative and positive outcome: for Joanne, although she initially struggled, she shaped her habitus to meet the needs of the field and gained the confidence to feel a part of it and a belonging; while Craig began to view himself against an idealised view of employee, who could read and write without support and embrace easily new technology. Not having the dominant cultural capital positioned him as being lacking. Interestingly, he drew on his muscle capital for empowerment, even when it had been replaced for a period of time by cultural capital aspirations.

Both Craig and Joanne were subjected to symbolic violence, but Joanne managed to take agency inside the field, while Craig took agency outside the field, by leaving the New Deal programme and entering the informal economy to secure a job he enjoyed and where he could also earn money.

The surprising part of the findings was the importance of social capital in facilitating the learners to generate a habitus that fits the needs of the field with its dominant symbolic power. For the women in the study, friendship was very important, and even more so for the lone mothers. Cynically, it may be argued that the bonds forged positioned friends as resources to be drawn upon to accrue the capital needed to navigate the fields they entered, for example, nursing. This would position friendship as something pre-meditated, individualistic and which fits a neo-liberalistic model. I would, however, suggest that these bonds were based on real emotion and support, rather than individualised re-invention in the field. Learners fed on the networks and friendships they formed and also fed back; there was a real feeling of the development of communities of support.

I would argue that the learners never really, even by proxy,[1] occupy the norms of any given field. The field, like their habitus, shifted in time and space. The habitus was also shaped by the way the learners used their bodies to fit into and shape the field. The body was used in gendered ways; consider the muscle and macho capital employed by the males as opposed to the glamour capital used by the females. The macho and muscle capital was used by Shammy for example to make changes, take control of his life and gain employment in the field of security and gain street credibility. The relationship between the male body and how that relates to the female was not mentioned. However, for the women, the glamour capital was related to looking attractive to males rather than getting work or having street credibility. Glamour capital was also linked to the security which they perceived a man would bring. Men were positioned as being commodities that could earn a wage so that the women would not have as much responsibility and have a more comfortable life. For the females there was also an awareness of the passing of time in the field of age; youth was something they wanted to hold onto by painting their faces and looking good. There was gendered symbolic violence in that the men took ownership of their bodies, while the females viewed their bodies as objects to please the male gaze.

Owing to the legalities of the learners exposing their involvement in the informal economy, my research does not expose the full impact on this illegitimate field. This may be viewed as a sign of how research collaborates with the dominant order. It would be beneficial to do further work into the area of the informal economy as a tool for empowerment as my research only touched on how it shapes the learners' lives. I would suggest that if we are to develop further understanding of the social practices of the working and under class, further inquiry and research needs to be done in this area. This would look to address how people are taking agency against the symbolic violence of the global economy to accrue illegitimate capital which makes their lives, often shrouded in poverty, more liveable – consider Mike, smoking marijuana and Raz, working long hours in restaurants to support his extended family while trying to get an education.

Personal reflections

Transferring my caring capital

I was able to relate to the learners and how they had transferred the caring capital accrued in childhood to gain a job in adulthood. Having helped my mam with the cleaning and looking after younger brothers, I felt that I could be a nurse and care for patients. I did not see myself as academic, but I knew I was a hard worker and was not squeamish. I suppose I was also keen to realise my mum's dreams: she had always wanted to be a nurse. I must say that when I did my training I was not based at the university, I was based in the hospital – on the job training, if you like.

There was a sense that when I was training to become a nurse I had become respectable. Gone was the girl who rarely went to school; here was a young woman who was committed and who was working towards a responsible job, a career that required three years training. I was ecstatic and couldn't believe my luck, me Vicky Duckworth, a nurse. Imagine if my old mates from school could see me, I was somebody now. At the age of 18 laying out my first dead body and washing it with dignity was a real wake up call to life and death and having respect for people in both.

Transitions

My transition from midwife to teacher was mediated by a degree. I never imagined I'd do a degree: like many of the learners I never thought about it, let alone considered it a real possibility, but I had thought about travelling, a lot. So after a year of working as a midwife and sister of a nursing home, whereby I was delivering babies at one end and laying out the elderly at the other, with four thousand pounds saved a friend and I went round the world. On my travels I met people from all walks of life, and through education and travel my world opened up. All walks of life merged together: the very wealthy who I'd called toffs, people who meditated early in the morning, waking me up with their chanting, people, all sorts who were, like me, looking for adventure. In the field of travel, we escaped the fields of our past and we were all on the same footing. For that time we shared the same hopes and aspirations, to see the beauty of the Taj Mahal in India, The

Golden Palace in Bangkok, The Barrier Reef in Australia and the list goes on. This connection in time and space bonded us. We were young and wanted to grab the future together. Travelling and meeting so many different people inspired me to do a degree and voluntary work in literacy. I suppose after going into the world I wanted to help others to reach their potential and question their beliefs and assumptions just like I had. I wanted to make a difference to the lives of people who had been brought up in communities like me. I still do. On listening to the learners' stories, many years after I travelled, I was reminded of how important the bonds of friendship are in shaping our habitus and our journeys across different fields.

Note

1 Consider Craig's wife carrying out the linguistic labour and plugging the gap in his linguistic capital when positioning it in the field of work and its dominant symbolic power.

Chapter 8

Violence in the private domain

His sin
How many times will the woman cope
In her brutal life with an armchair dope?
She wears a patterned dress stained by tears.

She stares at patterned paper stained by years
In her curtained parlour, curtailed of hope.
Now how many times will this woman cope?
(Vicky, 1990)

Overview

In this chapter I will explore the learners' experience of violence and trauma, as adults, in the private domain of the home. As in Chapter Seven I have taken the view that adulthood is not distinct from childhood, but an extension whereby the habitus shaped in childhood is taken into the field of adulthood. I call this 'scarring of the habitus' as the violence and trauma on the learners' lives both in childhood and adulthood can influence the way they view themselves, the choices they make in the relationships they form, the reasons they make for these choices and their views of motherhood, fatherhood and the family. WHO (2000a), highlight that most studies on violence against women indicate that:

- the perpetrators of violence against women are almost exclusively men;
- women are at greatest risk of violence from men they know;
- women and girls are the most frequent victims of violence within the family and between intimate partners
- physical abuse in intimate relationships is almost always accompanied by severe psychological and verbal abuse;
- social institutions put in place to protect citizens too often blame or ignore battered women.

(WHO 2000a: 2)

As such, going into the private domain is important in uncovering the violence and trauma which the learners in the study have experienced and in recognising the barriers that learners face in pursuit of their educational aspirations and dreams.

Motherhood and violence

Introduction

Motherhood is often painted as an idyllic time. It is a social space and field where women are expected to cope, be fulfilled and be good mothers. The emotional capital which embodies motherhood is thought to be in abundance in women. However, the notion of what a good mother is and the abundance of emotional capital is problematic. In western society it is very much linked to class – good mother being equated to dominant middle-class symbolic power/bad mother being seen as lacking and working class. Most recently Hey and Bradford (2006) carried out research on mothers involved in Sure Start programmes[1] and identified how working-class mothers are aware of being labelled as irresponsible and stigmatised. Walkerdine et al. (2001) highlight the surveillance gaze which working-class women experience, which can be compared to the legitimate lens (see Figure 5.1) and how they have to navigate through wider moralising discourses that locate the young working-class mother as 'the fecund Other' (Walkerdine et al. 2001: 187). I would extend this to not only encompassing young, but also older working-class mothers, and particularly single mothers. This is in contrast to being positioned as a 'yummy mummy' whereby the middle-class mother is privileged in the relatively new rhetoric of 'yummy mummy' which, in the press, McRobbie (2006) noted:

> In recent months the svelte figure of the high-income yummy mummy who can squeeze into size six jeans a couple of weeks after giving birth, with the help of a personal trainer, has become a favourite front-cover image in the celebrity weeklies. These glamorous mothers provide the fashion, beauty and lifestyle magazines with an ideal opportunity to extend the grip of consumer culture by suggesting that successful maternity now requires that mother and baby afford high maintenance pampering techniques as well as a designer wardrobe.

She goes onto note:

> Being poor within this new moral economy incurs the additional stigma of failed femininity.

Indeed on being stigmatised by the dominant legitimate gaze (see Figure 8.1) as being poor and having failed femininity, we can look to Tyler (2008) in her assertion that the discourse of the 'the chav' represent a new and insidious language of social class in the UK. She also asserts that the 'chav mum' is the contemporary expression of a historical vilification of white working-class femininity and motherhood. The learners in this study expressed a wide range of emotions in their roles as mothers.

The lacking is where Joanne, Tracy, Carol and Stella found they were positioned in their role as mothers.

Tracy

Tracy's experience of motherhood was overshadowed by the surveillance of the social workers whom she felt were judging her for not being good enough. She had called them and asked for help when she was having trouble managing her eldest son. The trouble lead her to begin to take prescribed medication for her anxiety which in turn caused her to put on weight and become very tired. It became a vicious circle. She got depressed because she felt a failure as a mother took the tablets and felt too tired to get out of bed. So the house and children were left untended.

Tracy described how she was judged rather than supported:

> I just didn't know what to do. It was like no one'd listen to a word I said. I'd nag him [son] to get out of bed and go to school but he wouldn't take a blind bit of notice. Then when he got up he'd be out of the house and I'd not see him for hours. My stomach was full of knots all the time.

While in the domestic sphere, Tracy has lost her confidence to go out to work and has great concerns about how she was judged by the social workers regarding the care of her children. It affected her to the degree that she suffered 'constant crying fits' when she knew they were coming and even though,

> I mopped and cleaned, I knew they'd pick holes in it, I just couldn't get it right. In their eyes I was no good just by the way they looked me up and down like dog dirt, yer know, I knew what they thought. That's how they made me feel, no good, useless.

When I asked Tracy why she felt she was being judged like this she explained, 'It's 'cos I live in a council house and can't afford, yer know, the best. They think I'm scum.' Tracy was clearly aware that she was being judged and blamed it on having little money (economic capital). She also felt that her role as mother was being questioned. Tracy compared these 'interrogations' to being 'proved guilty in a police cell'. Interestingly, the person whom she felt gave her the hardest time, was a man, 'a bit of a kid' is the way she describes him.

Tracy's situation may be viewed as an example of a surveillance system which favours the dominant discourse and pathologises working-class practices of motherhood as the 'other': something 'less than'. Figure 8.1 illustrates the cycle of middle-class surveillance (for example, social workers) and the symbolic violence the mothers experience because of being poor and having mothering practices which are pathologised.

The style of mothering she was advised about falls into the category that 'mothers were supposed to be tender, gentle, to protect their children above all from immoral influences, and the child savers considered yelling, rude language or sexually explicit talk to be forms of emotional cruelty' (Gordon 1994: 71). These 'culturally specific norms' of what constitutes a 'proper mother' were outside Tracy's vision of what being a mother is. Tracy said that 'yes, I did sometimes yell at the kids, but they deserved it. It stops 'em causing trouble.' The paradox is Tracy had telephoned the social services for support, 'to give me some support in tryin' to get the kids to behave. It's hard bein' on yer own, they don't listen to what I tell 'em and shout back.' Tracy felt that rather than strategies being put in place to support her, she was being judged. Tracy believes that the experience has left her a worse mother; 'less confident, more depressed'.

Drawing on Bourdieu's framework (1986), Puwar (2004) describes how a senior civil servant, by observing his peers, had acquired soft targets and thus 'practical knowledge' to 'fit into his job and rise up the ranks'. It is this 'practical knowledge' that Joanne is trying to establish in her nurse training, and Tracy is grasping for when the social workers scrutinise her mothering skills. Puwar,

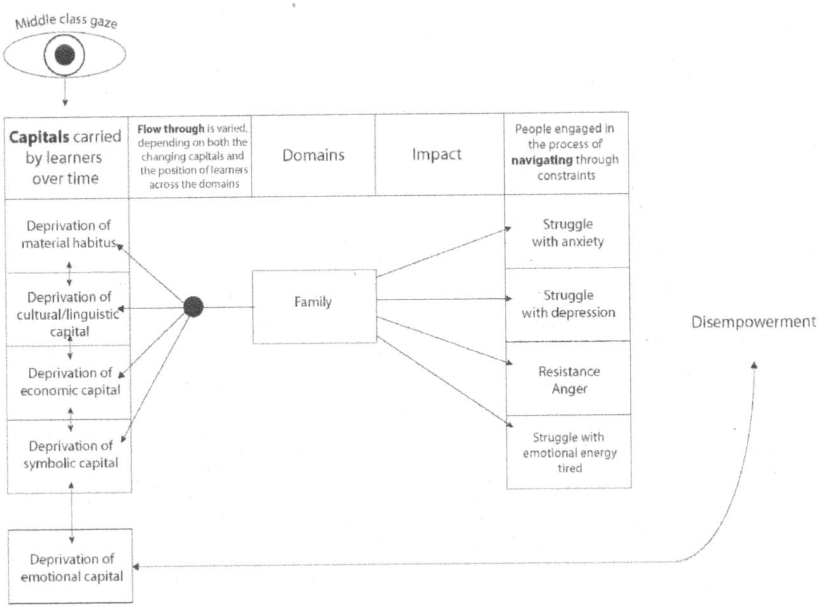

Figure 8.1 Cycle of middle-class surveillance gaze, deprivation of capitals, struggle and disempowerment in motherhood

identifies how 'we are more likely to become aware of the ways in which the dispositions are acquired when there is discordance between what one's habitus is and what one is required to be (Puwar 2004: 110–111).

However, this is too simplistic a notion for a number of the learners in my study. The civil servant could pull on cultural capital and so observe, reflect on what he needed to be to fit in. He had the cultural capital to draw upon in order to modify his behaviour to play the part within the normative culture mould. While, Tracy, having been brought up by a single mother who displayed the same ideas of what it is to be 'a mother' and living in a community which practices motherhood in a similar way, had no alternative role-models to follow. Despite, being 'othered' Tracy enjoyed being a mother, but whatever she did seemed to be incorrect and not right, no matter how much she tried to gain the approval of those who placed her under surveillance. She is blind to what is expected of her. Walkerdine and Lucey (1989: 30–31) assert how:

> Mothering is a very pleasurable activity and we are making it sound totally oppressive. We certainly agree that such pleasure is crucial and yet we would also argue . . . that such pleasure is also produced and regulated – correct and incorrect, normal and abnormal – and cannot be seen as given.

On visiting Tracy, I was aware that I also had ambivalent feelings towards her role as a mother. Seeing her children took me back to my childhood and released a confusion of emotions that left me reflecting deeply.

Journal extract

> I visited Tracy today. She sat on the on the settee with her friends around. They were all drinking spirits, the house was a mess and her youngest girl was sat on a chair, pale faced and in my view, being exposed to too much, too young. Looking at her sat there taking it all in, I remembered the overwhelming sense of being lost as a child. Surrounded by the chaos that alcohol brings. You go into yourself and smile on the outside, that's what the young girl seemed to be doing. She was eating the sweets that she said were her tea as she half listened to what was going on in between gazing at the music channel on telly that blasted into the room. Stuffy with cigarette smoke, I asked Tracy to open a window. T wasn't an aggressive drunk, she was welcoming and made a cup of tea for me. A woman called round named Gypsy A, 'she can't read and write' said T 'but I'm helpin' her'. Not yet seven in the evening, a week day, and the drink was being poured as I told 'em I'd bring some worksheets and paper round. When Gypsy A left, Tracy (T) told me how she [Gypsy A] had had all her eight kids taken off her 'cos she didn't clean up. 'She loved 'em though and it's cutting her up without 'em', she continued. Being a mother myself I know how strong and unconditional maternal love is. So when T got upset that she might also have her kids taken off her if she doesn't clean up

> more and take more responsibility, I felt for her. She seemed at her wits' end as she told me how she was up early mopping and cleaning but it got messy so quickly. She described how her eldest daughter and boyfriend were staying at the house, but they didn't help, she couldn't put them on the streets, though, either. T couldn't see a way out of the mess she said she was in. As I looked at her young daughter I had ambivalent feelings. I wanted to shout 'look at your daughter', put her first, stop drinking, pull yourself together or that young girl will end up with nowt but a broken childhood. Those kids of T's had no choice about being born into the chaos; but on the other hand neither did T. She had been brought up in a similar way as she was bringing up her kids. Depression had been passed on from mother to daughter and when it hit them it hit hard. 'You don't make me feel like shit, I feel as if I can do things when I speak to yer, move forward. When I speak to the social workers I feel like a no-hoper, I just wanna hide away. I wish they'd stop picking up what's bad about me and just see the good – I love me kids, that's summat innit. Love 'em I do' she told me. It seemed to be taking all her energy to get through the day. Rather than making judgement, which wasn't my place or my way, I did offer Tracy advice on how to get in touch with the council to sort out her cupboards, practical information that'd make the house more comfortable for her and the kids. She also gave me advice on where to buy some 'trendy' clothes at a good price for my daughter. The receiving and giving of advice is what it's about – valuing and sharing knowledge – no matter how seemingly trivial.
>
> (Journal extract, September 2007)

I was aware that Tracy's mental health issues had included bouts of depression and this was having an impact on her role as mother. As highlighted by WHO (2000b), 'women are more likely to suffer from depression, anxiety, psychosomatic systems, eating problems and sexual dysfunction. Violence may also affect their reproductive health' (WHO 2000b: 3).

Indeed, deprivation and poverty are strongly linked to the prevalence of mental ill health in communities. For Tracy this is having a huge effect on the stability of the household. With a family to care for and without a partner to offer any support she finds it 'worse than ever to cope'. Being a 'good mother' and providing for her 14-year-old son and her daughters is 'a day-on-day grind'. It is these conditions, which shape the learners' lives including Tracy, juxtaposed to the surveillance and expectations by those in positions of power.

On visiting Tracy regularly, I found that morally and ethically I needed to offer more than social support. Below is an extract from my journal, 24 June 2007:

> Visited Tracy at her house at about 2.20 pm. Her son, Mark had not been at school (second year of secondary school). He had his house coat on. Tracy's daughter was also not at college. I chatted to Mark and it turned out he had holes in his trainers – no shoes to wear and his tracksuit bottoms also had holes. He felt ashamed to go out. Tracy kept saying (in front of him)

> she wanted to get him assessed for his violent outbursts – for mental health issues. I discussed that he might feel like that because of his clothes. It was so tragic to see such a case of child poverty and how he was being labelled. He looked absolutely lost. I took Tracy, Laura (her youngest daughter) and Mark to a sports shop and bought him trainers, tracksuit bottoms and tee-shirt. He really needs a male role model to give him a chance. I will buy him a book (about a male role model) and drop it off for him.

The emotional energy which Tracy needed for her childhood, including surviving the bullying (see Figures 3.1 and 5.2) and now in motherhood (each having an impact on the other) was hard to conjure up, with the best will in the world. On medication for her depression she often felt lethargic and tired and angry about being labelled as mentally ill and an unfit mother.

Tracy is now afraid to contact the social services no matter how much help she feels she needs

Tracy: No way will I contact the social again, they're useless. They gave me no help. I'm still in shit street, but worse off with them knowing it.

Interviewer: Why?

Tracy: They're looking for one mistake, one move that they don't like and they'll take me kids from me. I won't let 'em though. They think they've got me sussed, have they bloody 'ell, I've got them sussed. A load of interferers, looking to point the finger where it suits.

Stella

For Stella, part of motherhood meant helping her children. However, when she was unable to help them with their reading and school work because she struggled to read and write, she felt ashamed and tried to hide it. Consider the shame of how Stella felt at school because of being poor (see Figure 3.3) and having a habitus out of sync with school which resulted in symbolic violence (see Figure 3.1b), the accumulation of symbolic violence (see Figure 5.2) and not having the legitimate linguistic capital (see Figure 5.3). Now as an adult it continued:

> It was easier to make out I could read when they were young. I'd know the story and pretend I was reading it from the book. But when they learnt to read they wanted to look at the pages when I told the story. Course what I was saying and what was written were miles apart. That's when I stopped reading to them. I felt embarrassed, yer know, being their mum and not being able to read, it's not right.

The shame had not gone, but raised its head again when her daughter experienced similar difficulty with spelling at school. Stella also felt upset because she was able to identify with the negative labels to which her daughter was subjected at school and felt unable to give her the support she needed. She describes how:

> Our A came home crying the one night, really upset she was. They'd singled her out in class because she got her spellings wrong. I thought 'no, the same's happening again', yer know, as what happened to me. I just felt hopeless like I was to blame.

Stella says that as she could not help her daughter with her writing or spellings she tried to put it to the back of her head and distance herself from it.

> It was like it was happening to me again. I just wanted to blank it out.

However, Stella was unable to carry on doing this and tackled the school about her daughter.

> I fought for our A to get extra help at school, kept going into see the teachers. She got it in the end. The one-to-one at school really helped her come on. I'm dead proud of her, she's cleverer than me.

The negative emotion Stella initially had did not result in a negative outcome. The negativity was subverted into the positive outcome of resistance capital and empowerment. The resistance was used for the next generation, in the push for Stella to get her daughter the help she needed, even if she had to fight for it. It was also the catalyst for her returning to college.

> Helping our A was like helping myself really. It got it out of me system. That's probably why I had the confidence to come back to college.

Figure 8.2 illustrates that empowerment and resistance within the family is not time bound and actions of empowerment can have a knock-on effect. Although, unable to help her daughter with literacy as a child, and feeling shame about this, as her daughter grew older Stella found resistance and empowerment to get her the dyslexia support she needed to progress at school. This led to Stella challenging her own illiteracy and returning to college which subsequently led to her acquiring linguistic capital and becoming empowered.

Joanne

Joanne voiced how she hadn't been able to help her eldest son when he was at school ''cos I didn't know how to do the things like spelling meself' and 'couldn't see a future out of the estate like I can now, I thought it was the right way to wag it an' that'. The estate with its own rules, its own field, fed into a habitus

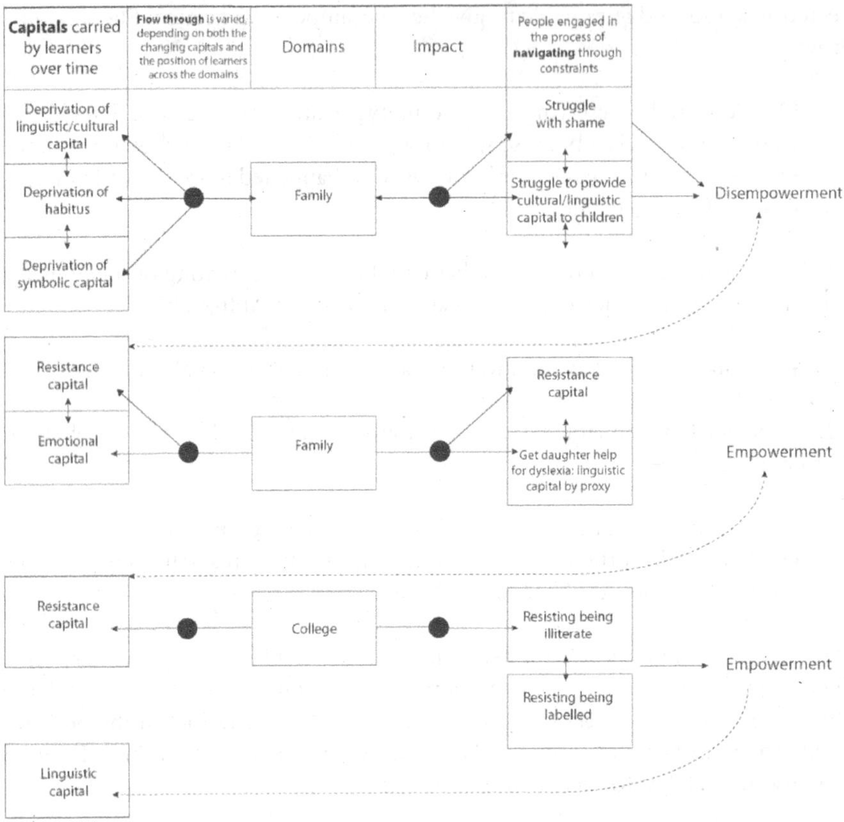

Figure 8.2 **Cycle of linguistic deprivation, motherhood, disempowerment and resistance**

in which 'respect was given to those who put their two fingers up at education' (see Figure 6). Tracy did not feel that it was important to help her eldest with his homework:

> I feel a bit guilty now, but with our L it was different than my two youngest. I never bothered helping him. It's not that I didn't think it was important, I didn't even think about it. I just wanted him to leave school and get a job like I did.

However, as Joanne accrued cultural capital at college (qualifications), her position in the field changed her view of what motherhood entails and the cultural support a child needs. Joanne's habitus on being a mother now fits into the dominant middle-class gaze (see Figure 8.1).

Joanne: It's my job to make sure our B and L do their homework. I sit with them and go through it. I'm really strict.

Interviewer: Why do you think it's important to help them with their homework?

Joanne: So they don't end up at my age with a load of wasted years behind them. No, I'd like them to get a decent job and do something with their life.

Joanne's behaviour and notion of motherhood has changed as her habitus has been shaped by the field of education (college and university) and job (nursing). This has resulted in higher expectations of the job her youngest children will progress to.

Figure 8.3 illustrates the cycle of linguistic deprivation and disempowerment across the domain of family. It also demonstrates how resistance capital (this time after the break-up of a relationship) can be a trigger to commencing college and gaining linguistic and cultural capital as well as empowerment.

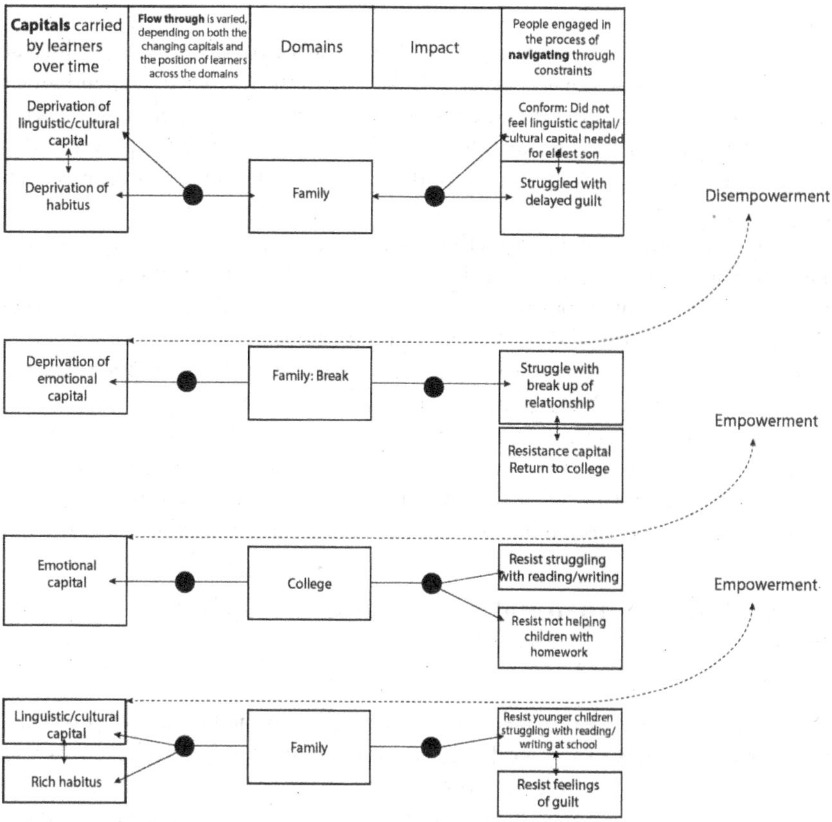

Figure 8.3 Cycle of linguistic deprivation, disempowerment, resistance and supporting children to gain linguistic capital

Joanne describes how this experience left her feeling:

> I thought I was thick. I left that school not being able to spell. I could read and write and I couldn't spell at all, as yer know, you taught me. I couldn't do maths, that's why I'm doin' the maths now. If I knew what I know now I'd 'ave made them teachers come to them lessons and teach me. But it's also made me who I am. I make the kids do their homework, they 'ave to do their homework and if a word comes up like 'to', I'll say is it a number two or is it to you or too much? And I make them explain which one they think it is and sometimes I feel like it's not fair and I'm pushin' them too much but I don't want them to 'ave the same experience I've had. Like, A, he always gets like 19 out of 20 and he's disappointed 'cos he wants 20 out of 20, 'cos he wants to please me. But I always go, like, 'that's brilliant' and he's spelling words that I can only just spell – honestly. He amazes me, he does. So really it's done me a favour 'cos I push me kids to do it. But the teachers 'ere, no they're good.

I would suggest that Joanne was able to address how she could support the children because she felt confident with her skills, unlike when she was a teenager and unlike Stella. Gaining cultural capital had enabled her to help her children to also accrue cultural capital at school. The knowledge that she now had symbolic power in that she was able to help her children impacted on her belief that she had become a better mother.

Clearly emotional capital is something that Tracy, Stella and Joanne needed to draw upon in order to fulfil their roles as mothers. This emotional capital may be viewed as being essential for opening up possibilities for educational success (Reay 1998b, 2000). Emotional capital includes the need to be a good mother, which includes caring for children; this includes educational care (O'Brien 2007) such as the support offered by Joanne and Stella. Reay (1998b, 2000) shows that investment of emotional energy in education by working-class mothers depletes their own emotional well-being. However, rather than depleting it for Stella it invigorated it and acted as a catalyst to Stella empowering herself and returning to college and Joanne finding satisfaction in helping her younger children to succeed at school.

Motherhood: emotional labour and transitions

Joanne

The emotional capital needed to make transitions into the field of work was difficult for the learners in the study. There were feelings of ambivalence. As well as caring for the children and supporting them in their emotional life, they were making difficult moves into a new field where in many cases they were anxious. Balancing the need to ensure that the family's emotional needs were met and transitions into new fields of work was difficult.

Joanne wrote in our journal on 20 January 2006:

> Sat having a curry with Vicky and the rest . . . I start uni in March and I'm dreading it, but at the same time I'm looking forward to it. I've got a lot to do! My biggest fear is that when I start uni, I don't enjoy it. If I don't, what then? I want to really enjoy going to uni and the placements because I really think you should enjoy doing what you do. Beccy [Joanne's daughter] keeps on asking when do I start uni. She thinks that when I start nursing 'as she calls it' she won't see much of me and she keeps crying. I have to keep reassuring her.

Rachel also wrote in the journal (7 February 2006) about how the caring she had invested in her family had stopped her pursuing her transition into the world of work and the field of administration.

> I started the course in administration in 2004, but had to pull out in May 2005 as my son became ill with pneumonia, even though I did come off the course, I did get some certificate. My eldest son got married at the end of May and then my mother had a stroke, which resulted in her being in hospital for a number of weeks and [my] visiting every day willing her to pull through. She had to learn to eat and walk again and I was there every day helping to feed her.

While for Stella, moving from a cleaning job to working in a care home, as a nursing assistant meant she had to work nights. She describes how:

> I enjoy working nights, but feel bad not being there for them all. My husband looks after the house, when I get home he goes to work. We're like a pair of yo-yos.

The women can see that the practices of caring, which Stella later transferred to working as a nursing assistant become 'inseparable from personal dispositions' (Skeggs 1997: 56). They have learned these skills by their selflessness, in the intimate social relations with those they have cared for, including their children and wider family. These are skills which they have been able to transfer into the workplace to gain respectability and make choices. For Stella and Joanne it is escaping heavy labour intensive work.

Making ends meet

Sally's story

While all the learners struggled to make ends meet when they were at college, only Sally, who has a husband who earned a good wage had the luxury of being able to give up work for college. Driving to college in a BMW and wearing expensive clothes, she maintained an expensive lifestyle which continued throughout college and on into university. Sally writes her comments in our journal on a night out with the research group:

> I have ten weeks off before starting uni. So I have joined the gym to try and tone up and to become healthy.

Rather than having or feeling the necessity to work prior to continuing college, unlike the other women and men in the study she was able to indulge in caring for herself and meeting her own needs. This was something Sally expected, prior to marriage she had been supported by her parents and on getting married and moving into a private house her husband had continued this role. She has the freedom to pursue a career, with economic support and security provided by her husband. Figure 8.4 illustrates how Sally has the legitimate capitals and symbolic power they offer to travel with ease across the domain of family and college, very much in the same way that she has travelled with ease across the field of schooling. Only this time, rather than her parents providing the economic capital, it was her husband.

College and choice

If we compare Sally's freedom from economic struggle to pursue her interests we see a stark contrast to Raz's situation. As identified previously, Raz worked long

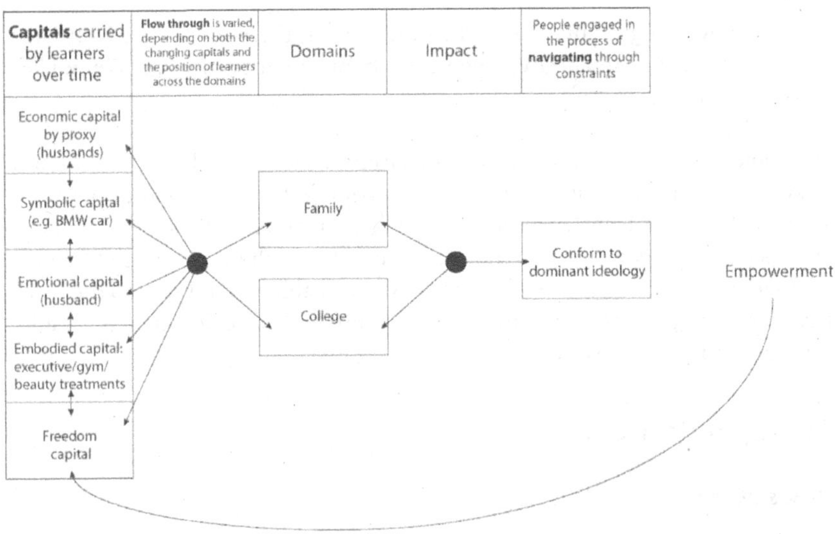

Figure 8.4 Cycle of capitals, education, freedom and empowerment

and unsociable hours. He was often tired when he came to class. However, by underground working and gaining informal economy capital he was able to continue on the FE course and progress. However, unlike Sally who had economic support and completed her course, Raz had to eventually leave and give up his dream of being an accountant in order to satisfy the immediate need of bringing a substantial wage to support an extended family. For many learners the prospect of being full-time students is unachievable because they do not have the economic capital. For Joanne who lived off social benefits when she was at college, she often wondered whether she should give up college for short-term economic benefits. This was compounded by the fact that she has three children to care for. She noted that:

> Sometimes I just think I may as well give it all up. When I've got the kids on at me because they want this and that and I can't afford it, I feel rotten.

Being poor

For a number of the learners in the group, as discussed, being poor led to participating in the informal economy (see Figure 7.5). For example, for Raz it provided the extended family with economic capital. However, the need to provide for the family, rather than being provided for led to responsibility and a lack of opportunity for self-improvement to pursue university and follow dreams of becoming an accountant. Figure 8.5 illustrates the struggles Raz had across the domains of his

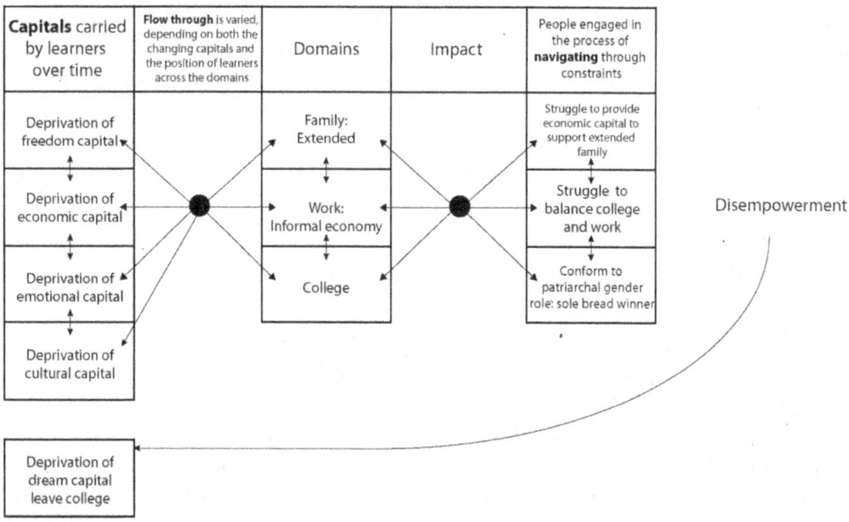

Figure 8.5 Cycle of deprivation of capitals, balancing college and work, struggle and disempowerment

life and how this led to a deprivation of dream capital of progressing to university.

For other learners, economic restraints also threatened to stop the freedom of following their dreams. To resist this, support was also accrued through awards and prizes. For example, because she was struggling financially I put Joanne forward for the NIACE Adult Learners Award[2] of £250 and the status of the achievement and a Helena Kennedy Foundation award,[3] which consisted of a £1500 bursary provided in instalments during her time in higher education. Joanne used the first instalment of £500 from the Helena Kennedy prize to buy her children a school uniform. Making sure her children were clean and smart was important to Joanne. She describes how:

> If I had a choice between the kids being turned out a mess and me getting a career, the kids come first.

Financial support

The teacher's role can therefore support the accruing of economic capital and the subsequent freedom this can offer learners to pursue their learning trajectory as well as support motherhood. Without recognition of the roles learners have in the private domain, including motherhood and the responsibilities this brings, offering the support they need may not be possible. Part of this recognition is linked to teaching being aligned to caring (see Noddings 1984, 1992; Feeley 2007). I would extend this caring to caring for the community and being involved in community activism.

For example, the research allowed me to work with the learners and community initiatives, such as publishing, to set up awards to support future learners. Following Marie McNamara qualifying to be nurse, rather than receiving the royalties for her book, *Getting Better*, she has donated them to the Gatehouse Getting Better Award. This is awarded each year to an adult learner who is overcoming significant barriers to learning in her/his life. We are both on the judging panel. As a result of this prize I have worked with Gatehouse further to set up the Gatehouse Books Prize. This is awarded to a student of Edge Hill University who has shown excellence in the teaching of literacies or vocational studies and who, during the course of their teaching experience, has encouraged learners to write as part of their personal development.

The research also allowed me to apply for scholarships for myself and the learners. For example, Marie and I were awarded the Adult Higher Education Alliance (AHEA) International Professional Award and AHEA International Graduate Student Award (jointly awarded). This included financial support for us both to travel to the USA and deliver a joint paper at the AHEA conference 'Animating Change in Adult Higher Education', was held in Mobile, Alabama, 1–4 October 2008. Marie contributed to writing a research article (Johnson et al. 2010). 'Tracy' and 'Carol' also received funding to deliver a paper on widening participation, at the Widening Participation conference, held at Edge Hill which resulted in a jointly written paper. Here they shared their stories and brought some creative images and words that had been produced in literacy lessons. They sought to get the participants to explore how they could find space to develop and deliver a creative curriculum aimed at empowering learners.

Motherhood and money

Tracy, Emily, Stella and Joanne's identity in motherhood was linked to having money. Part of having the money was being able to buy their children the basics, but also to save up for birthdays and Christmas presents.

Both Tracy and Stella got into debt with loan sharks to pay for things. In today's consumerism society there are many pitfalls when striving for 'distinction' in the field (see Bourdieu 1984) particularly for the working class. Credit cards, loan sharks and overdrafts add more debt as people, including members of the research group, try to distinguish themselves as respectable (see Skeggs 1997).

Tracy describes how:

Tracy: It started off a tenner here and there, before I knew it I owed over three hundred quid. I sometimes don't answer the door, but he's back an hour later. They must be making a ton.

Interviewer: What did you spend the money on?

Tracy: Nowt really, presents when it was our J's birthday. I took them all for a pizza, too. Once you start it mounts up dead quick. They bounce loads of interest on it an all.

Stella also describes how she took a loan from a loan shark:

> I bought me daughter some proper glasses, not the cheapo ones. I didn't want her to be called names or owt. They call every week for the money I owe them. It was worth it, my daughter loved 'em.

For both Stella and Tracy motherhood was about finding the money to buy their children what they needed. It was also about protecting them from the stigma and labelling they had as children for being poor (see Figures 3.3 and 5.2). This meant Stella taking out money from a loan shark to buy her daughter designer glasses, which reflected respectability rather than National Health Service free glasses. They were aware of the markers on the body which signify being poor. For Tracy she wanted to make sure that she could buy her children presents and take them for a meal. Both were unable to get a credit card from the bank, so chose to borrow money from a loan shark whose interest is double that charged by credit card companies. In many cases they were paying back double what they had borrowed. However, rather than being put off by this, they recognised it but considered it a necessity. Their poverty was being exploited by the loan sharks and putting them in further debt.

Spouse violence

A number of the mothers in the study were left to care for the children without the support of a partner. For Tracy the fathers left before the children were born or when they were babies. She felt abandoned by them and describes how:

> I was stupid; I thought with J's dad it'd be different. I really cared about him, nice to me he was. We had our arguments like everyone, but he'd always come back to ours. Then, after I brought the baby home he got narked at everyone, grumpy all the time. He was also shouting at the baby to shut it when he was crying, so I told him to shut it and fuck off.

Tracy was angry at her partner's behaviour towards her and the baby and told him to leave. The abuse and violence also included him shouting at Tracy. He played no part in her son's life and did not contribute any money to his upkeep. While she looked after the baby he could lead the life of a single man without any of the responsibilities Tracy had. She described how:

> I hated being angry all the time. I loved my baby but it didn't seem fair that he'd pissed off and left it all up to me. I felt like a useless mum on me own. Dickhead he was, it was probably for the best though, know what I mean?

Walby and Allen (2004) highlight how, 'In any one year, there are 13 million separate incidents of physical violence or threats of violence against women from partners or former partners.'

For some of the learners, violence and intimidation were a real threat that scarred their life and the choices they made. For the women the physical and psychological violence and trauma continued even when their partners left the home.

Joanne

Joanne's partner had taken drugs and visited prostitutes when they were in a relationship:

> He'd come home wrecked, off his face. Talk to me like crap and not give a toss about mine or the kids' feelings. He made me feel like shit most of the time.

He went missing for days on drink and drug binges, while Joanne was left alone to care for the children. However, rather than hating or falling out of love with her partner, she was full of ambivalent feelings, describing how:

> It was really hard to tell him to go. Every time I seen him I wanted to ask him to come back. Yer can't just switch off yer feelings like that. I can't anyway. I really loved him and wanted it to work out proper with us. After he left I couldn't even get out of bed. I felt useless, it was a horrible feeling. Like feeling ill all the time.

For both Tracy and Joanne, being left by their partners had an impact on the way they viewed themselves. Joanne was left feeling useless and Tracy, 'like shit'. While Tracy had no contact with her ex, for Joanne, her ex would occasionally see the kids. Both collecting the kids and living on the estate gave him the opportunity to continue to carry out physical and psychological abuse throughout the FE course and when she started nursing. She felt she could not turn to her family because of the pain they had caused her and spoke of how:

Joanne: He tried to stop me getting anywhere.
Interviewer: How did he do that?
Joanne: Where do I start? He'd tell me he'd pick the kids up from school and then I'd get a call at uni telling me they were waiting. It made me look like a crap mother, but I was doing it all for them. He just told lies and strung me along.
Interviewer: Did anything help you get through all that?
Joanne: Having the research group really helped me. I looked forward to the nights. It also made a difference knowing I could call you and chat.

The continual verbal abuse culminated in physical abuse at Christmas 2006. Below is an extract from our journal:

Christmas 2006

> Joanne's husband attacked her in the pub. She went to the pub and he cornered her and hit her at the bar. When I rang her she was distraught. She said he was drunk and angry at her, she put it down to her now being independent and doing something with her life. She said it's given her strength and made her more determined to succeed.

However, it wasn't always easy to keep the resolve to succeed. Joanne looked forward to the get-togethers with the group, but on more than one occasion her plans were thwarted due to being let down by her former partner. Below is an extract from our journal from October 2007:

> Joanne was supposed to come round and have a meal [at my house]. She said she was looking forward to it. She needed someone to talk to. However her X, ended up going on a binge with the drink and couldn't look after them

> [the children]. When I rang her on Saturday she was really upset. I met her in Woodhouses, had lunch. Then we went to Asda. She explained how it was really hard for her to do the course [nursing] with no support and no one to pick the kids up from school.

Craig

The lone women in the group were pulled in all directions, with the primary responsibility and most cases all the childcare being theirs. However, Craig would have liked more responsibility for his son, but the courts had allocated more time to his ex-wife and limited visiting to Craig. He did not describe how his wife felt about this, he seemed too broken up about the marriage breakdown and the effect it had had on him and his son. He did describe how his son wanted to spend more time with him. Symbolic violence was being carried out here, with the dominant stand being that women are the better carers and Craig and his young son allowed limited access with each other. Craig felt very upset that he was not allowed to be closer to his son when he was growing up. He described how:

> It's hard to get your head round. One minute you're in the house with him, you know there to watch him have his meals, watch the telly and all that, then I'm stuck on my own without him.

Craig also felt ashamed about bringing his son back to the council flat where he was now living.

> I don't want him to think his dad's a loser, living in a doss house. I've tried to smarten it up but there's nothing much you can do, soon as you step through the door, it's a shithole.

Shame had clouded Craig's changing position in the field and location he lived. As identified by Parsons and Bynner (2008) 'Both men and women with Entry level skills were also the most likely to live in disadvantaged housing conditions – rented and/or overcrowded accommodation – at age 34.'

As an adult Craig had turned the cycle of living in poor housing around, moving away from his childhood estate which was in a very deprived area to a private and suburban housing complex in Tameside. The avoidance of being a statistic, as outlined by Bynner and Parsons (2008) and living in disadvantaged housing was due to being promoted up the career ladder, gaining a managerial position which brought economic capital and buying a private house for his family. However, on losing his job due to not having the linguistic capital (see Figure 7.4) he and his family lost everything. Because Craig was not given custody of his son, he was given a one bedroomed flat in a very deprived area of Oldham which mostly housed teenagers and young adults. Craig described how:

> The music is banging out all night, it drives me mad, like, I want to sleep, but with the noise you can't.
>
> (Craig, speaking in 2007)

Spouse violence to children

The violence which Joanne and Tracy's partners aimed at them also had an impact on their children. The mothers were left to care for their own and their children's emotional needs. For Tracy's daughter, the dad had abandoned her and rarely visited. Tracy describes how:

> I feel really guilty sometimes that there's no dads around. They ask me what happened, what can you say, they don't give a shit about us.

Tracy's daughter wrote the poem about her relationship with her father which was published in *Write About . . . Bullying* (2008). She described how it helped her to come to terms with the pain she had felt:

Tracy's daughter, C: Them awful feelings that made me feel sick got a bit better.
Interviewer: How's that?
Tracy's daughter, C: It's like when I write I can talk things through on the page that I'd normally keep to myself. It helped me get rid of really hurtful stuff. Do you know what I mean?

What do I do?

My whole world is crashing down on me
Everyone that used to care . . . GAVE UP
Everyone I could turn to . . . RAN AWAY
Everyone I love . . . SIMPLY IGNORES
I don't know what to do
I just sit in my corner
The same corner I was in many times before
The corner that knows it all
The corner that has been flooded . . . and dried up a million times
The corner that doesn't judge me
Those walls just join together to enclose me
A safe place where I can be me
I can let it all out
I can cry . . .
And Cry
Until no more tears will fall from my lonely eyes
Have you ever had a time

Where you had no idea what to do?
I have those times all the time
I believe it's almost time
To GIVE UP.

C also spoke of how it had given her the confidence to believe she was good at something. History was repeating itself with C experiencing bullying like her mum, Tracy, had years previously.

> I didn't like school I got bullied. I also had an eating disorder which made me really self-conscious. Knowing that my poem was good enough to get published in a book gave me confidence somehow.

Tracy wanted to help but did not know what to do.

> I feel like I've let our C down, like I should have done something more. I don't know sometimes I think is it all worth it.

Overcoming patriarchy

As identified by Walby and Allen (2004):

> Women are much more likely than men to be the victim of multiple incidents of abuse, and of sexual violence: 32% of women who had ever experienced domestic violence did so four or five (or more) times, compared with 11% of the (smaller number) of men who had ever experienced domestic violence; and women constituted 89% of all those who had experienced four or more incidents of domestic violence.

With these statistics, overcoming patriarchy is an issue which needs to be taken seriously. However, the theory of overcoming it and the reality of the lives of the women in the study are very different. It was hard for a number of the women to overcome patriarchy. Even when they had left their partners the abuse continued. There were also ambivalent feelings of love and loss. For Joanne, she knew that she loved her partner but could not live with him because he dragged her down. It took a lot of strength to make it on her own, especially when she was lonely. Simple things like someone making a cup of tea for you were missed. The gap was partly plugged by focusing on a career, but the knocks still came.

Female friendship as a means of overcoming patriarchy was also a theme of the research. The nature of patriarchy determines access to the role in, and the use of, networks. Addressing the gender relations and inequalities is necessary for making useful statements about the link between social networks and vulnerability.

> Women are more likely than men to have experienced all types of intimate violence (partner abuse, family abuse, sexual assault and stalking) since the ages of 16. And nearly half the women who had experienced intimate violence of any kind were likely to have been victims of more than one kind of intimate abuse.
>
> (Coleman et al. 2007)

I would also add that a study on intimate violence on those girls under 16 would add to the debate and praxis. For the women in the study, the violence by men had left them looking for friendship to help them heal the scars of symbolic, physical and psychological violence and trauma. Rachel describes how friendship helped her heal and resist the ongoing anxiety and emotional upset it had caused her and continued to cause her after her divorce:

Rachel: I get really down sometimes and having people who care around me makes a big difference.
Interviewer: Who are these people?
Rachel: My friends, the girls who I see at college.

However, for Rachel there was also the re-visiting of, and conforming to, the ideals of youth and femininity as she mourned for the glamour capital (see Figure 6.2). She had possessed this in her youth and used its power in attracting a man who could provide for her. The need to attract a male seemed to negate the fight for patriarchy:

Rachel: I was pretty when I met my ex.
Interviewer: Yer still are.
Rachel: No, I feel washed out now. I still put my make-up on to try and look nice, but men don't want an older bird. It's frightening yer know, being on yer own and looking after yourself.

While Joanne and Tracy had been single mothers and had to provide for themselves, Rachel had had the economic capital provided by her husband. Unlike the other women in the study she had not needed to work when the children were growing up and took on the role of housewife. However, when her husband met another woman on his business trips abroad and pursued the relationship, Rachel then filed for a divorce. The woman her husband left Rachel for was a lot younger and this made Rachel feel like she was no longer attractive or desirable. She describes how:

> He must have gone off me because she was younger and attractive. I kept myself nice but that wasn't enough for him.

Youth was a capital that the women spoke of as being important in both attracting men and also keeping them. Youth was equated to being pretty and it equated to using this to attract a man. However, for men youth was not mentioned as a capital for attracting or keeping a partner. It was about offering opportunities outside relationships, for example, for Craig youth equated to re-building his life and gaining self-esteem when he lost his job.

Interestingly, middle-class women and those with economic support/capital can buy youth capital by having cosmetic treatments and surgery to maintain their 'beauty'. For example, when I asked Sally about what she would do when she was waiting to go to university to study midwifery, she explained how she would spend time taking care of herself. This included having facials and treatments to get her skin back in good condition as it had come out in spots with the college exams. She described how:

> I like to look after myself. X doesn't want to look at me looking a mess. My skin always feels tons better when I've had a facial, it takes all the dead skin away.

The other women in the study were unable to afford luxuries of beauty treatments. I would argue that they pined for the loss of what McRobbie and Garber's (1976) early work referred to as a 'bedroom culture' where they can cultivate their beauty for finding a husband. Sally had replaced the 'bedroom culture' with the beauty treatment room which was now used to create a look (soft skin) to please and what she considered important in keeping her man. Joanne spoke of the importance of female friendship.

Joanne: After the split up men were the last people I wanted to spend any time with. It's having the other women in the class to chat to who'd been through the same crap.

Interviewer: How does it help?

Joanne: Takes away the sort of idea that it's me that made it happen. I used to think if I'd have been different he would've stayed, he'd love me more. All them daft thoughts 'cos really I loved him and wanted him to love me back. A daft word, 'love', but it cuts yer up if you don't have it. Sharing our up and downs helps. Makes yer realise like, it's not me it's the fella who's got it wrong. It's his problem, not mine

Interviewer: Was it men and women you spoke to?

Joanne: No, always women. You'd never tell a man. Couldn't trust 'em. If they were listening it's probably 'cos they want to get into your knickers. Or if you showed 'em you're vulnerable yer might as well put a sticker on yer head sayin' hit me an all. When I meet someone I fancy I pretend how I've been treated alright off me ex. I want to start afresh and have him respect me, yer see. Who wants someone who's been knocked around, unless yer after a bit of rough.

Joanne also spoke of needing glamour capital (see Figure 6.2) to attract a man.

Joanne: I don't like looking at myself sometimes.
Interviewer: Why
Joanne: Sounds stupid, but I don't like seeing I'm losing my looks. Getting older it's scary when you're on your own. At least when you're younger you can go out and meet someone. It's not that easy now, especially if you're after a decent bloke.

Although the women were trying to overcome patriarchy, there was still the idea that they needed to look pretty and have youth on their side to attract a man. Glamour and looking nice was a means to attract a male and get security (economic capital) and love (emotional capital). The paradox is that when youth and glamour were on their side they had attracted a man, but had only been given snatches of emotional and economic capital from them; with the relationships came instability and violence. The notion of re-claiming glamour capital was made more poignant because it was only the women who were approaching 40 and over who spoke of it with such longing. They had hope that economic and emotional capital could be gained from using their looks to get a relationship, this was linked to being able to give up work, have a comfortable life with less responsibility. They had dreams and linked these dreams to soap operas on the television. Rachel describing how:

Rachel: Look at all the fellas Audrey [from *Coronation Street*] has had and they all worship her, don't they?
Interviewer: Didn't one leave her?
Rachel: But she soon got another 'cos she looks good for her age.

They were also lonely and had not excluded the prospect of a decent man coming into their lives to fill a gap. Their hope and belief in males was still there after all they had been through, perhaps this was reinforced by the soaps and the romance that took place on them. The group spoke a lot about what was going on in *Coronation Street* and *Eastenders*; this sometimes seemed as real as what was going on in reality. I did not pursue this line of research, but it would be worth following up the impact of television and the representation of romance on the learners' dreams and hopes for the future.

However, while they voiced their hopes and fears to me, the reality was that they were single and remain single. They exchanged telephone numbers. It offered them the opportunity to contact someone if they needed support. Many incidents which happened in the learner' lives were not predictable and being able to telephone at weekends and in the evening created an on-going dialogue that they could initiate. I regularly received telephone calls from the group and regularly called them. This offered the opportunity for the group to support each other and stay in touch at busy times. The social events were also described as being important social occasions. We would meet up each month and go to the local Indian restaurant. Although the males, Craig, Robert, Raz, Shammy and Martin, would sometimes come along to the events, the women and men tended to gravitate together. This did not however stop them having a laugh together. A number of the female learners told me that this was the first time they had formed friendships with males which were not sexual but platonic. Joanne described how:

> It gives me the chance to get a bit dressed up and meet everyone. It makes a change seeing them out of my jeans.

The social networking with the males in the study was a means for the women to form platonic male friendships. It also helped the learners' resilience to continue in learning. This was particularly the case for Joanne, Sarah, Tracy and Stella.

> After a drink, I don't know we all just opened up. When Joanne told me she struggled with the assignments on her access course it didn't make me feel so stupid. It, like, keeps you going, knowing others have their doubts too.
>
> (Sarah, speaking in 2007)

> I was planning at stopping at the NVQ Two but when I seen what Joanne had done, I thought, well, I can do it too. It really helps chatting about what we're all up to.
>
> (Stella, speaking in 2007)

Conclusion

The findings demonstrate how the violence and trauma experienced in the private domain and public domain of the learners' lives work to feed each other, from childhood through to adulthood. The violence and trauma the learners have experienced in childhood marks them both metaphorically and literally and is further marked on their bodies by the symbolic representation and physical injury experienced in adulthood.

The cycle of gendered divisions of labour in the private domain from childhood is subsequently re-enforced in adulthood, for example, the girl's role in domesticity and caring and the boys in physicality, for example, 'muscle capital' continues into the private domain of adulthood. It is the female learners in this study who were left by their male partners to care for the children as lone mothers. Their male partners often used their physicality to exert violence and oppress the women. As such when the women broke free from violent relationships it resulted in them receiving very little or no emotional or economic support from the fathers to the children. In contrast to the constraints the women had on their time, energy and other resources when caring for children, they described how their partners were able to continue their life without the responsibilities of parenthood. The men were able to pursue their own interests without responsibility of domestic obligations as they had done as children. Craig was the only separated male parent in the study, and he rebuked this as he wanted more responsibility for his son than the courts had allowed. Craig's experience may have been different because he had played an active part in his son's baby years and childhood up until the divorce, while the lone-mothers described how even when they were still with the father of their child, the father had not supported them in caring for the baby/child. They were expected to carry out this role without any support.

Ideas about the 'norm' and 'right' kind of parent are extremely pervasive in today's society. What constitutes good or bad parenting is fuelled by representations and media discourses, images of couples in stable relationships. This is further fuelled by notions of good and bad mothering being informed in images such as the 'yummy mummy' and its antithesis 'the chav' mother as highlighted in this chapter. Mothering discourses are influenced, restrained and informed by culture and society's thinking about women's mothering (Giddens 1992) which, for example, under the dominant gaze of the social workers (see Figure 8.1), led to feelings of anxiety and guilt as mothers' habitus struggled to conform to the dominant norm.

However, rather than just a cycle of struggle and disempowerment (see Figure 8.1) there was also resistance and empowerment. For example, Stella subverted the negative emotions she experienced as a mother associated with deprivation of linguistic/cultural capital into empowering herself and her family (see Figure 8. 2). This demonstrated how the cycle of disempowerment can transform not only the individual but those around them in new and exciting ways.

The emotional and economic capital needed for the learners to make transitions through education and into the field of work was difficult for most of the learners in the study. As identified above, some were restrained in the resources they had available to them because of being carers to children. This caring role had continued from childhood, for example, caring for siblings and as adults, caring for their children. Although their maternal habitus appeared deprived to the middle-class gaze (see Figure 8.2) the irony was that they were able to use their caring habitus for resistance and symbolic power by resisting labour intensive jobs which held no security and instead moving into caring jobs such as nursing. This validated the importance of their caring capital in the public domain and with it brought economic reward, stability and self-worth.

However, it is important to recognise that most learners struggled to reach the point that they could enter nursing roles due a lack of economic capital and emotional back-up from home to support them through college. The contradiction to this was Sally (see Figure 8.4) who had the emotional and economic support of a husband. The role of the teacher in offering resistance against the barriers the learners faced and, what is important, caring enough to do this was highlighted. The result was the sourcing of alternative funding to support the learners and facilitate the accruing of economic capital (see Figure 4.1) and work towards social justice and empowerment for the learners.

Most of the female learners longed for the return of their 'glamour capital', an embodied cultural capital that was time set to their teenage years and early 20s (see Figure 6.2). Glamour capital was linked to security from a man. There was gendered symbolic violence in that the men took ownership of their bodies, while the females viewed their bodies as objects to please the male gaze.

For Sally, using her husband's economic capital, she was able to invest time in cultivating her body and looks serving to accumulate cultural capital in the embodied state (see Figure 8.4).

There was a paradox as the women struggled to overcome patriarchy. Some of the learners longed for a return of their glamour capital, conforming to the ideals of youth and beauty, while they also struggled with and resisted spouse violence. For example, Joanne had told her partner to leave their home, but she also struggled with the strong feelings she had. She described how attending college had given her the strength not to go back to his abuse:

> If it wasn't for the good friends I made at college I would have probably gone back to him, had more kids hanging off me and been in a lousy relationship.
>
> (Joanne, speaking in 2010)

In their resistance against patriarchy the social network of friendship and care was important. Interestingly, this is a theme that has also been important in aspects of the learners' working lives (see Figure 7.2). The networks forged at college and in the research group offered the female and the male learners resistance in continuing at college against the backdrop of economic and emotional deprivation. For a number of the learners, the research group and their peers were a lifeline against feelings of isolation. The research group became like family or indeed a 'wish family' where each learner cared for the others, offering support and encouragement. However, even the power of the support was not enough for some learners to have the freedom to pursue their educational dream. For Raz, the pull for extra economic capital to care for his extended family was too strong for him to have the freedom to pursue going to university and becoming an accountant. In many ways Raz was restrained by the patriarchal culture that his family firmly believed was the norm. While the female relatives were also restrained by the expectation that they would do domestic chores, Raz had the burden of providing for them all and was expected to bring the money into the house. This is in sharp contrast to Sally, who was not expected to fulfil the domestic role and was given the freedom to pursue her education. However, she did expect her husband to carry on working and provide for her. Sally was able to manipulate a power position in the patriarchal system where she could pursue her dreams.

Personal reflections

My positioning

The clothes and jewellery I wear may be deemed as having symbolic power (see Bourdieu 1994) positioning me both as an 'insider' and 'outsider' (see Warren and Hackney 2000; Bourdieu 1990b). Most of the female learners had been in broken relationships and wore no marital ring. As they spoke of their anger at the men who had 'let 'em down' and their desire to meet someone who was 'different' who would treat them better, I felt both an 'insider', having recognition of the chaos an abusive relationship can give rise to and an 'outsider' as I no longer returned home to abuse. My marital rings also positioned me as an outsider. The jewelled engagement ring, bought second-hand, signified indulgence, luxury, respectability and suburbia, moving me into an uncomfortable position. Respectability was important to the learners (see Skeggs 1997) and while I didn't want to shed my identity, I also didn't want markers on my body to position me as 'the other' and maybe cause a psychological division.

Trying to find a balance was something I developed and I have to say that once I had a wedding band on my finger somehow I felt safer. I realise that's not how it should be, but as a woman put in vulnerable positions, that's the fact of it. With the band on I was treated differently by the male learners. Of course, older now, without the wedding ring, I probably wouldn't face the same issues of amorous remarks. However, on interviewing the male learners, who were keen to ask about my husband and family, I do believe that this positioning lent me respectability. For example, when I telephoned their homes and their parents/partners answered, I am a married tutor partaking in research, not a single woman with a man's telephone number.

Taking into account the above, I kept on my wedding band and removed my engagement ring – which I now consider to be an ostentatious label. It was liberating and helped me to feel closer to the learners.

Wearing respectability

For a couple of the learners, the idea of respectability was closely linked to buying clothes from brand-name shops. Although stretched financially, they dressed themselves and their children in 'designer gear'. This placed me as an outsider when I told them that I bought my children's clothes from less prestigious supermarkets and accepted secondhand clothes from friends. Some, who had worn secondhand clothes years ago, felt that they were now 'bettering themselves' and put plainly: 'buying cheap' and 'secondhand clothes' was for 'mingers'. Yet there were others with whom there was a close bonding because we shared similar experiences, for example, buying clothes for ourselves and our family from the local second hand shops as kids.

Changes in the private domain

In the private domain of my life, time has helped me see my mum and dad differently. Bits of kids when they had me, we've grown up together. I have no doubt I have been a puzzle to them as much as they were to me. What they were, how they were, I hit out against, hoping for change, wanting them to conform to my ideals, rather than allowing what is.

I understand them more now, maybe not always agreeing, but understanding.

Notes

1 Launched in 1998, under New Labour, the programmes seeked to integrate and expand health, childcare, early education and family support services to families with young children living in economically deprived areas. The emphasis was on outreach and community development.

2 Adult Learners' Week Awards recognise extraordinary individuals who have had inspirational learning journeys that have helped them transform their lives, often beyond what they ever thought was possible. The Awards are also given to learning projects that give adults the opportunity to learn and improve their lives.

3 The awards scheme, which has been running since 1998, is aimed at providing much needed support to students from the further education sector who have overcome significant obstacles, both financial and personal, to complete their further education. Helena Kennedy Foundation Awards are designed to support students in their progression to Higher Education, to improve chances of success in Higher Education and to increase employability when students move from higher education to work.

Chapter 9

Literacy and transformation

Getting better

Going back to education
was changing all our lives.
History was not going to repeat itself,
I was making sure of that.
I took another course
called Access to Heath and Nursing.
I realised I wanted to be a nurse,
but needed more qualifications.
(McNamara 2007: 9–10)

Overview

In this chapter, I will explore the learners' experience of literacy in relation to shame, blame, respectability and empowerment. Juxtaposed to this I will examine how tutors, PAR and the strong caring bonds formed between the teacher and the learners can help address and challenge negative emotions, by developing and delivering more egalitarian approaches to pedagogy based on care and mutual respect. This includes exploring how critical reflection and dialogue can facilitate the move from a competence-based model to a holistic approach which empowers the learners and their communities. I will also explore how creativity in the curriculum, community projects, dissemination of the research in the local, national and international domain, and consciousness-raising, can engage learners and communities in mutual learning and development of knowledge which offers the potential for raising hope and working towards social justice.

Introduction

Prior to discussing the impact of critical curriculum on the learners, it is worthwhile considering literacy and transformation. Adult Literacy education can often be a critical space to support and empower learners (and indeed tutors against the dominant discourse) to take agency, no matter what their trajectory so far. With regard to the learners' transformation, it is important to consider the journeys they have taken (for example, see Figures 7.1 and 7.2). The previous chapters have explored their sometimes difficult journeys in the public and private domains of their life (see Figures 7.1 and 8.2) which included being labelled and stigmatised (see Figures 5.2). As a result of the often painful histories, many learners had low self-esteem (see Figure 3.1) and experienced feelings of failure when they began the literacy course. This was exacerbated because of the shame many felt because they struggled to read and write (see Figure 5.3).

Adult literacies: shame, respectability and empowerment

On arrival at college there was a strong feeling that, mirroring their experiences at school, they would be judged and pathologised by others (see Figure 3.1). This learner marginality related to the dynamics of symbolic violence (Bourdieu 1991). In the discussion with the learners there was a link between what they considered their 'poor' literacy skills and viewing themselves as childlike because of that. This is hardly surprising when in all aspects of society including entering learning, basic skills learners are labelled as lacking and in many case put to the bottom of the list when it comes to the hierarchy of employment and courses offered in college. Further to this, the dominant discourse that runs through Adult Education (like that of compulsory education) is often constructed on a deficit model which positions the learners as lacking in relation to what are widely deemed as the norms of literacy. Indeed, literacy is not simply about mastering a code, but within a dominant framework, about developing power over literacy practices that are recognised as 'legitimate', that is, situationally defined, arbitrarily sanctioned forms of reading or writing with legitimate audiences (Bourdieu 1991). Without legitimate literacy, Stella described how:

> You just feel thick. The worst is when you've got to read something in front of someone. I hate that.

While Craig noted:

> I'm ashamed, really, of not being able to spell properly. It's okay as a kid, but at my age it's not right, it's not. I'd be mortified if my mates down the pub knew.

A key driver for all the learners attending the basic skills classes, whether they attended voluntarily or were compulsory attendees on New Deal programmes, was to become literate. The classes were also viewed as means to gain respectability and what they considered normality. Joanne described how:

> People look at you differently when you can't spell, like you've got two heads. I just want to be normal.

While Stella described how:

> As soon as I feel confident enough with my writing I'm doing my Level 2 in Care. The ones who are doing it in the rest home now are treated more professionally somehow. Like they get to help with the medicine round.

The development of literacy skills, confidence and self-esteem was linked to the learners seeing other possible choices in their lives. For many of the learners the adult literacy classes were their last hope of education. At the beginning of the course Stella described how:

Stella: My aim is to get on the Level Two NVQ in Care.
Interviewer: That would be great. Have you ever considered that you could go further than that?
Stella: What, you mean take the Level Three?
Interviewer: Yes.
Stella: Not really. You've got to be really bright to do that. No I'll just about manage Two. A few people I know are on it and there's a lot of writing and that.

There was a transformation in the belief that she could just about 'learn to read and write properly' (Stella, speaking in 2006) to aspiring for and realising her dreams. Working in a collective was a way for the learners to begin to see themselves differently as individuals, and question their positioning in unbalanced power relationships that have marginalised them and their practices of literacy, and act to change them. Stella progressed onto the Level Two and completed the Level Three in Health and Social Care. The cultural capital Stella developed led to resistance and empowerment for her family and self (Figure 8.3).

While Raz, who worked in the informal economy and was sent on a New Deal programme by the careers centre, shared:

Raz: I'm hoping to go onto the book-keeping class. I'll be able to do that and work in the restaurant 'cos it's run in the afternoons.
Interviewer: Do you have a long-term plan?
Raz: Not really.
Interviewer: Is there anything you'd like to do with your life in the future?
Raz: I used think I'd like to go to uni', but that's not really a goer.
Interviewer: Why not?
Raz: 'Cos I missed too much school and that. I'm too behind in what I need to know. It's not for the likes of me.

From this interview, I was able to work with Raz on a personalised pathway. In the planning, he expressed that his dream goal would be to go to university. We discussed the stages of learning and necessary steps he would require to achieve that goal. Like Raz, many non-traditional learners dismiss their dreams as being unrealistic and so dismiss the possibility of achievement beyond learning literacy and Level Two courses. The assumptions, beliefs about HE and the decisions which form the prospect of whether a person goes onto HE is linked to the habitus. Raz did not consider partaking in a degree was for someone like him. Providing the opportunity to consider higher learning goals in the light of essential qualifications to achieve ambitions hitherto only on a wish list, can help learners challenge the symbolic violence and consider strategies to succeed in steps. Raz progressed from the book-keeping course to a Foundation Business course. From here, he progressed onto the intermediate and advanced level, hoping to progress to university. The realisation that he could go to university was a shift in his earlier beliefs and aspirations. He may have followed these steps without the planning and reflection of the routes he could take, but many learners lack the social capital of a network of peers to share the knowledge of how to navigate through the educational system. However, he still faced the constraints of needing economic capital, to support his extended family. Raz had to abandon his studies and dreams in order to take on the role of provider. Accruing economic capital through the informal economy, allowed Raz to support his extended family and maintain some control over his life, whereby he could work within his community as a waiter and around his family. He hopes to complete a degree in the future.

When Joanne arrived at college, she struggled to read and write and sat at the back of the class, she avoided eye contact and spoke neither to me nor to the other learners. After Joanne joined the research group, we began to spend more time together. This allowed me the opportunity to speak to Joanne in detail about the barriers she had faced and her hopes and aspirations for the future. Initially, she described why she had come to college:

> I want to be able to fill in forms on me own and be more confident in me spelling.

However as Joanne's confidence increased in both herself and her writing skills, there was a simultaneous shift in aspirations. We spoke of the pathways she could take following Level Two. Like Shammy, this was the first time she had planned for the future. She began to make choices that she had previously thought were deemed as not for people from her back ground. She began to speak about a career rather than a job, with a determination and optimism:

> I want to be a good role model for my children, getting a career can give us all a better future.

Joanne was breaking down the barriers that had held her back for so long and was now on her way – successfully completing a Level Two course in Literacy and Numeracy; she progressed onto an Access to Nursing Course then to Salford University to pass her diploma and is now a qualified staff nurse working in Rochdale, in the north of England.

Below, Joanne tells her story in her own words. This was part of the writing she shared with me when she began to explore writing an autobiography about her learning journey (see McNamara 2007):

> Do you know, three years ago, if I had to fill in anything like a form, I couldn't, it may as well have been written in another language. In the end I did not even bother looking at any forms that were sent to me. I would just go to my sister and ask her to fill them in for me and I would just sign them. There are so many other things that I could tell you about how not being able to read, write and spell has affected my life, but the chances are that if you're reading this you already know about most of them.
>
> Through learning to read and write, etc., I now see life differently. Now when my children bring homework home I'm right onto it. I sit down with them and we go through their work together. For example, my son A is only eight and he has 20 spellings a week to learn. This week he had words such as exhibition, examination and electrocution. Before returning to education I would never have been able to help him with words like this, so the chances are he would not have learnt them. He would have gone to school, had his spelling test. Maybe he got 4 or 5 out of 20, if he was lucky, felt a bit daft in front of the children who had got most them right and slowly but surely before you know it, it's a knock-on effect, history is repeating itself. But because I can now sit down with A and help him with his homework he gets marks like 17 out of 20, which to me is pretty amazing. I really feel that in my case because I'm all my children have, if I'd not have returned to education the chances are that my children would have ended up experiencing difficulties in their education. I'm not saying that they won't, but if they do, like I did, I can now help them.
>
> In today's world qualifications are needed in most jobs, again proving how important learning is.
>
> I just want to say that returning to education for me was one of the most frightening things that I have ever done, but one of the best. There have been times when I have wanted to quit because I found it too hard and believe me I have cried in frustration. There are two things that have kept me going, one is my beautiful children, they are depending on me and the other is my teacher, who is always on my case – only messing! She has been amazing. She is the one who when I've thought, 'What's the point?', has kept me going. She made me believe that I can achieve my goal if I work hard enough and so far she has been right.

The transformation of her aspiration and her life had an impact on her children's progression and the transformation in the dynamics of the family. She no longer felt childlike but empowered to support her children. Their grades improved and Joanne felt much more confident and valued in her role as a mother (see Figure 8.3).

Curriculum design and working with learners

The PAR led to the negotiation of the structure and content of the curriculum and was a key part of my drive as a research practitioner (see Figure 4.1). There was an emphasis on facilitating the learners to view themselves as sharing power with myself where they felt confident enough to express themselves. A key drive of the curriculum design was to recognise the socially situated literacies the learners brought to the classroom. The PAR facilitated this, allowing us to explore our lives in the public as well as private domains. Moving from a deficit model, this legitimised the experiences and knowledge of the learners across the domains of their life.

The shift in the power position in relation to my role as teacher and researcher, allowed the learners to be co-investigators in the research and from the findings, to be co-constructors of the curriculum. The pedagogy allowed critical discussions where we were able to unpick the themes of the research and see how this could be further expanded on and illuminated in the lesson. One theme that came up was having the space to plan for the future and looking at the steps they needed to take (as discussed earlier). This involved developing activities that valued the learners' everyday practices within the classroom (for example, Barton and Hamilton 1998; Barton et al. 2006). With the learners, we looked at different people's experiences and learning from each other, identified different steps which could be used to reach our goals.

This allowed us to reflect on the barriers we had and how we could address them to move forward. The sharing of the barriers provided the opportunity to critically discuss the violence and trauma the learners had experienced in their lives. Issues related to addressing violence and trauma were then embedded into the lesson and are now part of a set of national resources. The resources are also embedded into the teacher education programme, offering trainee teachers examples of more critical approaches to curriculum design which include opening up opportunities to address issues of violence which permeate through many learners' lives. Stories, poetry and images were used as foils to represent the generative themes in the lives of the learners. An example is of Marie McNamara's easy reading autobiography (McNamara 2007).

It talks about how 'coming back to education was the hardest decision I have ever made'. Marie's book looks at the motivation for returning to education and part of the resources looks at goal setting. The other themes that arose from Marie's narrative included exploring experiences of violence, poverty and illiteracy which many learners face, how these problems exist and what could be done to address them. The resources encourage learners to consider their own life situation, their hopes for the future and aims to help them identify a series of actions which they can take towards achieving their goals. The sharing of ideas and the dialogue between the learners and me, led to a sharing of experiences which was framed within a social praxis that included reflection and action (Macedo 1994).

Creativity and transformation

Poetry and art was used as a way to engage the learner in critical dialogue. An example was using Linda Lucas's poem as resource (Lucas 2001). A former literacy learner and cleaner at the college, Linda composed the poem in class when the race riots were active in Oldham. Delivering to an ethnically diverse class, where there continued to be tensions around race and gender, I used the poem as a discussion piece and for consciousness-raising. This facilitated the group to shape their assumptions about identity and racism. It also opened up a space to use poetry as a means for emotional expression.

Up until seeing the poem, Carol thought that reading and writing poetry was for those with 'qualifications and, yer know, good jobs'. She described how she felt scared of exploring the possibilities of language, believing it was 'not for someone like me'. Carol was experiencing symbolic violence and the: 'Universal adopted strategy for effectively denouncing the temptation to demean oneself is to naturalise difference, to turn it into second nature through inculcation and incorporation in the form of the habitus' (Bourdieu 1994: 123).

However, on reading Linda's poem she seemed totally amazed that people who lived on the same streets as her had written such 'magic'. She described how her position in the field changed. She soaked up the lessons, even asking for poetry. Inspired rather than running from words, she began to embrace language as something she had the right to use. She described how on shaping sentences it really helped her to:

> Deal with those lousy feelings that have crammed my life too often, like doubt, failure and fear.

Discovering she had a flair for writing poetry helped her realise that:

> I used to think everyone was better, now I know we're all the same, equal, like.

Taking control of language empowered Carol and the belief that she can use words to express herself. She turned the symbolic violence she had initially experienced, into symbolic power. Carol's confidence developed together with her self-esteem. The writing of poetry was very much linked with her view of self. She gained respectability from writing her thoughts and feelings:

Carol: When I read out my poems I feel like the class is really listening to me. That makes me proud.
Interviewer: How does it do that?
Carol: It's being able to share some painful memories rather than hiding them away. I've got the guts to do it now; I'm not frightened; like I used to be.

Below is an extract from an initial interview based on Carol's view of how the course has affected her view of 'self':

Carol: Like I said, it's given me more confidence to express myself in words and in writing, how I feel about the past and the present and my future.

Interviewer: And how does that, being able to express yourself better in your writing and also expressing about your future. How does this make you feel being able to do this?

Carol: It makes me feel good.

Interviewer: And how have you been expressing yourself, what forms?

Carol: Just poetry really, about depression and negative things yer know.

Interviewer: And when you're writin' about these negative things, what effect does that have on you?

Carol: It makes me feel better. It gets it out of my system. It's on paper and if I want to read it then I can do. Just gives me positive feedback.

Interviewer: And has this affected how you view yourself? So, do you think you've changed from starting the course 'til now?

Carol: Definitely. I'm a lot more confident. I might make mistakes sometimes but I'm learning from the mistakes I make, so I can go back and rectify it all.

Figure 9.1 illustrates how the cycle of deprivation of capitals across the domains of education and family can be transformed though education and creative expression. This can lead to empowerment, ownership of language and creative expression, a rich habitus and the empowerment of communities.

Below is one of a collection of many that Carol has written over the course of the research. A poignant reminder that research is not merely pages of dead ink; it is a means to give voice to those whose words, whose voices, are often hid from the public domain.

My mask

Take a look at my face,
What do you see
do you see happiness,
do you see glee.

Am I frightening
is it all an act,
you will never know,
unless you ask.

Have you got time,
do you really care,

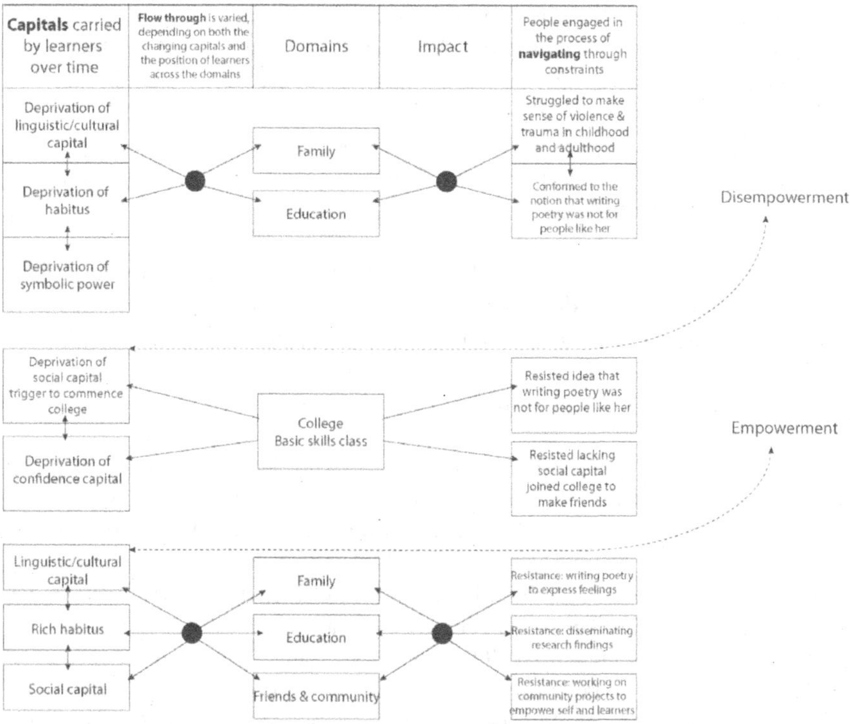

Figure 9.1 **Cycle of deprivation of capitals, transformation though education and creative expression, empowerment and ownership of language**

are you too wrapped up,
in your own affairs.

Most of the time I wear a mask,
pretending to be happy and jolly,
but deep down inside,
I'm full of doubt and worry.

Take off my mask,
what do you see
Nobody of importance,
just sad and silly me.
(Carol March 2007)

Carol's daughter Tracy found the classes gave her the motivation to pursue painting and drawing. Tracy came to the College with no formal qualifications. She was very nervous about starting a course and she describes how, 'It was a huge step to come through the front doors and back into the classroom, a place

I hadn't been since I left school.' A single mother with three children and a full-time job, learning wasn't without its hiccups and getting to college on cold harsh winter nights required some grit and determination. Joining a night-class in literacy made her realise that she wasn't on her own. There were other like-minded people keen to top up their skills and this gave her the hope, enthusiasm and commitment for her future. Below is an extract, from an initial interview, based on how the course has had an impact upon Tracy's view of 'self'. Below she describes this in our conversation:

Tracy: I'm more confident, I'd say, yeh, more positive. If I can do this, I know I can do whatever I want really, if I set my mind to it. But it is, it's just like freeing the wheels, init, and turning them on.
Interviewer: Yeah.
Tracy: I'm a lot more confident now, definite.

Along with her mother, Carol, they made it through the tough times and Tracy went on to paint pictures of animals and nature. When I visited her home for an interview they were displayed on her living room walls. Tracy described how:

Tracy: It's something that I have just for me. When the kids are playin' up which is like twenty four seven, I paint.
Interviewer: Have you painted all these on your wall?
Tracy: Yep. My favourite is the dolphin. I'd never have believed I'd be painting, let alone doing all these. Coming back to college changes you somehow, makes you believe you can do things. It has for me, anyway.
Interviewer: How?
Tracy: I don't know. It just gives me the confidence not to bother what anyone thinks and do it. I was always one of these that'd say 'tomorrow'. Well, yer know what, Vicky? Tomorrow doesn't come – you've got to go and get it.

The result of mother and daughter having a positive and productive creative experience at college has had a further knock-on effect on the third generation in their family. Due to persistent bullying, C, Tracy's teenage daughter was reluctant to return to school at 14 and, instead, engaged in learning on-line at home. However, when C was 16, her mother contacted me via my mobile phone to express her concerns about C's education. A week later, sharing 'a brew', Tracy further explained how she really wanted her daughter to 'Make summat of herself' and 'Get a career, rather than just working in factories, grateful for cleaning jobs or owt, to earn enough to do more than get by.' I took the opportunity to discuss this with C, her setbacks and hopes for the future. The meeting led to a number of actions being implemented to help facilitate C's next step. Subsequently, she enrolled on a Childcare programme.

The creativity opened a space for transformation. This transformation saw a shift in Carol and Tracy's habitus. Bourdieu positions the habitus as a socially constituted system of cognitive and motivating structures which produce and organise practices and their representations for the social agents. The lessons offered a critical space for them to explore their creativity and their literacy practices. The hierarchy of taste and style which are embedded in culture are useful when considering Carol and Tracy's attitude towards creativity. Poetry and art were classed for 'people not like us'. Bourdieu (1984) suggested the ways in which apparently distinctive and individualised consumption and leisure practices tend to betray their class origins. In order to challenge this hegemony of distinction which serves to oppress the working classes, judgment of taste must hold open a future that goes beyond the culture of the dominant or dominated.

This move towards embedding creativity into the curriculum is often difficult, as college curricula often do not acknowledge the creativity that learners bring into the classroom. Their creativity is often masked in a process of symbolic violence where their hopes, desires and practices outside the class are not explored and instead, a dominant competency-based model of literacy is delivered. Using multimodal approaches which includes poetry and images, can be a move towards reflection and transformation. Shifting the habitus systems of dispositions that generate behaviours, including perceptions, expectations, beliefs and actions in a particular context, in this case creativity, can arise from sharing creativity and encouraging learners to think beyond a competence-based approach to literacy. The confidence that arises for creativity can help the learners in other fields.

> I never thought I could do it, write a poem; it was too posh really.
>
> (Carol)

> It was like coming to the class and seeing me mam write her poems gave me the confidence to paint. It sort of gave me the permission.
>
> (Tracy)

> I feel more confident in myself and being a mother when I paint. It's something the social services can't take from me.
>
> (Tracy)

Seeing and acting

Rather than watching the learners leave the course and having no idea of the outcome of their journey, the research facilitated close observation of the drawbacks and leaps the learners have made. For example, the relationships formed also facilitated on-going support and guidance. Although on another course, Sally brought her UCAS form for university and asked me to support her on writing a personal statement.

Informal interviews also took place on nights out. This allowed the group to share each other's experiences and celebrate success. However, this wasn't always straightforward. Sharing experiences of struggles and the obstacles that they had overcome and continue to fight against created a more cohesive group which was able to offer mutual support. It was extremely empowering for the group to be offered the space and opportunity to share each other's experiences and find tactics and strength drawn from coping with adversity. These occasions provided an opportunity for consciousness-raising. This was particularly evident in the stories the women told each other, many involving the physical and psychological abuse they had regularly encountered from fathers, brothers, uncles, partners, sons and strangers. As identified by (Dominelli 2006: 109) this was a key concern and one which had led to obstacles being put in their way and hindered their progress.

Resources, community projects and consciousness-raising

PAR is rooted in the cultural tradition of the participants and builds on strengths and resources in the community. Actively involving learners and the community in PAR increased the likelihood of developing interventions and resources that are culturally relevant and address the learners' needs, as well as promoting the continuation of community engagement and initiatives when the research ended. The consciousness-raising and storytelling led to the development of resources and participating in the community activities which included Write About . . ., which was founded in the north west of England by like-minded people who were inspired by those people they taught or supported and wanted to help them get their work published.

As a member of Write About . . ., the learners expressed how it had helped to give them confidence. Tracy spoke about the experience of having her story published (see Dolan 2008), describing how:

> It felt unreal; to see my words in print. It made me proud that I'd got through it. It also felt good that I could help others who were in the same boat.

Her daughter C wrote the poem about her relationship with her father. This was also published in Write About . . . (2008). She described how it helped her come to terms with the pain she had felt (see Chapter Eight).

They also spoke about how membership allowed the writers, which included Joanne, Carol, and Tracy's daughter, C, the opportunity to gain cultural capital by drawing on this social network. This led to cultural participation and personal empowerment. Tracy spoke about her experience of reading her story out at the launch of the book, held at the Zion Centre in Hulme, as being 'great'.

Tracy:	I felt really nervous at first, really embarrassed. But when I got up there I felt great.
Interviewer:	Why did you feel great?
Tracy:	You know, because I had the guts to stand up and speak out about bullying. I didn't feel ashamed. I felt proud I'd got through it. It was my story not the bullies that everyone was listening to.

Following the successful publication of *Write About . . . Bullying* in May 2008, Write About . . . turned their attention to the subject of inspiring people. We hoped that the learners we work with on a daily basis, who regularly inspire us with their courage, determination and sheer effort, could tell us about the people who had inspired them. *Write About . . . Inspiring People* was produced after working with students across the North West which included the Manchester College, a photography group at Loreto College, Manchester, workshops at Stockport College, community groups in Oldham and the Zion Centre in Hulme, Manchester. There were even contributions from the photography website, Flickr.

Offering a space both in the classroom and the community for the learners to share their narratives allowed the sharing of obstacles and solutions to overcome them. In this capacity the narratives are themselves a capital which can be pulled on by others to inspire and offer strategies to move forward. For example, Tracy's story offered strategies for dealing with bullying (Dolan 2008), while Joanne's narrative offered an inspirational narrative related to her learning journey and overcoming obstacles, such as being poor, being in an abusive relationship and the power of education to transform her and her children's lives for the better. This provided what Tedder and Biesta (2009: 89) referred to as effective 'narrative learners' expanding on this as:

> By narrative learning we mean that learning can take place as a result of articulating stories from one's life, through the process of talking about and reflecting on life experiences, in other words from the very *narration* of one's biography; and can take place as a result of presenting stories from one's life, by having stories with content and structure, by *having a narrative* that says something about what and how you have learned.
>
> (Tedder and Biesta 2009: 89)

The learners were able to be actively involved in decision making and dialogue with the positive outcome of a democratic environment and culture being co-constructed both inside and outside the classroom. For many of the learners, this inclusive approach to education and community action was the antisthesis to what they had experienced previously. The research group facilitated the power of the collective over individual approaches. These bonds helped the learners to overcome the violence and trauma of school experiences, where they were judged by the dominant culture for being poor and not being successful within the educational system. Interestingly, the consciousness-raising facilitated the learners to begin to shift the habitus they had in their dreams of what the future could hold, to ground it in realty. Stella described how:

Stella: I'm over the moon I'm doing my Level Three NVQ.
Interviewer: Did you always know you could do it?
Stella: No way, didn't think I stood a chance 'not with my spelling an' that.
Interviewer: What changed you to believe you could do it?
Stella: Confidence, really, and getting better with my writing. I suppose I've always secretly hoped I'd do it, but I didn't say owt to anyone in case they thought I was daft. I put it to the back of my mind.

Community projects can challenge the discourse of a neo-liberal approach to learning societies which privileges individual over collective learning. This positions education as a commodity and pays no regard to issues of economic, political and social equality.

College, local and national and international dissemination

PAR challenges not only the status of researchers as experts but also raises questions about how knowledge is generated. By definition, 'emancipatory' research should be judged by its ability to empower people – both inside and outside the actual research process. Dissemination of research findings to communities, which include those which are marginalised, requires innovative and meaningful approaches.

Throughout the research the learners' progress was followed by the media department of the college where they enrolled for basic skills courses. Joanne, Tracy, Sally and Raz's learning journeys were placed in the prospectus together with their images to motivate other learners. Their stories were also hung in the college admission area. These were used as motivational narratives and images for adults contemplating joining a basic skills class.

The findings from the research were also published in national women's magazines and the local media. The impact of this was that a number of the learners were stopped by people in their community and asked about their progress and in many cases how they could enrol for college. Joanne described how a neighbour had stopped her in local fish and chip shop and asked what she needed to do to enrol at college. A single mum, with young children, Joanne took her under her wing and, as well as directing her, became a friend and mentor. She would visit the neighbour and offer support on a regular basis.

Joanne: I connected with X right away. I suppose she reminded me of how it was for me when the kids were younger. Havin a bit of support really makes a difference like.
Interviewer: How?

Joanne: Having someone to gab to who knows where you're coming from. She had no confidence in her reading and writing, like me. She could see I'd got on and that helped give her the push, like, to go to college. If it wasn't for her seeing me in the paper and letting on to me in the chippy we probably wouldn't have got chatting.

Tracy described how:

> The neighbours are dead surprised about what I've done, I've given X loads of help with her English.

Carol voiced that:

Carol: X is on her own, like me, and getting on a bit. She's gonna start a course with me next year.
Interviewer: What's made X want to do this?
Carol: Seeing I can do it, I suppose. I've kept all the newspaper clippings to show her.

Clearly the newspapers were offering images of community role models which the community could pull on to consider options that they had not previously considered, for example, completing a basic skills course and progressing to university. The media tracked the learners' progress and this knowledge fed into and empowered the communities. The images offered social capital, by proxy, in that the community could draw on the accounts to motivate them to take their own learning journey (see Figure 9.2).

The learners were also involved in the dissemination of the research findings on a local, national and international stage. This involved collaborating on writing projects from the research findings to local, national and international audiences (for example, Duckworth and Taylor 2008; Johnson et al. 2010). It also involved disseminating the findings in academic text books for teacher educators (Duckworth and Tummons 2010; Tummons and Duckworth 2012; Ingle and Duckworth 2013; Duckworth 2013), resources (McNamara 2007; Duckworth 2008a) and vocational resources (Duckworth 2009), to reach wider communities and a wider audience.

Carol described sharing her story to a national audience:

> I really enjoyed the day. It made me feel confident that what I had to say was important. I felt really proud of myself.

While Joanne described how:

> I never thought I'd have an audience listening to me and what I had to say. Going to America and sharing my story was amazing. It just made me feel kinda, like, I can do anything. I can now.

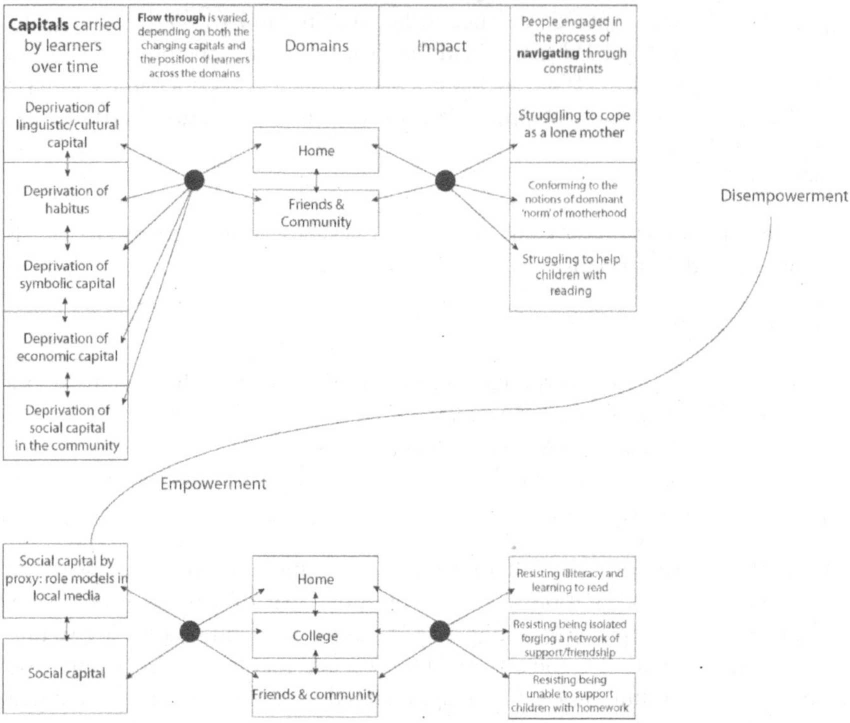

Figure 9.2 Cycle of media role models

Here we can see how the telling of the narrative is empowering and this can again be linked to the narrative as a capital for resistance against the barriers they have faced, for example, being poor, labelled and stigmatised (see Figure 3.3). Rather than the stories being hidden in shame, the learners took ownership of them. They reclaimed them as stories of success recognising the structural inequalities they have challenged and resisted to become empowered to take agency in their lives. The very words that they had feared and struggled with when they commenced the literacy classes are now tools which they use to re-claim identities that are not stigmatised by struggling with a lack of linguistic capital but are celebrated for using linguistic capital to tell their story and put their voices in the public domain. Again, they offer accounts that communities can pull on to resist structural inequalities and a lack of flow of capitals across the domains of their lives.

Conclusion

The potential for resistance and counter hegemonic practice remains a challenge to teachers. Teachers need to be aware of how their beliefs and practices may be inclined by perceptions of learners' ability tied to class, gender and ethnicity and to challenge the reproductive tendencies these perceptions involve. The PAR facilitated the development and delivery of a critical curriculum. It allowed me to address the conflict for basic skills tutors between enacting the dominant ideologies of individualism and exploring the structural inequalities which have had an impact on the learners' lives, so they can challenge these inequalities. To explore these structural inequalities, I needed not only a theoretical framework (see Chapter Three) to explore and explain them, but also an alternative pedagogical approach. As identified in Chapter One, Freire engaged in alternative approaches which refute neo-liberal models based on individualism and competitiveness, models of academic success, which resist the inequalities played out in many of the compulsory classrooms of the learners in this study, which for many of the learners in this study led to violence and trauma in child and adulthood.

Critical educators/researchers reflect a critical pedagogy, providing a curriculum which is culturally relevant, learner driven and socially empowering (Freire 1993; Barton et al. 2000 and 2006). Dialogic communication between teachers and learners was the key to actively involving learners in their own education; this active participation included the co-creation of the curriculum whereby learners' needs, motivations and interests were the driving factors (see McNamara 2007; Duckworth 2008a; Johnson et al. 2010). Assessment was measured by each learner's own goals and aspirations and the distance they had travelled in relation to their learning journey. Offering an egalitarian model takes into consideration the cultural, psychological and educational factors related to the learner. This values their history, present and future narrative, rather than fitting all learners into one learning narrative and prescriptive framework. It facilitated the learners to make their own connection with historical, social, economic and political structures that privilege the dominant ideologies. As they gained confidence and were facilitated on their learning journey within a supportive and holistic learning environment, they were encouraged to strive for their dreams. Linked to the learners' progress was the joint designing of an emancipatory curriculum[1] which embedded critical reflection and recognition that:

> among all the solutions put forward throughout history to the problem of the transmission of power and privilege, there surely does not exist one that is better concealed, and therefore better adapted to societies which tend to refuse the most patent forms of hereditary transmission of power and privileges, than that solution which the educational system provides by contributing to the reproduction of the structure of class relations and by concealing, by an apparently neutral attitude, the fact that it fills this function.
>
> (Bourdieu 1973: 72)

Opening up a space for critical reflection and dialogue the learners challenged notions of what literacies are. It was this move from a competence-based model to a holistic approach (see Morrish et al. 2002) and care (see Feeley 2007) which was strengthened as a result of the PAR and the strong bonds formed with the learners that allowed a critical space for me to fully explore the learners' motivations and barriers. Both the approach of the research and the lessons also worked to encourage the learners to reflect. This was a tool for 'consciousness-raising' (Freire 1996) and praxis. The praxis was linked with social action (see Habermas 1974: 113) and emancipation (Kemmis and Wilkinson 1998). The critical spaces which were provided in the research and the class moved towards a deepened consciousness in which the learners recognise that they are products of history and as such challenge the structural conditions of oppression (see Freire 1996).

Part of challenging the structural oppression included the dissemination of the research as highlighted in Figure 4.1. Basis skills learners' voices are seldom heard, and in many cases not taken seriously. Embedding their voice in the research validated their experience and also allowed a more egalitarian approach not only in the research design but the whole process from start to finish.

The learners' lives and experiences were embedded into the curriculum using their narratives and poetry, etc. This validated their experience and deconstructed the old knowledge, where they blamed themselves for being 'thick' and 'stupid' because they struggled in literacies and substituted it with the construction of new, shared knowledge where they were able to see the inequalities and violence in their lives from which this had stemmed. Using Bourdieu's theoretical framework has allowed me to explore the part played by symbolic culture and violence as an embodied identity. As such, the learners were able to recognise the discourses which shape them and interpret the landscape of their lives, exposing the structures of domination in the learners' lives and how they embody these structures in their everyday practices in the public and private domains of their life. In doing so the research has illuminated how symbolic culture and structure feed into each other to reproduce education and social inequality in the learners' lives.

Social capital is not a homogenous resource equally available and accessible to all members of communities. For the learners in this group, who had been constrained by class, gender and ethnicity, both they and their communities benefited from the media and specifically from the local media following their trajectories. For the single mothers who had themselves faced barriers prior to and while at college, their stories inspired the lone mothers in the community they live. The media stories allowed the single mothers to come together and offer mutual support and to construct identities that challenge negative representations, such as 'chavs' as identified in Chapter Eight, and instead offer representations that take agency and aspire to achieve educationally and build a future for them and their families.

Personal reflections

I knew at an early age that words had power. I formed a relationship with words from songs that would lead me into other times, places and emotions away from the erratic nature of my childhood and reassuring me as I entered adulthood that the future promised better things. Unlike the learners in this study, Carol, for example, I never thought that words were not for me. However, what I did believe was that no one else would be interested in them or anything that I wrote. As the learners' narratives are validated by this study and the dissemination of the research, so are mine. My habitus has become richer by struggling to write this study and resisting giving it up.

Note

1 See, for example, Duckworth 2008a and 2008b.

Chapter 10

Conclusion

Introduction

In the final chapter of the book, I have drawn the main conclusions from the findings of the research, which was driven by the strong relationship between the learners and me and the impact of this in the personal and public domains of our lives. This study adds to the debate on the impact of violence and trauma on learning and its link to class, gender and basic skills. It explored the ways in which symbolic and physical expressions of violence are used to reinforce the dominant class and gender norms against which participants struggle, across the 'fields' in their lives. In doing so it offers a qualitative, longitudinal, feminist, ethnographic and PAR approach, applying Bourdieu's theoretical framework and concepts to expose and explore the structural determinants such as class and gender on the constraints and choices available to the learners on their trajectories. Bourdieu's concepts of habitus, field and symbolic domination have helped me to better understand how mechanisms of power that enable inequalities are embodied in places, people, historical and social existences, and as such are difficult to remove.

The concepts of capitals and habitus provided a useful tool for illuminating the strong link between the impact of the flow, or lack of flow, of capitals in the fields the learners inhabited/navigated across in childhood and as adults, and their experiences of violence and trauma. It has also provided an insight into how the learners' habitus was shaped by the capitals (or lack of capitals) they had and how these were legitimised or not legitimised by the dominant legitimate lens (for example, see Figure 8.1) and the illegitimate lens (for example, see Figure 7.1).

In this study, Bourdieu's conceptualisation of habitus and symbolic violence has further helped me explore the learners' awareness and understanding of the fields they inhabit and highlight what it is that shapes their behaviour and movements in those fields. It offers an insight into the restraining and conforming factors they faced, together with exposing critical spaces for resistance and empowerment in the struggle to transform habitus, despite neo-liberalist claims of an apparently egalitarian social field.

The experiences of violence and trauma in childhood, its subsequent impact on the learners' trajectories and opportunities for agency

Throughout the chapters I have exposed the ways in which the learners' habitus was shaped in relation to access to capitals and their position in the field. Their journeys were classed and gendered. During childhood, legitimate capitals enabled a construction of self which was congruent in the fields they travelled and equated to symbolic power; a lack of capitals led to an incongruous habitus that constrained the learners and resulted in symbolic violence, for example, with symbolic power in the field of education, the learners were able to gain skills and the feelings of being valued by their teachers and peers; this was contrasted with a lack of legitimate capitals which led to a cycle of symbolic and physical violence (see Figure 5.2). In the public domain of schooling, the people in a position of symbolic power labelled and stigmatised the learners, often without regard to the learners' emotions (such as hurt, pain, anxiety, dignity), influenced by the symbolic capital, such as class capital and self-certainty (Reay 1997).

The learners in this study have been disadvantaged for a long time; just as many of these have experienced social and economic inequality most of their lives. Bourdieu (1990a) states that habitus, embodied in agents and inherited through time, is difficult to change. Using the habitus was an excellent tool to explore the potential for change, resistance and empowerment against the symbolic violence that permeated their lives and shaped their identities. It also allowed insights into what the individuals were born into, their legacies, and the socio-economic and political landscapes that frame the fields they enter and travel through. Many of the learners found it hard to move on from their labelled and stigmatised past (for example, see Figures 5.3, 8.2), especially when the violence and trauma had continued in adulthood. There seemed to be recognition of the habitus being at an unconscious level of response, whereby the actions of the learners were pre-reflective (see Sayer 1984). The habitus had durability which was ever-present. However, despite its durability, Bourdieu (2002: 29) (original emphasis) asserted the habitus 'may be *changed by history* that is by new experiences, education or training (which implies that aspects of what remains unconscious in habitus be made at least partially conscious and explicit)' and although 'it is difficult to control the first inclination of the habitus . . . reflexive analysis, which teaches us that we endow the situation with part of the potency it has over us, allows us to alter our perception of the situation and thereby our reaction to it' (Bourdieu and Wacquant 1992: 136).

Indeed, many of the learners were reflexive and had well-developed habitus; with heightened awareness that they did not have the 'right' legitimate capitals across the sites they travelled (for example, see Figures 8.2 and 9.1). Although they struggled with anxiety and pain, they realised that they could resist and alter their personal encounters with symbolic violence (for example, see Figure 7.5). As a consequence, experiences of rupture of the habitus and change occurred across the lives and domains of the learners. The learners' narratives show how the habitus is always in process, in that socialisation into different classed and gendered identities is never complete. The learners took agency and shaped their habitus so that it was not incongruent with the field (for example, see Figures 8.2 and 8.3). I would suggest, however, that this process was not simplistic. Indeed, for the learners in this study there was often a contradiction between how they appeared to the public gaze and how they appeared to their internal gaze. This incongruence caused great anxiety when appearances were in conflict with inner feelings of emotional ambivalence and feeling like an 'outsider' and 'unworthy'. Consider Joanne's perceived lack of linguistic capital and how this positioned her in the field of nursing. The habitus had a durability that even the acquisitions of capitals could not make congruent within the field of nursing. The learners' narratives offered me an insight into their habitus that reflected what was seen as well as unseen. It is these narratives which allowed a deep awareness of the impact of past experiences of symbolic violence and trauma on the learners' changing positions across the domains they travelled.

Distinctions and symbolic power across the fields

The research has demonstrated that, as asserted by Bourdieu, domination, whether class or gender, is secured through a symbolic universe that defines categories of distinction and thereby baffling the core reality of structural inequality that the learners faced in this study in their daily lives. To be dominant is to be able to define what a society values as distinction which, in turn, corresponds to what the dominant classes possess and display; thus reproducing their own dominance as 'legitimised distinction'. We see this at work clearly in notions of distinction where underlying class domination is transposed into an assertion of cultural superiority which the dominated accept as an innate attribute of the dominant in motherhood (for example, see Figure 8.1) education (for example, see Figure 5.3) and work (for example, see Figure 7.4). Moreover, as asserted by Bourdieu, the state holds the domination of legitimate symbolic violence, the state agents, for example, social workers, teachers and workplace managers, and these distinctions, defining what it is to have legitimate symbolic capital to be a 'good' mother, learner and worker. What constituted a family was made legitimate by the dominant gaze of the social workers (see Figure 8.1), teachers (see Figure 3.1) and workplace managers. Learners were pathologised across the fields they travelled, by those in a position of power for not having what are considered legitimate capitals or enough of them, for example, lone parents were considered as not having parenting practices and ways of being which adhered to what was considered the dominant taste in the mediation between the agents of the state (social workers) and the parents. Practices and the way they are unequally viewed in the public and the private domain of the learners' lives were significant across the fields. The social and cultural practices in the fields regulated and shaped hierarchies of social order. The cultural capitals across the fields, when viewed through the dominant lens (for example, see Figure 5.1) privileged the middle classes.

The learners' experience of symbolic power asserted on them was not hidden, they had a strong awareness of where they were positioned in terms of legitimate capital and were aware that they were being labelled and stigmatised, for example, being poor and struggling to read and write at school (see Figure 5.3). The familiarity by which they were pathologised did not become naturalised to them and they were not passive. Although they struggled with low self-esteem and anxiety they took agency and offered resistance against the labels (for example, see Figures 6.1, 6.2, 7.3, 7.4 and 7.5), a counter culture that allowed them symbolic capital in the context of their own communities.

Gendered divisions of capitals in the private and public domains on the learners' lives

The study allowed me to analyse the gendered divisions of capitals in the learners' lives and how these shaped their habitus. It also opened up possibilities for resistance and transformation. The analysis revealed that the learners conformed to patriarchal gender norms across childhood and adulthood. The duality of these two roles was linked in their habitus and both roles were seen as gendered. The notions of what it means to be female and male were entrenched in trajectories. As adults, the females took the caring and domestic roles which they had established in childhood; while the males rarely partook in what they considered to be female roles and responsibilities. Indeed, even when the roles were not carried out according to traditional gender norms, the learners' habitus was still aligned to them, for example, the lone mothers combined their caring role with what they viewed as the traditional male breadwinner role. And though the reality saw them challenging the patriarchal gender norms, their habitus was still deeply aligned to them. Rather than seeing the strength of fulfilling both of these sites and acknowledging the strength in their capacity, they considered their lone mother position second best to that of the traditional family. The mothers did not challenge this symbolic violence, even though the role of mother and carer constrained them and their freedom in ways that the males in their relationships did not experience. However, these mothers were aware of the fulfilment and enrichment that being a mother brought to their lives, which outweighed the constraints.

The study has revealed that the deep alignment to patriarchal gender norms that the learners' habitus initially had, was malleable. The accruing of cultural capital in the form of qualifications and social capital at college and beyond was a means to re-shape the habitus and change both the perceptions of what motherhood was and empower the learners and their families to take agency (for example, see Figures 8. 3 and 8.4). Furthermore, the resistance and empowerment was not always linear, time or field bound, for example, the symbolic and physical violence experienced at school for being poor and not having the considered legitimate linguistic/cultural capital (see Figures 3.1, 3.2 and 5.3) was later transformed to empowerment in the field of motherhood and family to empower both the learners and their families (see Figure 8. 2).

The findings from the research also exposed how gendered capitals can be transformed into powerful capitals outside the private domain. The learners had an awareness of expectations for them to go into unskilled and unstimulating jobs. Rather than their habitus being congruous with this route, they resisted this pathway by pulling on gendered capitals which offered them alternative choices. The male habitus was strongly aligned to notions of masculinity and power which 'muscle capital' provided and without the dominant cultural capital, they drew on their gendered capital to find work. They also found spaces to challenge and resist the dominant lens of legitimate work for that of the informal economy. This allowed them empowerment, autonomy, economic capital, stimulation and street capital (for example, see Figure 7.5). For the females the caring capital accrued was also reframed as a valuable transferable capital which could be exchanged for stimulating work, and offer symbolic capital and power (for example, see Figure 7.3) in jobs which included healthcare work.

This study has drawn attention to how gendered capitals are drawn upon in the workplace. Although the exploration of these has been important in highlighting the gendered practices in the workplace, I am aware that gendering capitals can lead to essentialism of labelling such practices 'male' and 'female', however by placing the learners' trajectories into a historical context my aim has been to emphasise how gender is a cultural construct that is played out in the fields which the learners inhabit.

Violence, trauma, gender and hidden secrets

Throughout the analyses and interpretation I have attempted to show the importance of considering the impact of gender related violence and trauma, which was experienced in childhood (for example, see Figures 6.1, 6.2) and adulthood (for example, see Figures 7.2 and 7.3) in the private domain of home. The constraints, challenge and resistance to violence was gendered. A number of the female narratives have been removed at the request of the learners. These exposed the sexual violence and trauma they experienced. This violence sapped the women's energy, undermined their confidence and left them struggling with the stigma of shame in adulthood. Though the secrets of sexual violence remain unchallenged, it is hardly surprising that it provoked the strongest feelings in the learners who had experienced it. This anxiety and pain shaped their habitus in relation to their self-worth. The learners spoke of having black days and feelings of being brokenhearted. This loss of innocence was compared to a death. Their sexual exploitation had left a scar that seemed to refuse to heal. The strength of the learners' resistance to live with this scarring and pain and still build a life is evidence of their resilience. However, in their struggle to deal with emotions they did not challenge the patriarchy which had objectified and sexualised them in childhood. The abusers were not made accountable for the pain they had caused through the judiciary system. Their silence may be viewed as conforming to the constraints. However, I would argue that the silence was a weapon of empowerment whereby they could protect their identity from being soiled by the public gaze, rather than leaving it open to shame. Their silence is about them taking ownership and dealing with their emotions on a personal level, whether these emotions of pain will ever be resolved remains to be seen.

Resistance and empowerment against the impact of violence and trauma in childhood was also gendered. Although the men had struggled with the shame of childhood violence and trauma, they were able to re-claim a spoiled identity to one of empowerment by converting the muscle capital they had acquired to resist the physical violence into street capital (see Figure 5.1) and labour capital (see Figure 6.1). The females' identity was shaped by the shame of the sexual violence and trauma, and it continued to influence their habitus. The prospect of the women re-claiming their identity from stigma seems impossible while the sexual violence remains invisible and unchallenged.

The field of education

The research findings have allowed the analyses of the learners' experiences in the field of education. This has further enabled me to explore the impact of schooling and how this both shapes and is shaped by the habitus. Rather than school being a meritocratic site, it exposed it as a site for intergenerational marginalisation, social exclusion, and labelling by teachers and peers (Figures 3.1 and 3.3). With the learners reduced access to the cultural capital of the dominant, they were at a disadvantage in the classroom, suffering educational repercussions for having a cultural capital which was in the wrong currency (Gewirtz et al. 1995).

The literacies the working-class children brought to school, and adults brought to further education, afforded little symbolic value in that they could not be used in class to pass exams (Figure 5.3), for example, the domestic and caring literacy which has been traditionally carried out by girls and women seldom enters the public domain and often remains invisible and unrecognised. The working-class practices, which were often gendered, were not valued. Wrapped in notions of literacies, were domination and symbolic violence. Oral and written linguistic capabilities were not equally valued in schools (or the workplace), and even within the oral tradition, the codes of the upper classes were prioritised over the codes of working class and ethnically diverse learners (Bernstein 1971b; Labov 1972). This inevitably meant that learners who were not proficient in the linguistic skills required in schools and colleges were defined as failures or lacking in intelligence simply by virtue of the way they relate to and know the world. The wheel of symbolic power (Figure 4.1) illustrates how many of the learners were positioned in the field of education and the accumulation of symbolic violence (Figure 5.2). While the lack of dominant literacies (see Figure 5.3) had an impact on their progress through the field of education, all the aforementioned caused them to struggle through the educational system. It had an impact on the choices or lack of choices they made (for example, see Figures 3.1a and b). This, juxtaposed to being poor and having little social capital to support them to break out of their conditions, left many anxious, with low self-esteem and a belief that they were stupid and failures.

As they struggled with symbolic and physical violence in their navigation within and out of the field of education, they were aware the capitals they took to the classroom were not valued by the legitimate lens of symbolic representation of cultural domination. Rather than being passive, there was a rupture in their habitus whereby they challenged the status quo and offering resistance took agency. To escape the oppression of labelling and stigma, they played truant and left school. They also found alternative capital, for example, accruing street capital and symbolic representation which was valued in the context of their communities (Figure 5.1). This allowed them to take back ownership of their identity and empower themselves by replacing dominant cultural capital of schooling, for example, qualifications with situated gendered embodied cultural capitals of muscle for the males (see Figure 6.1) and glamour capital for the females (see Figure 6.2).

Self-worth and esteem were very much tied up in outward appearance. However, the accruing of embodied capital was done for more than notions of self-improvement, it was a means to take ownership of capitals within the learners' grasp and offer resistance to re-claim an identity of shame. They were used in the struggle against the violence and trauma which the learners experienced in both childhood and adulthood in their struggle against symbolic and physical violence.

The study revealed that when the learners joined the adult basic skills class, there was a shift in the learners' habitus. The habitus became more aligned with notions of dominant cultural capitals which had marginalised them in childhood. In an educational environment where they were valued and their socially situated literacies acknowledged and used, they were able to challenge the cycle of domination and symbolic violence. They re-claimed spoilt identities of failure and transformed them to ones of success. In the process the feelings of self-worth and identity that were previously linked to gendered embodied capital of glamour and muscle capital saw a shift to the acquisition of linguistic capital for empowerment (see Figure 7.4). This process was, however, not one or the other, the gendered capitals the learners had were complex and robust; they constrained and empowered depending on time and space, and not necessarily in a linear way, for example, the teenage glamour capital had a durability that the older women learners longed to re-visit as their own faded. They conformed to the patriarchal norms of women being equated to the body, hoping to squeeze out the last bits of glamour capital to find a partner for love, caring and financial security to put an end to their struggles.

Sharing of capitals

In the interrogation of the data I have aimed to show the importance of the distribution and sharing of capitals in the communities. While the learners struggled in and across the fields in the public and private domains of their lives, lacking capitals, such as economic capital, disempowered them. Since the realisation that even the necessity of a pair of decent hole-free shoes is a luxury, when on benefits or a low wage, a challenge for me was to find ways to address poverty. The sharing of capital is vital to my participation in the research. Together with the learners we put a number of actions to address the poverty and the impact of this that the learners faced. I nominated the learners for monetary bursaries and prizes, for example, Joanne was awarded the Helena Kennedy award[1] and we collected and distributed clothes, shoes and household goods among the research group. I spent a couple of evenings each week visiting members of the group and, where possible, providing mechanisms of support. The research group also offered mechanisms of support for each other.

I also contributed to the meal and always bought the alcohol on our evenings out. As the learners' position in the field changed, they began to pay for themselves and to support other members of the group and their community, for example, when Joanne found employment as a nurse, she gave her neighbour, who was a single mother like herself, the money to buy her children's school uniforms.

The study put forward strategies for positive networks to examine and understand inequalities affecting our lives and the lives of others and the principal causes of these inequalities. However, without acting on the impact of these inequalities, which include poverty, the study would not have examined the real challenges that the learners face on a day-to-day basis. These were real and having the opportunity to live fulfilled lives, free from continued struggle had a profound effect on them.

Friendships and trust

The research analyses and interpretation have revealed the importance of social capital in supporting the learners into education and on their trajectory. While the women's friendships would have been traditionally located in the community, such as neighbours, the community cohesion was weak in the areas in which many learners lived and being without work left men without this network. Many of the learners were isolated in their communities. The friends they made at college and on their trajectory became their family (Roseneil and Budgeon 2004). It was where the learners went to for support and care. Social capital is a resource which was accumulated through the relationships formed across the field of education. It offered many of the learners a support mechanism throughout their trajectories and beyond.

Trust was something that many of the learners had lost due to their experiences of violence and trauma and the breaking of trusts by those in positions of power. The social capital they accrued from the new and old bonds can be viewed as a production factor consisting of 'networks, norms, and trust that facilitate coordination and cooperation for mutual benefit' (Putnam 1993: 35–36). The sharing of friendship and the building up of trust was a positive outcome of the research; it was a social capital that was strengthened as the research progressed which allowed them to offer each other on-going support. The learners found the courage to empower themselves to navigate through the flows of capitals through the bonds of friendship (see Figure 7.3).

The habitus of the learners was informed by the social networks and experiences they encountered, which allowed them to go beyond their previous experiences which had often resulted in violence and trauma (see Figure 3.1). The relationships were based on trust, commitment, energy and enthusiasm; capitals which were vital in sustaining them on their journey. The PAR allowed these bonds to be further strengthened.

The research has also demonstrated that research goes beyond peers; it is also part of the learner and teacher relationship. As a member of the community, I shared my struggles and strategies for attempting to overcome these. The relationships formed were meaningful and strong; they continue socially.

The power of PAR and a critical curriculum

The learners in this study have shown that they wanted to improve their social and economic positioning and wanted to improve their life chances and those of their children. Education plays a role in their ability to gain the cultural and social resources that they need to organise an upward mobility shift; just as it serves as a site in which the inequalities that already exist are reproduced (Bourdieu and Passeron 1977). PAR led to the negotiation of the structure and content of the curriculum and a model of teaching that embraced caring between the teacher and learner. This facilitated the learners to view themselves as sharing power with myself, where they felt confident enough to express themselves. The sharing of ideas and the dialogue between myself and the learners, led to a sharing of experiences which was framed within a social praxis that included reflection and action (Macedo 1994). This 'commitment to giving back allowed them to reconcile difficult contradictions between wanting to escape, while seeking to preserve, their working class identities' (Reay 2003: 306).

As a teacher and researcher I was able to utilise the research findings to inform my classroom practice and create a holistic curriculum which recognises the socially situated literacies which the learners bring into the classroom (see McNamara 2007; Duckworth 2008a). This was important, particularly to offer learners who do not fit with dominant ideologies (the school's invisible curriculum and New Labour's individualism) a voice and to validate their literacies, leading to the development of more meaningful knowledge. Subsequently, this knowledge was generated from the lived experience of the group rather than thrust upon it; resulting in explanatory power in the public and private domains of their lives (for example, Write About . . . 2008, 2009). Partaking in emancipatory action research (see Figure 4.1) also offered space for learner transformation and consciousness raising in adult literacy classes and the community (see figure, 9.2).

Commitment to addressing violence and trauma

Bourdieu argues that violence inherent in symbolic domination lies in agents' complicity (Bourdieu 2001b). The points of consideration presented here aim to expose and redress the misrecognition of certain held dispositions that 'legitimatize' classed and gendered inequalities. As educationists and community members, I would argue that we need to look at the violence and trauma, such as the ones above, not as isolated accounts, but relate them to the structural inequalities in people's lives (for example, see Figures 3.1, 3.2, 3.3, 5.2 and 5.3). It offers an indicator of the relationship of the learners to the state and the social values which uphold this. Violence and trauma had an impact on the learners in many ways which include mental and physical well-being, economic and social capitals or lack of capitals. It shaped their experiences and was not something that they threw off but something that cut deep and scarred. However, that is not to say that the learners were passive, many offered resistance or took agency (for example, see Figures 7.1, 7.3, 7.4 and 7.5).

Blame and guilt

This 'blame and 'guilt' is hardly surprising in today's neo-liberalist society, where myths of everyone having equal choice and options permeate through institutions and public life. In the spotlight was the media's fixation with the wedding between Kate Middleton and Prince William and most recently the birth of their child. Here the press saturate images of Kate and narratives which hail her as an 'ordinary' girl, the narratives and images harking back to fairytale notions that allude to even 'ordinary' girls being able to meet and marry a prince. Indeed, according to the media, anything is possible if we just believe. One newspaper journalist describing it thus: 'By unveiling a bride whose social background is not too unlike that of many *ordinary* Britons, Prince William has taken a gigantic step towards rekindling the long love affair between Crown and country' (Sandbrook 2010).

The idea that her social background is not unlike many Britons feeds into the idea of a meritocratic society where anything is possible.[2] What it fails to take account of is the rich capitals which have supported Kate in her private and public trajectory from 'ordinary' girl to princess, for example, she was schooled at Marlborough College, a £30,000-a-year boarding school. This is hardly the schooling of many ordinary Britons who do not have the opportunity to accrue the dominant capitals which such public schooling so readily provides. Indeed, it may be argued Kate Middleton's Marlborough education helped give her the rich habitus that offered her an ease around the upper classes, polished manners and a genteel accent to match those of her royal fiancé and the institution into which she has since married. Accent is still a key class signifier and Kate's bears no resemblance to an ordinary accent.

It is in this climate where learners are expected to succeed against the odds and if they do not, the fault is their own (after all even 'ordinary girls' become princesses) and not structural inequalities, many are up against each step of their learning journey and indeed life. It is this lack of awareness that leads to the fact that: 'even the most disadvantaged tend to perceive the world as natural and to find it surprisingly acceptable, especially when one looks at the situation of the dominated through the eyes of the dominant' (Bourdieu 1990: 131).

The ideas of choices and opportunities for all was compounded by New Labour's rhetoric about responsibilities (and now the coalition's notion of the Big Society) which, when considering social pathologies, failed to address the largely structural explanations of poverty and deprivation and instead placed significant emphasis upon the lifestyle, culture and choices of the poor and marginalised. As the course and the research progressed, learners began to discuss the barriers they faced and the guilt and blame they felt for being poor, unemployed and struggling with literacy. This fed into the notion that individuals can rise above the barriers, such as the violence and trauma experiences by a number of the learners in this study, and if they don't they are to blame.

Conclusion

Throughout the previous chapter I have highlighted the learners' experiences of violence and trauma across the fields they navigated and that their habitus was shaped by these experiences. The learners' accounts of their experiences showed that access to capitals and positioning in the field they inhabit can influence symbolic capital and power and also influence the possibilities open for their future trajectories. I have illustrated the learners' capacity for agency and flexibility, showing the habitus is involved in resistance and reflexivity as well as compliance. The cycle of violence and trauma was played out at home and when they went to school. As adults it was a similar picture with violence in the home and at work. The links between the learners' experience of violence across the domains was important in offering a more meaningful landscape of their lives and the barriers they face in education (for example, Figure 3.1, 3.2 and 5.2). The link between the learners' experiences was important in demonstrating the pervasive and dominant nature of symbolic capital and violence on the poor and those who struggle with literacies (for example, see Figure 5.3).

The research has shown the ways in which the learners' experiences are shaped through classed and gendered processes which result in different dispositions in the public and private domains and differ in their trajectories. Histories, while always social, are also distinct enough to merit closer attention to the details that contribute to significant differences in learners' habitus and choices or lack of choices across the fields they inhabit, especially in such cases where the product being examined (capitals) is defined by the dominant lens of distinction from the start (for example, see Figure 5.1). Learners are tied to their physical space which, in turn, is reflected in their positioning in social space (Bourdieu 1999). The learners have described the difficulties they encounter when trying to move outside their space, for example, returning to college. The learners' stories challenge notions of a meritocratic society, where everyone is on an equal footing across the fields they enter, and where, specifically, education is problematic.

The depth of misrecognition within the dominated means that unmasking domination cannot be conducted at a distance and, as a practitioner researcher adopting PAR, it allowed me a close engagement with the learners and their communities:

> It is not a question of the truth or falsity of the unsupportable image of the working-class world that the intellectual produces when, putting himself in the place of a worker without having the habitus of a worker, he apprehends the working-class condition through schemes of perception and appreciation which are not those that the members of the working class themselves use to apprehend it. It is truly the experience that an intellectual can obtain of the working-class world by putting himself provisionally and deliberately into the working-class condition, and it may become less and less improbable if, as is beginning to happen, an increasing number of individuals are thrown into the working-class condition without having the habitus that is the product of the conditionings 'normally' imposed on those who are condemned to this condition. Populism is never anything other than an inverted ethnocentrism.
>
> (Bourdieu 1984: 374)

Bourdieu's theoretical model has provided an important argument against perspectives which see these issues simply in terms of personal choice and meritocracy based on neo-liberal discourse. I would argue that what is needed is dialogue on the freedom and the constraints learners in their daily life experience and offer equal weight to both of these. This allows notions of agency while also recognising structural inequalities that have an impact on this. I would argue that the relevance of class and gender on the learners' trajectories has continued importance in the era of individualising modernity (Beck 1994). Further to this, the concept of capitals and how they are accrued and valued used in this study are important in facilitating a more detailed analysis of different relations of power which can remain hidden and implicit in concepts such as 'individualism', 'choice' and 'mobility' (for example, Giddens 1992; Beck 1994). Critics of the theories of individualisation point to the persistence of class, gender and ethnic stratification in the field of employment (for example, see Furlong and Cartmel 1997; Skeggs 2004). Despite attempts to rewrite their own history and to mould a different life trajectory through education, the learners were still bound by the significance of class through both cultural process and the reproduction of position through their capitals or lack of them.

The learners' narratives have exposed the contradiction, complexities and ambivalences they experience in their daily lives and how they try to make sense of them from their structural positioning as basic skills learners in a society based on inequality of opportunity and choice. Situations of rupture and transformation occur when there is no longer acceptance of the rules of the game and the goals proposed by the dominant class. So while some will seek to preserve the status quo, others will strive to challenge and transform existing hierarchies.

The analyses of the learners' past experiences was crucial in explaining the interconnectedness of violence and trauma and how it had an impact on the learners in the private and public domains they inhabited and through which they travelled. Childhood experiences of being poor, being subjected to violence in the home and at school, left many learners scarred and desperate with low self-esteem and low confidence both in childhood and adulthood (see Figures 5.2, 5.3, 8.3 and 8.5). As well as struggle, resistance against violence and trauma was present in their school and home life. The learners hit back by truanting, leaving school early and leaving abusive homes to escape the symbolic and physical violence.

Reflections

It is by working together as learners practitioners, policy makers and researchers that we can build a better society for all, and not just for the privileged few, based on justice, equality and hope for the future.

Being political, I would argue, is less of an option, but more of a need in the field of education today. Hegemony seeps through the very fabric of an education system which is deeply aligned to a global neo-liberal market place, with competition at its helm.

Since I started teaching I have seen a lessening in any political activity, for example, many trainee teachers and new teachers refuse to join the teachers' union seeing it not as a means of solidarity but as radical activity which will single them out as 'trouble-makers'.

The lifelong learning sector is not an easy landscape to navigate through. Often the emotional labour which teachers invest in their job can be draining (Avis and Bathmaker 2004). This labour often includes 'underground working' (Gleeson 2005), such as supporting learners' needs in unaccounted time slots, for example, breaks and lunchtimes. The time, energy and commitment of a working week based on extra hours, compounded by work environments where job security is unstable due to redundancies and restructuring, often leaves practitioners fearful of their job security, exhausted and reluctant to challenge the hegemony which is ever present in a curriculum based on quantifiable outcomes such as skills for life (SfL) end tests. These outcomes are what the lifelong learning sector uses to measure performance, pull down funding and reach national benchmarks.

New Labour has left a legacy of a meritocratic system, supported by theories that assume 'choice' paradigms in exploring education and choice career trajectories. These fail to see the impact of capital, or the lack of capitals on choice, and the impact of this on symbolic violence. As the gap between the rich and poor widens, it is time for a change in the way education is delivered and the curriculum implemented if we are to address the needs of working-class learners. Adult education needs to dis-entangle itself from neo-liberal fusion to create space for contextualised and emancipatory learning. As Freire outlines, this has to occur in a learner-centred and grounded way through dialogic pedagogy and critical transivity. Critical education can open up spaces for a more equitable approach where a more level playing field is established for those from disadvantaged backgrounds. We need to recognise and address the historical and contemporary disparities that exist in the structural inequalities between the learners and their lives, for example, class, gender and ethnicity. A way to address this is for educators and society to recognise and value the cultural dimensions which the learners bring with them and work with these to create a curriculum which is meaningful to their lives. Working with models of NLS and critical approaches has enabled me to provide a holistic and emancipatory curriculum which seeks to facilitate the learners to reflect on their world in order to transform it (Freire 1972).

Future research

The current research has identified a number of other possibilities in the field of basic skills, violence and empowerment. An area for development would be further research into sexual violence and its impact on the learners' trajectories in the private and public domains of their life. Many of the learners' stories of sexual abuse remain invisible. My research has cut out the narrative the learners did not want included, the silences are as important as what is said. And yet, the impact this experience of violence has had on their lives is enormous. It would also be interesting to extend the research to other curriculum areas, for example, vocational subjects such hairdressing and bricklaying. This would enable an exploration of vocational learners' experience and allow a broader analysis of the learners in the further education sector.

When the coalition government came to office, there seemed to be little cause for celebration or optimism given the recent cuts and the divide between the academic achievements of learners from private and state schools. Recent statistical studies have identified that social class remains the greatest predictor of educational attainment in Britain (National Equality Panel 2010; Kerr and West 2010). In this massively socially-divided society, the Cameron–Clegg-led Britain of today, I would argue that it is more important than ever to recognise social class and identity and how this shapes educational experiences and social lives. While middle-class parents have the capitals to help ensure that their children have a privileged education, working-class children face further exclusion and fewer prospects of accessing Higher Education. The impact that the above and the increased tuition fees will have on choice and learners' trajectories is worth further research.

Hope, class, faith and education is something that needs further exploration. Without hope there is little optimism for social justice and a future based on choice for all, regardless of the communities into which they are born.

Notes

1 Each year the Helena Kennedy Foundation invites Further Education and Sixth Form Colleges and Adult Education Centres across the UK to nominate up to five students for a Helena Kennedy Foundation Award. The awards scheme, which has been running since 1998, is aimed at providing much needed support to students from the further education sector who have overcome significant obstacles, both financial and personal, to complete their further education.

2 Which is ironic considering the man and indeed the institution into which she is marrying is that of wealth, privilege and title, which is certainly not meritocratic.

Appendixes

Appendix 1, Table 1 Learners' biographical information

	Gender	Ethnicity	Occupations prior to commencing course	Residence	D.O.B.		Course
Craig	M	White British	Unemployed	Oldham	1963	Dyslexia	FT New Deal
Stella	F	White British	Cleaner	Oldham	1959	Dyslexia	PT literacy
Sally	F	White British	Nursery Nurse	Rochdale	1982		PT literacy
Emily	F	White British	HW	Oldham	1954		PT literacy
Rachel	F	White British	Unemployed	Oldham	1954	Dyslexia	FT New Deal
Sarah	F	White British	Carer	Oldham	1980		PT literacy
Joanne	F	White British	Unemployed	Oldham	1968	Dyslexia	PT literacy
Martin	M	White British	Student	Oldham	1968	mental health issues	PT literacy
Robert	M	White British	Unemployed	Oldham	1957		PT literacy
Jack	M	White British	Unemployed	Oldham	1956		PT literacy
Tracy	F	White British	Factory Work	Oldham	1968		PT literacy
Raz	M	British Asian	Unemployed	Oldham	1985		FT New Deal
Mike	M	White British	Unemployed	Oldham	1982		FT New Deal
Melanie	F	White British	Unemployed	Oldham	1965	Dyslexia and Bi-Polar	PT literacy
Carol	F	Irish	Unemployed	Oldham	1957		PT literacy
Shammy	M	British Asian	Unemployed	Oldham	1982	Dyslexia	FT New Deal

Appendix 2, Table 2 Themes and topics generated from questions

Schooling	Peers	Experience	What makes a 'good' and 'bad' teacher	Impact of Labelling
College	Motivation and commencing college	Ongoing experience	Barriers faced	Progress
Work Life	Work history	Occupations	Why Chosen	Job satisfaction
Home Life	Role models in the family?	Books, magazines, newspapers in the house	Value placed on learning	Support given
Family Life	Wife/Husband (Support offered)	Role as parent	Any change from the way their parents were? How? Why?	Spirituality

Table showing the core questions (highlighted in bold) used to promote a learner led approach to further data collection, leading to learner led sub topics (non bold)

Bibliography

Ahmed, S. (2000) *Strange Encounters: Embodied Others in Post-Coloniality*. London: Routledge.

Ahmed, S. (2004) *The Cultural Politics of Emotion*. Edinburgh: Edinburgh University Press.

Alaszewski, A. (2006) *Using Diaries for Social Research*. London: SAGE.

Alvesson, M. and Skoldberg, K. (2000) *Reflexive Methodology: New Vistas for Qualitative Research*. London: SAGE.

Apple, M. (2000) 'Can critical pedagogies interrupt rightist politics?', *Education Theory*, 50 (2) pp. 229–253.

Appleby, Y. and Duckworth, V. (2009) 'Sustaining learning over time: it looks more like a Yellow Brick Road than a straightforward path for women experiencing violence', University of Wales, Newport: Sustainable Literacies, Research and Practice in Adult Literacy Conference RaPAL.

Archer, L. and Hutchings, M. (2000) '"Bettering yourself?" Discourses of risk, cost and benefit in ethnically diverse, young working-class non-participants' constructions of HE', *British Journal of Sociology of Education*, 21 (4): 555–574.

Archer, L. and Leathwood, C. (2003) 'Identities, inequalities and higher education', in L. Archer, M. Hutchings and A. Ross (eds) *Higher Education: Issues of Inclusion and Exclusion*. London: Routledge Falmer.

Archer, L., Hutchings, M. and Ross, A. (2003) *Higher Education and Social Class: Issues of Exclusion and Inclusion*. London: Routledge Falmer.

Arnot, M. and Weiner, G. (eds) (1987) *Gender and the Politics of Schooling*. London: Hutchinson.

Atlas, R. S. and Pepler, D. J. (1998) 'Observations of bullying in the classroom', *Journal of Educational Research*, 92: 86–99.

Avis, J. (2005) 'Beyond performativity: reflections on activist professionalism and the labour process in further education', *Journal of Education Policy*, 20 (2): 209–222.

Avis, J. and Bathmaker, A. M. (2004) 'The politics of care: emotional labour and trainee further education lecturers', *Journal of Vocational Education and Training*, 56 (1): 5–20.

Back, L. (1993) 'Gendered participation: masculinity and fieldwork in a south London adolescent community', in D. Bell, P. Caplan and W. J Karim (eds.) *Gendered Fields: Women, Men and Ethnography* (pp. 215–233). London: Routledge and Kegan Paul.

Ball, S. J. (1981) *Beachside Comprehensive: A Case Study of Secondary Schooling*. Cambridge: Cambridge University Press.

Ball, S. J. (2003) *Class Strategies and the Education Market: The Middle Classes and Social Advantage*. London: Routledge Falmer.

Ball, S. J. (2008) *The Education Debate*. Bristol: The Policy Press.

Ball, S. J. (2010) 'New class inequalities in education: why education policy may be looking in the wrong place! Education policy, civil society and social class', *International Journal of Sociology and Social Policy*, 30 (3/4): 155–166.

Ball, S, J., Roew, R. and Gerwitz, S. (1995) 'Circuits of schooling: a sociological exploration of parental choice in social class contexts', *Sociological Review*, 43 (1): 52–78.

Ball, S., Maguire, M. and Macrae, S. (2000) *Choice, Pathways and Transitions Post-16: New Youth, New Economies in the Global City*. London: Falmer Press.

Barton, D. (1994) *Literacy: An Introduction to the Ecology of Written Language*. Oxford: Blackwell.

Barton, D. and Hamilton, M. (1998) *Local Literacies: Reading and Writing in One Community*. London: Routledge.

Barton, D., Hamilton, M. and Ivanic, R. (2000) *Situated Literacies: Reading and Writing in Context*. Abingdon: Routledge.

Barton, D., Ivanic, R., Appleby, Y., Hodge, R. and Tusting, K. (2004) *Adult Learners' Lives Project: Setting the Scene, Progress Report*. Lancaster University: NRDC.

Barton, D., Ivanic, R., Appleby, Y., Hodge, R. and Tusting, K. (2006) *Relating Adults' Lives and Learning: Participation and Engagement in Different Settings*. London: NRDC.

Barton, D., Ivanic, R., Appleby, Y., Hodge, R. and Tusting, K. (2007) *Literacy, Lives and Learning*. London: Routledge.

Bauman, Z. (1987) *Legislators and Interpreters: On Modernity, Postmodernity and Intellectuals*. Cambridge: Polity Press.

Bauman, Z. (1998) *Globalization: The Human Consequences*. Cambridge: Polity Press.

Beck, U. (1992) *Risk Society: Towards a new modernity*. London: SAGE.

Beck, U. (1994) 'The reinvention of politics', in U. Beck, A., Giddens and S. Lash (eds) *Reflexive Modernisation: Politics, Tradition and Aesthetics in the Modern Social Order*. Cambridge: Polity Press.

Beck, U. and Beck-Gernsheim, E. (2001) *Individualization*. London: SAGE.

Becker, H. (1963) *Outsiders: Studies in Sociology of Deviance*. New York: Free Press.

Becker, H. (1973) 'Labelling theory reconsidered' in H. Becker (ed.) *Outsiders: Studies in the Sociology of Deviance* (pp. 177–212). New York: Free Press.

Beresford, P., Green, D., Lister, R. and Woodard, K. (2002) 'The effects of poverty', in B. Bytheway, V. Bacigalupo, J. Bornat, J. Johnson and S. Spurr (eds) *Understanding Care, Welfare and Community: A Reader*. London and New York: Routledge.

Bernstein, B. (1971a) *Class, Codes and Control: Theoretical Studies towards a Sociology of Language*, Vol. I. London: Routledge and Kegan Paul.

Bernstein, B. (1971b) 'On the classification and framing of educational knowledge', in M. F. D. Young (ed.) *Knowledge and Control: New Directions for the Sociology of Education*, pp. 19–46. London: Collier-Macmillan.

Birchal, J. (1994) *Co-op: The People's Business*. Manchester: Manchester University Press.

Bourdieu, P. (1973) 'Cultural reproduction and social reproduction', in R. Brown (ed.) *Knowledge, Education and Cultural Change*. London: Tavistock.

Bourdieu, P. (1974) 'The school as a conservative force: scholastic and cultural inequalities', in J. Eggleston (ed.) *Contemporary Research in the Sociology of Education*. London: Methuen.

Bourdieu, P. (1977) *Outline of a Theory of Practice.* Cambridge: Cambridge University Press.

Bourdieu, P. (1984) *Distinction: A Social Critique of the Judgement of Taste* (R. Nice, trans.). Cambridge, MA: Harvard University Press.

Bourdieu, P. (1985) 'The social space and the genesis of groups', *Social Science Information*, 24 (2): 195–220.

Bourdieu, P. (1986) 'The forms of capital', in J. G. Richardson (ed.) *Handbook of Theory and Research for the Sociology of Education*, pp. 241–258. New York: Greenwood Press.

Bourdieu, P. (1987a) 'What makes a social class? On the theoretical and practical existence of groups', *Berkeley Journal of Sociology*, 32: 1–17.

Bourdieu, P. (1987b) *In Other Words: Essays Towards a Reflexive Sociology.* Stanford CA: Stanford University Press.

Bourdieu, P. (1987c) 'What makes social class?', *Berkeley Journal of Sociology*, 22: 1–18.

Bourdieu, P. (1990a) *In Other Words: Essays Towards a Reflexive Sociology.* Cambridge: Polity Press.

Bourdieu, P. (1990b) 'Social space and symbolic power', in P. Bourdieu (ed.) *Other Words*, pp. 123–139. Oxford: Polity Press.

Bourdieu, P. (1990c) *The Logic of Practice* (R. Nice, trans.). Polity Press: Cambridge.

Bourdieu, P. (1991) *Language and Symbolic Power.* Cambridge, MA: Harvard University Press.

Bourdieu, P. (1993) *Sociology in Question.* London: SAGE.

Bourdieu, P. (1994) *Language and Symbolic Power.* Cambridge: Polity Press.

Bourdieu, P. (1996) *The State Nobility: Elite Schools in the Field of Power* (L. C. Clough, trans.). Cornwall: Polity Press.

Bourdieu, P. (2000) *Pascalian Meditations.* Stanford, CA: Stanford University Press.

Bourdieu, P. (2001a) 'The forms of capital', in M. Granovetter and R. Swedberg (eds) *The Sociology of Economic Life*, pp. 96–111. Cambridge, MA: Westview Press.

Bourdieu, P. (2001b) *Masculine Domination* (R. Nice, trans.). Stanford, CA: Stanford University Press.

Bourdieu, P. (2002) 'Habitus', in J. Hillier and E. Rooksby (eds) *Habitus: A Sense of Place.* Aldershot: Ashgate.

Bourdieu, P. (2004) *Science and Reflexivity.* Cambridge: Polity Press.

Bourdieu, P. and Passeron, J. (1977) *Reproduction in Education, Society and Culture.* London: SAGE.

Bourdieu, P. and Wacquant, L. (1992) *An Invitation to Reflexive Sociology.* Chicago, IL: University of Chicago Press.

Bourdieu, P. and Wacquant, L. (2002) *An Invitation to Reflexive Sociology.* Cambridge: Polity Press.

Bourdieu, P., Passeron, J. C. and Saint-Martin, M. (1994) *Academic Discourse, Linguistic Misunderstanding and Professorial Power.* Cambridge: Polity.

Bowles, S. and Gintis, H. (1976) *Schooling in Capitalist America.* London: Routledge.

Bowles, S. and Gintis, H. (1982) 'The crisis of liberal democratic capitalism: the case of the United States', *Politics and Society*, 11 (1): 51–93.

Briggs, A. (1979) *The Age of Improvement 1783 –1867.* London: Longman.

British Educational Research Association (BERA) (2004) *Revised ethical guidelines for educational research.* Southwell: BERA.

Brownridge, D. A. (2009) *Violence Against Women: Vulnerable Populations.* London and New York: Routledge.

Burke, P. J. (2006) '"Fair access?": Exploring gender, access and participation beyond entry to higher education', in C. Leathwood and B. Francis (eds) *Gender and Lifelong Learning: Critical Feminist Engagements*, pp. 40–53. London: Routledge.

Bush, M. (2005) *The Casualties of Peterloo*. Bath: Carnegie.

Bynner, J. and Parsons, S. (1997) *It Doesn't Get Any Better*. London: Basic Skills Agency.

Bynner, J. and Parsons, S. (2003) 'Social participaton, values and crime', in E. Ferri, J. Bynner and M. Wadsworth (eds) *Changing Britain, Changing Lives*. London: Institute of Education Press.

Bynner, J. and Parsons, S. (2005) *New Light on Literacy and Numeracy*. London: National Research and Development Centre for Adult Literacy and Numeracy.

Bynner, J. and Parsons, S. (2006) 'New light on literacy and numeracy', reflect on-line, Issue 4, available at www.nrdc.org.uk/content.asp?CategoryID=922.

Bynner, J. and Parsons, S. (2008) 'Insights into Basic Skills from a UK longitudinal study', in S. Reder and J. Bynner (eds) *Tracking Adult Literacy and Numeracy Skills*. New York: Routledge.

Bynner, J. and Steedman, J. (1995) *Difficulties with Basic Skills: Findings from the 1970 British Cohort study*. London: The Basic Skills Agency.

Bynner, J., McIntosh, S., Vignoles, A., Dearden, L., Reed, H. and Van Reenan, J. (2001) *Improving Adult Basic Skills: Benefits to the Individual and to Society*. London: DfEE.

Byrne, D. (2005) *Social Exclusion*. Buckingham: Open University Press.

Canal, G, O. (2004) 'Photography in the field', in S. Pink, L. Kűrti and A. I. Afonso (eds) *Working Images: Visual Research and Representation in Ethnography*, pp. 31–46. London and New York: Routledge.

Cannadine, D. (2000) *Class in Britain*. London: Penguin Books.

Carr, W. and Kemmis, S. (1986) *Becoming Critical: Education, Knowledge and Action Research*. London: Routledge Falmer.

Casey, H., Jupp, T., Grief, S., Hodge, R., Ivanic, R., Lopez, D., Cara, O., Eldred, J. and McNeil, B. (2006) " *You Wouldn't Expect a Maths Teacher to Teach Plastering . . .". Embedding Literacy, Language and Numeracy in Post-16 Vocational Programmes: The Impact on Learning and Achievement*. London: National Research and Development Centre for Adult Literacy and Numeracy.

Clarke, S. (2002) 'Class struggle and the working class: the problem of commodity fetishism', in A. Dinerstein and M. Neary (eds) *The Labour Debate: An Investigation into the Theory and Reality of Capitalist Work*, pp. 41–64. Aldershot: Ashgate.

Clough, P. and Nutbrown, C. (2002) *A Student's Guide to Methodology*. London: SAGE.

Coare, P. and Johnston, R. (2004) *Adult Learning, Citizenship and Community Voices: Exploring Community Based Practice*. Leicester: NIACE.

Cohen, D. and Prusak, L. (2001) *In Good Company: How Social Capital Makes Organizations Work*. Watertown, MA: Harvard Business School Press.

Cohen, L., Manion, L. and Morrison, K. (2007) *Research Method in Education*, 6th edn. London: Routledge.

Coleman, J. S. (1988) Social capital in the creation of human capital, *American Journal of Sociology*, 94 (Supplement) S95–S120.

Coleman, K., Jansson, K., Kaiza, P. and Reed, E. (2007) *Homicides, Firearms Offences and Intimate violence 2005/6 (Supplementary Volume 1 to Crime in England and Wales 2005–6)*. Home Office Statistical Bulletin 02/07: Office for National Statistics.

Collins, R. and Makowsky, M. (1993) *The Discovery of Society*. New York: McGraw Hill.

Crequer, N. (2001 1) *Whispers of Talent that Built Up to a Crescendo*, available at www.tes.co.uk/article.aspx?storycode=349734.

Crowther, J., Hamilton, M. and Tett, L. (2006) *Powerful Literacies*. Leicester: NIACE.

Davies, C. A. (2008) *Reflexive Ethnography: A Guide to Researching Selves and Others*, 2nd edn. London: Routledge.

De Coulon, A., Meschi, E. and Yates, M. (2010) *Education, Basic Skills and Health-related Outcomes Research Report*. London: NRDC.

Denzin, N. K. (1989) *Interpretive interactionism*. Newbury Park, CA: SAGE.

Department of Health (DoH) (2002) *Women's Mental Health: Into the Mainstream – Strategic Development of Mental Health Care for Women*, p. 16, available at www.dh.gov.uk/assetRoot/04/07/54/87/04075487.pdf.

Department for Education and Employment (DfEE) (1998) *The Learning Age: A Renaissance for a New Britain* (Green Paper CM 3790). London: The Stationery Office.

Department for Education and Employment (DfEE) (1999) *A Fresh Start: The Report of a Working Group Chaired by Sir Claus Moser*. London: Department for Education and Employment.

Department for Education and Employment (DfEE) (2001) 'Executive Summary', *Skills for Life: The National Strategy to Improve Adult Literacy and Numeracy Skills*. Nottingham: DfEE Publications.

Department for Education and Skills (DfES) (2002) *Success for All*. London: DfES.

Dillabough, J. and Arnot, M. (2001) 'Feminist sociology of education: dynamics, debates and directions', in J. Demaine (ed.) *Sociology of Education Today*. London: Palgrave.

Doherty, K., 'Marie's epic journey is certain to inspire', available at www.gatehousebooks.co.uk/news/21.

Dolan, M. (2008) 'Marie's story', in Write About (ed.) *Bullying*. Warrington: Gate House Books.

Dominelli, L. (2006) *Women and Community Action*. Bristol: Policy Press.

Duckworth, V. (2006) 'Extraordinary achievements', *Research and Practice in Adult Literacy*, 60: 5–6.

Duckworth, V. (2007a) 'Freeing the wheels and moving on: the impact of Basic Skills on the learners' progression', paper present at *The times they are a changin'*, 4th Centre for Research in Lifelong Learning International Conference, 22–24 June, University of Stirling.

Duckworth, V. (2007b) 'The impact of practitioner research on: self, learners and teachers in training', *Research and Practice in Adult Literacy*, 62: 18–21.

Duckworth, V. (2008a) *Getting Better Worksheets, Adult Literacy Resources*. Warrington: Gatehouse Books.

Duckworth, V. (2008b) 'Embracing the community: increasing the influence of research findings', paper presented at *Engaging with Research: Developing a New Future*, LSRN and NIACE conference, 6 December 2007.

Duckworth, V. (2009) *On The Job: Car Mechanic Tutor Resources*, On The Job 14–19 Series. Warrington: Gatehouse Books.

Duckworth, V. (2010) 'Sustaining learning over time: it looks more like a Yellow Brick Road than a straightforward path for women experiencing violence', *Research and Practice in Adult Literacy*, 71: 19–20.

Duckworth, V. (2011a) 'Developing a curriculum which opens up spaces for empowerment and dialogue between tutors and for basic skills learners', paper presented at British Educational Research Association (BERA) Annual Conference 2011.

Duckworth, V. (2011b) 'Basic skills, curriculum design and learner empowerment: using practitioner research to inform practice and emancipatory approaches to curriculum design', paper presented at *Prioritising Teaching in an Age of Austerity*, Research Day: College Research Network. Liverpool: Liverpool Community College.

Duckworth, V. (2013) *How to be a Brilliant FE Teacher: A Practical Guide to Being Effective and Innovative*. Abingdon: Routledge.

Duckworth, V. and Taylor, K. (2008) 'Words are for everyone', *Research and Practice in Adult Literacy*, 64: 30–32.

Duckworth, V. and Tummons, J. (2010) *Contemporary Issues in Lifelong Learning*, 1. Lifelong Learning Sector. Buckingham: Open University Press.

Duckworth, V. and Cochrane, M. (2012) 'Spoilt for choice, spoilt by choice: long-term consequences of limitations imposed by social background', *Education and Training*, 54 (7): 579–591.

Duckworth, V., Gelling, C., Sheridan, B. and Shiel, C. (2010) *I teach: Journeys into Teaching*. Warrington: Gatehouse Books.

Elliott, J. (1991) *Action Research for Educational Change*. Buckingham: Open University Press.

Etherington, K. (2004) *Becoming a Reflexive Researcher: Using Our Selves in Research*. London: Jessica Kingsley.

Farraday, A. and Plummer, K. (1979) 'Doing life histories', *Sociological Review*, 27 (4): 773–798.

Feeley, M. (2007) *Adult Literacy and Affective Equality: Recognising the Pivotal Role of Care in the Learning Relationship*. Dublin University: unpublished PhD.

Field, J. (2000) *Lifelong Learning and the New Educational Order*. Stoke-on-Trent: Trentham Books.

Field, J. (2008) *Social Capital*. London: Routledge.

Field, J., Gallacher, A. and Ingram, R. (2009) *EDS Researching Transitions In Lifelong Learning*. London: Routledge.

Finch, J. (1984) '"It's great to have someone to talk to": ethics and politics of interviewing women', in C. Bell and H. Roberts (eds) *Social Researching: Politics, Problems, Practice*, pp. 166–180. London: Routledge and Kegan Paul.

Franklin, B. (1995) 'The case for children's rights: a progress report', in B. Franklin (ed.) *The Handbook of Children's Rights: Comparative Policy and Practice*. London: Routledge.

Freire, P. (1993) *Pedagogy of the Oppressed*. New York: Continuum.

Freire, P. (1996) *Pedagogy of the Oppressed*. London: Penguin.

Freire, P. (2004) *Pedagogy of Indignation*. London: Paradigm Publishers.

Furlong, A. and Cartmel, F. (1997) *Young People and Social Change: Individualization and Risk in Late Modernity*. Buckingham: Open University Press.

Furlong, A. and Cartmel, F. (2006) *Young People and Social Change: New Perspectives*. Buckingham: Open University Press.

Furlong, A., Cartmel, F., Biggart, A., Sweeting, H. and West, P. (2003) *Reconceptualising Youth Transitions: Patterns of Vulnerability and Processes of Social Exclusion*. Scottish Executive: Edinburgh.

Gee, J. P. (1996) *Social Linguistics and Literacies: Ideology in Discourses*, 2nd edn. London: Routledge Falmer.

Gee, J. P. (1999) *An Introduction to Discourse Analysis: Theory and Method*. London: Routledge.

Gee, J. P. (2000) 'Discourse and sociocultural studies in reading', in M. L. Kamil, P. B.

Mosenthal, P. D. Pearson and R. Barr (eds) *Handbook of Reading Research, Volume III*. Mahwah, NJ: Lawrence Erlbaum.

Gee, J. P. (2004) *Situated Language and Learning: A Critique of Traditional Schooling*. London: Routledge.

Gee, J. P. (2005) *Education for Critical Consciousness*. New York: Continuum International Publishing Group.

Gewirtz, S., Ball, S. J. and Bowe, R. (1995) *Markets, Choice and Equity in Education*. Buckingham: Open University Press.

Giddens, A. (1991a) *Modernity and Self-identity: Self and Society in the Late Modern Age*. Cambridge: Polity Press.

Giddens, A. (1991b) *The Consequences of Modernity*. Cambridge: Polity Press.

Giddens, A. (1992) *The Transformation of Intimacy: Sexuality, Love and Eroticism in Modern Societies*. Stanford, CA: Stanford University Press.

Giroux, H. (1997) *Pedagogy and the Politics of Hope: Theory, Culture, and Schooling*. Boulder, CO: Westview.

Glaser, B. G. (1978) *Theoretical Sensitivity*. Mill Valley, CA: Sociology Press.

Glaser, B. G. and Straus, A. L. (1967) *The Discovery of Grounded Theory: Strategies for Qualitative Research*. Chicago, IL: Aldine.

Gleeson, D. (2005) 'Learning for change in further education', *Journal of Vocational Training and Education*, 57 (2): 239–244.

Goffman, E. (1959/1971) *The Presentation of Self in Everyday Life*. New York: Doubleday and Anchor Books; 2nd edn (1971) London: Penguin.

Goffman, E. (1963) *Stigma: Notes on management of spoiled identity*. London: Cox and Wyman.

Goffman, E. (1969) *Asylums*. Harmondsworth: Penguin.

Goffman, E. (1970) *Stigma*. Harmondsworth: Penguin.

Goffman, E. (1981) *Forms of Talk*, Oxford: Blackwell.

Goldthorpe, G., Llewellyn, C. and Payne, C. (1986) *Social Mobility and Class Structure*. Oxford: Clarendon Press.

Goldthorpe, J. H. (1996) 'Class analysis and the reorientation of class theory: the case of persisting differentials in educational attainment', *British Journal of Sociology*, 47 (3): 481–512.

Goodley, D., Lawthom, R., Clough, P. and Moore, M. (2004) *Researching Life Stories: Method, Theory and Analyses in a Biographical Age*. Abingdon: Routledge.

Goodson, I. (1992) 'Studying teachers' lives: an emergent field of inquiry', in I. Goodson (ed.) *Studying Teachers' Lives*, pp. 1–17. London: Routledge.

Goodson, I. F. and Sikes, P. (2001) *Life History Research in Educational Settings: Learning from Lives*. Buckingham: Open University Press.

Granovetter, M. S. (1973) 'The strength of weak ties', *American Journal of Sociology*, 78 (6): 1360–1380.

Greer, S. (2007) 'Help us to turn off the red light', *Oldham Advertiser* (5 December), available at http://menmedia.co.uk/oldhamadvertiser/news/s/1027065_help_us_to_turn_out_red_light.

Grenfell, M. and James, D. (eds) (1998) *Bourdieu and Education: Acts of Practical Theory*. London: Falmer Press.

Grenfell, M. and James, D. (2004) 'Change *in* the field – chang *ing* the field: Bourdieu and the methodological practice of educational research', *British Journal of Sociology of Education*, 24 (4): 508–523.

Gurr, D. and Hunt, J. (1998) *The Cotton Mills of Oldham.* Oldham: Arts and Heritage Publications.

Habermas, J. (1974) *Theory and Practice.* London: Heinemann.

Hamilton, M. (1996) 'Literacy and adult basic education', in R. Fieldhouse with Associates (eds) *A History of Modern British Adult Education.* Leicester: NIACE.

Hamilton, M. and Hillier, Y. (2006) *Changing Faces of Adult Literacy, Language and Numeracy: A Critical History.* Stoke-on-Trent: Trentham Books.

Hamilton, M., Davies, P. and James, K. (2007) *Practitioners Leading Research: A Report of Action Report Projects from the NRDC Practitioner-led Research Initiatives.* London: NRDC.

Hanley, L. (2007) *Estates: An Intimate History.* London: Granta Publications.

Harding, S. (1987) 'Introduction: is there a feminist method?', in S. Harding (ed.) *Feminism and Methodology*, pp. 1–14. Bloomington, IN: Indiana University Press.

Harding, S. (1991) *Whose Science? Whose Knowledge? Thinking from Women's Lives.* Ithaca, NY: Cornell University Press.

Harding, S. (2004) 'Introduction: standpoint theory as a site of political, philosophic and scientific debate', in S. Harding (ed.) *The Feminist Standpoint Theory Reader: Intellectual and Political Controversies.* New York: Routledge.

Hargreaves, A. (1986) *Two Cultures of Schooling: The Case of Middle Schools.* Lewes: Falmer Press.

Hargreaves, D. H. (1967) *Social Relations in a Secondary School.* London: Routledge and Kegan Paul.

Hargreaves, D. H. (1982) *The Challenge for the Comprehensive School.* London: Routledge and Kegan Paul.

Hargreaves, D. H., Hester, S. and Mellor, F. (1975) *Deviance in Classrooms.* London: Routledge and Kegan Paul.

Harker, R., Mahar, C. and Wilkes, C. (1990) 'The basic theoretical position', in R. Harker, C. Mahar and C. Wilkes (eds) *An Introduction to the Work of Pierre Bourdieu: The Practice of Theory.* London: Macmillan.

Heath, A. (1981) *Social Mobility.* London: Fontana.

Heath, S. (1983) *Ways with Words: Language, Life and Work in Communities and Classrooms.* Cambridge: Cambridge University Press.

Hey, V. and Bradford, S. (2006) 'Re-engineering motherhood? Surestart in the community', *Contemporary Issues in Early Childhood*, 7 (1): 53–67.

Hobsbawm, E. J. (1990) *The Penguin Economic History of Britain Industry and Empire: Volume 3.* London: Penguin.

Hochschild, A. (1983) *The Managed Heart: Commercialization of Human Feeling.* Berkeley, CA: University of California Press.

Home Office (2002a) *Secure Borders, Safe Haven: Integration with Diversity in Modern Britain*, CM5387. London: The Stationery Office.

Home Office (2002b) *Community Cohesion.* London: The Stationery Office.

Home Office (2002c) *Building Cohesive Communities.* London: The Stationery Office.

Hooks, B. (1994) *Teaching to Transgress: Education as the Practice of Freedom.* New York: Routledge.

Horsman, J. (1991) 'The problem of illiteracy and the promise of literacy', in M. Hamilton, D. Barton and Ivanic, R. (eds) *Worlds of Literacy.* Clevendon: Multilingual Matters.

Horsman, J. (1999) *Too Scared to Learn: Women, Violence and Education.* Toronto: McGilligan Books.

Horsman, J. (2004) 'What did they learn? Legacies of schooling: how literacy programs can support learners affected by violence', *Literacies*, Fall: pp. 11–13.

Hymes, D. (1996) *Ethnography, Linguistics, Narrative Inequality: Towards an Understanding of Voice*. London: Taylor and Francis.

Ingle, S. and Duckworth, V. (2012) *Enhancing Learning through Technology in Lifelong Learning: Fresh Ideas: Innovative Strategies*. Buckingham: Open University Press.

Ivanic, R. et al. (2008) 'Harnessing everyday literacies for student learning at college', *Teaching and Learning Research Programme (TLRP)*, Research briefing No. 50, available at www.tlrp.org/pub/documents/IvanicRB50final.pdf.

James, N. (1989) 'Emotional labour: skill and work in the social regulation of feelings', *Sociological Review*, 37: 15–42.

Johnson, C., Duckworth, V., McNamara, M. and Apelbaum, C. (2010) 'A tale of two adult learners: from adult basic education to degree completion', *National Association for Developmental Education Digest*, 5 (1): 57–67.

Kelly, L., Burton, S. and Regan, L. (1994) 'Researching women's lives or studying women's oppression? Reflections on what constitutes feminist research', in M. Maynard and J. Purvis (eds) *Researching Women's Lives from a Feminist Perspective*, pp. 27–48. London: Taylor and Graham.

Kemmis, S. (1993) 'Action research', in M. Hammersley (ed.) *Educational Research: Current Issues*. London: Paul Chapman.

Kemmis, S. (2001) 'Exploring the relevance of critical theory for action research: emancipatory action research in the footsteps of Jürgen Habermas', in P. Reason and H. Bradbury (eds) *Handbook of Action Research: Participative Inquiry and Practice*, pp. 91–102. London: SAGE.

Kemmis, S. and McTaggart, R. (eds) (1988) *The Action Research Planner*. Geelong, Vic: Deakin University Press.

Kemmis, S. and Wilkinson, M. (1998) 'Participatory action research and the study of practice', in B. Atweb, S. Kemmis and P. Weeks (eds) *Action Research in Practice: Partnerships for Social Justice in Education*. London: Routledge.

Kenney, A. (1924) *Memories of a Militant*. London: Edward Arnold.

Kerr, K. and West, M. (eds) (2010) *BERA Insight: Schools and Social Inequality*. London: BERA.

Kidd, A. (1996) *Manchester*. Keele: Keele University Press.

Kidd, A. and Roberts, K. W. (1985) *City, Class and Culture*. Manchester: Manchester University Press.

Labov, W. (1972) *Language in the Inner City: Studies in the Black English Vernacular*. Philadelphia, PA: University of Pennsylvania Press.

Lacey, C. (1970) *Hightown Grammar, Manchester*. Manchester: Manchester University Press.

Lacey, C. (1976) 'Problems of sociological fieldwork: a review of the methodology of "Hightown Grammar"', in M. Hammersley and P. Woods (eds) *The Process of Schooling*. London: Routledge and Kegan Paul.

Lankshear, C. (1997) *Changing Literacies*. Buckingham and Philadelphia, PA: Open University Press.

Lankshear, C. (1993) 'Functional literacy from a Freirean point of view', in P. McLaren and P. Leonard (eds) *Paulo Freire: A Critical Encounter*, pp. 90–118. New York: Routledge.

Lankshear, C. and McLaren, P. (eds) (1993) *Critical Literacy: Politics, Praxis, and the Postmodern*. Albany, NY: State University of New York Press.

Lauder, H., Hughes, D., Watson, S. et al. (1999) *Trading in Futures: Why Markets in Education Don't Work*. Buckingham: Open University Press.

Lave, J. and Wenger, E. (1991) *Situated Learning: Legitimate Peripheral Participating*. Cambridge: Cambridge University Press.

Lawler, S. (2004) 'Rules of engagement: habitus, power and resistance', in L. Adkins and B. Skeggs (eds) *Feminism after Bourdieu*, pp. 110–128. Oxford: Blackwell Publishing.

Lawler, S. (2005) 'Disgusted subjects: the making of middle-class identities', *The Sociological Review*, 3 (3): 429–446.

Lawthom, R. with Stamford, C. (2004) '"I'd never met a vegetarian, never mind a lesbian": Coleen's life story', in D. Goodley, R. Lawthom, P. Clough and M. Moore (eds) *Researching Life Stories: Method, Theory and Analyses in a Biographical Age*, pp. 15–25. London: Routledge Falmer.

Layder, D. (1994) *Understanding Social Theory*. London: SAGE.

Leathwood, C. (2006) 'Gendered constructions of lifelong learning and the learner in the UK policy context', in C. Leathwood and B. Francis (eds) *Gender and Lifelong Learning: Critical Feminist Engagements*, pp. 40–53. London: Routledge.

Leitch, S. (2006) ' *Prosperity for All in the Global Economy: World Class Skills*. Final report of the Leitch Review of Skills. London: HMSO/HM Treasury, available at www.official-documents.gov.uk/document/other/0118404792/0118404792.pdf.

Light, D. (2010) 'The final stage? Writing up ethnographic research', in J. Scott Jones and S. Watt (eds) *Ethnography in Social Science Practice*, pp. 173–186. Abingdon: Routledge.

Lincoln, Y. and Guba, E. G. (1985) *Naturalistic Inquiry*. Beverly Hills, CA: SAGE.

Lucas, L. (2001) 'Whispers', *Times Educational Supplement*, 13 July, available at www.tes.co.uk/article.aspx?storycode=349734.

Lucey, H. and Reay, D. (2002) 'A market in waste: psychic and structural dimensions of school-choice policy in the UK and children's narratives on "demonised" schools', *Discourse*, 23 (3): 253–266.

Luttrell, W. (1997) *School-smart and Mother-wise: Working-class Women's Identity and Schooling*. New York: Routledge.

Lynch, K., Lyons, M. and Barry, U. (eds) (2008) *The Gendered Order of Caring: Women in Contemporary Ireland*. Dublin: New Ireland Press.

Macedo, D. (1994) *Literacies of Power: What Americans are Not Allowed to Know*. Boulder, CO: Westview.

Maguire, P. (2001) 'Uneven ground: feminism and action research', in P. Reason and H. Bradbury (eds) *Handbook of Action Research and Participatory Inquiry and Practice*. London: SAGE.

Mallows, D., Chester, A. with Duckworth, V. (2008) 'Seeing yourself in print', *Reflect: National Research and Development Centre*, 10: 26.

McGee, R. (2002) 'The self in participatory poverty research', in Karen Brock and Rosemary McGee (eds) *Knowing Poverty*, pp. 14–43. London: Earthscan.

McKernan, J. (1996) *Curriculum Action Research: A Handbook of Methods and Resources for the Reflective Practitioner*. London: Routledge.

McNamara, M. (2007) *Getting Better*. Warrington: Gatehouse Books.

McNiff, J. and Whitehead, J. (2007) *Action Research: Principles and Practice*. Abingdon: Routledge Falmer.

McNulty, M. A. (2003) 'Dyslexia and the life course', *Journal of Learning Disabilities*, 36 (4): 363–381.

McRobbie, A. (2000a) 'Feminism and the Third Way', *Feminist Review*, 64, pp. 97–112.

McRobbie, A. (2000b) *Feminism and Youth Culture*, Palgrave Basingstoke (3rd edn, a compilation of earlier work).

McRobbie, A. (2004) 'Notes on "What Not to Wear" and post-feminist symbolic violence', in L. Adkins and B. Skeggs (eds) *Feminism after Bourdieu*. Oxford: Blackwell/The Sociological Review.

McRobbie, A. (2006) 'Yummy mummies leave a bad taste for young women', *Guardian*, 2 March, available at www.guardian.co.uk/world/2006/mar/02/gender.comment.

McRobbie, A. and Garber, J. (1976) 'Girls and subcultures: an exploration', in Stuart Hall and Tony Jefferson (eds) *Resistance Through Rituals: Youth Subcultures in Post-War Britain*, pp. 209–222. London: Hutchinson.

Maynard, M. and Purvis, J. (1995) *Researching Women's Lives from a Feminist Perspective*, pp. 1–9. London: Taylor and Francis.

Mercer, N. (1995) *The Guided Construction of Knowledge: Talk Amongst Teachers and Learners* Clevedon, Philadelphia, PA: Multilingual Matters.

Metcalfe, H. (1997) *Class and Higher Education: The Participation of Young People from Lower Social Classes*. London: CIHE.

Mezirow, J. (1991) *Transformative Dimensions of Adult Learning*. San Francisco, CA: Jossey-Bass.

Mezirow, J. (2000) *Learning as Transformation: Critical Perspectives on a Theory in Progress*. San Francisco, CA: Jossey Bass.

Mies, M. (1999) 'Towards a methodology for feminist research', in M. Hammersley (ed.) *Social Researching: Philosophy, Politics and Practice*, pp. 64–82. London: SAGE.

Miles, M. B. and Huberman, A. M. (1984) *Qualitative Data Analysis: A Source Book of New Methods*. Beverly Hills, CA: SAGE.

Mills, C. (2008) 'Reproduction and transformation of inequalities in schooling: the transformative potential of the theoretical constructs of Bourdieu', *British Journal of Sociology of Education*, 29 (1): 79–89.

Moore, R. (2004) 'Cultural capital: objective probability and the cultural arbitrary', – *British Journal of Sociology of Education*, 25 (4): 445–456.

Morrish, E., Horsman, J. and Hofer, J. (2002) *Take on the Challenge: A Sourcebook from the Women, Violence, and Adult Education Project*. Washington, DC: United States Department of Education, Women's Educational Equity (WEEA) Program.

Murdock, G. P. (1949) *Social Structure*. New York: Macmillan.

Narayan, U. (1989) 'The project of feminist epistemology', in S. Bordo and A. Jaggar (eds) *Gender/Body/Knowledge: Feminist Reconstructions of Being and Knowing*, pp. 256–272. Rutgers, NJ: Rutgers University Press.

National Equality Panel (NEP) (2010) *An Anatomy of Economic Inequality in the UK*. London: Government Equalities Office.

Nicholson, L. (1997) 'The myth of the traditional family', in H. L. Marsh (ed.) *Feminism and Families*, Routledge: New York.

Noddings, N. (1984) *Caring: A Feminine Approach to Ethics and Moral Education*. Berkeley, CA: University of California Press.

Noddings, N. (1992) *The Challenge to Care in Schools*. New York: Teachers College.

Oakley, A. (1994) 'Women and children first and last: parallels and differences between children's and women's studies', in B. Mayall (ed.) *Children's Childhoods Observed and Experienced*, pp. 13–32. London: Falmer.

O'Brien, M. (2005) 'Mothers as educational workers: mothers' emotional work at their children's transfer to second-level schooling', *Irish Educational Studies*, 24 (2–3): 223–243.

O'Brien, M. (2007) 'Mothers' emotional care work in education and its moral imperative', *Gender and Education*, 19 (2): 159–178.

Office for National Statistics (ONS) (2007) Office Statistical Bulletin 02/07, available at www.neighbourhood.statistics.gov.uk/dissemination.

Office for National Statistics (ONS) (2009) available at www.statistics.gov.uk/cci/nugget.asp?id=2193andPos=1andColRank=2andRank=224.

Oldham Metropolitan Borough (2008) Coldhurst Community Council minutes, available at www.oldham. gov.uk/2008.03.12_-_coldhurst_cc_notes. pdf.

Oldham Chronicle (2009) A NIACE chance for adult learners. Available at www.oldham-chronicle.co.uk/news-features/8/news/30732/a-niace-chance-for-adult-learners.

Oldham Council www.oldham.gov.uk/downloads/file/712/concise_version_of_oldhams_jsna.

Oldham Education and Leisure (1997) *Ferranti: An Oral History*. Oldham: Oldham Arts and Heritage Publications.

O'Rourke, R. (2005) *Creative Writing: Education, culture and community*. Leicester: NIACE.

Park, P. (1999) 'People, knowledge and change in participatory research', *Management Learning*, 30 (2): 141–157.

Parsons, S. (2002) *Do I Want to Improve my Reading, Writing and Maths?* London: The Basic Skills Agency.

Parsons, S. and Bynner, J. (1998) *Influences on Adult Basic Skills*. London: The Basic Skills Agency.

Parsons, S. and Bynner, J. (2002) *Basic Skills and Social Exclusion*. London: The Basic Skills Agency.

Parsons, S. and Bynner, J. (2005) *Measuring Basic Skills for Longitudinal Study: The Design and Development of Instruments for Use with Cohort Members in the Age 34 Follow-up in the 1970 British Cohort Study (BCS70)*. London: National Research and Development Centre for Adult Literacy and Numeracy.

Parsons, S. and Bynner, J. (2006) 'Measuring basic skills for longitudinal study: the design and development of instruments for use with cohort members in the age 34 follow-up in the 1970 British Cohort Study (BCS70)', *Literacy and Numeracy Studies*, 14 (2): 7–30.

Parsons, S. and Bynner, J. (2007) *Illuminating Disadvantage: Profiling the Experience of Adults with Entry Level Literacy and Numeracy Over Their Life Course. Summary Report*. London: National Research and Development Centre for Adult Literacy and Numeracy.

Payne, G. (2006) 'Re-counting "illiteracy": literacy skills in the sociology of social inequality', *The British Journal of Sociology*, 57 (2).

Pidgeon, N. (1996) 'Grounded theory: theoretical background', in J. T. E. Richardson (ed.) *Handbook of Qualitative Research Methods for Psychology and the Social Sciences*, pp. 86–101. Leicester: The British Psychological Society.

Pink, S. (2007) *Doing Visual Ethnography: Images, Media and Representation in Research*. London: SAGE.

Plummer, G. (2000) *Failing Working-Class Girls*. Stoke-on-Trent: Trentham Books.

Prosser, J. (1998) *Image-Based Research: A Sourcebook for Qualitative Researchers*. London: Falmer Press.

Prus, L. (1996) *Symbolic Interaction and Ethnographic Research: Intersubjectivity and the Study of Human Lived Experience.* New York: State University of New York Press.

Putnam, R. D. (1993) 'The prosperous community: social capital and public life', *The American Prospect*, 13: 35–42.

Putnam, R. D. (2000) *Bowling Alone.* New York: Simon and Schuster.

Puwar, N. (2004) *Space Invaders: Race, Gender and Bodies out of Place.* Oxford: Berg.

Ramazanoglu, C. and Holland, J. (2004) *Feminist Methodology: Challenges and Choices.* London: SAGE.

Reason, P. (1994) 'Three approaches to participative inquiry', in N. Denzin and Y. Lincoln (eds) *Handbook of Qualitative Research*, pp. 324–339. Thousand Oaks, CA: SAGE.

Reason, P. and Bradbury, H. (2001) *Handbook of Action Research: Participative Inquiry and Practice.* London: SAGE.

Reay, D. (1997) 'Feminist theory, habitus and social class: disrupting notions of classlessness', *Women's Studies International Forum*, 20 (2): 225–233.

Reay, D. (1998a) 'Rethinking social class: qualitative perspectives on class and gender', *Sociology*, 32 (2): 259–275.

Reay, D. (1998b) *Class Work: Mothers Involvement in their Children's Primary Schooling.* London: University of London Press.

Reay, D. (2000) 'A useful extension of Bourdieu's conceptual framework?: emotional capital as a way of understanding mothers' involvement in their children's education', *Sociological Review*, 48: 568–585.

Reay, D. (2001) '"Spice Girls", "Nice Girls", "Girlies" and "Tomboys"; gender discourses. Girls' cultures and femininities in the primary classroom', *Gender and Education*, 13 (2): 153–167.

Reay, D. (2003) 'A risky business? Mature working-class women students and access to higher education', *Gender and Education*, 15 (3): 301–317.

Reay, D. (2004a) '"It's all a habitus"; beyond the habitual use of habitus in educational research', *British Journal of Sociology of Education*, 25 (4): 431– 444.

Reay, D. (2004b) 'Exclusivity, exclusion, and social class in urban education markets in the United Kingdom', *Urban Education*, 39 (5): 537–560.

Reay, D. (2004c) 'Gendering Bourdieu's concept of capitals?: emotional capital, women and social class', in L. Adkins and B. Skeggs (eds) *Feminism after Bourdieu.* Oxford: Blackwell.

Reay, D. (2005) 'Beyond consciousness? The psychic landscape of class?', *Sociology*, 395: 911–928.

Reay, D. (2006) 'The zombie stalking English schools: social class and educational inequality', *British Journal of Educational Studies*, 54 (3): 288–307.

Reay, D. (2007) 'Unruly places: inner-city comprehensives, middle-class imaginaries and working-class children', in *Urban Studies: Special Issue on The Geography of Education*, 44 (7): 1191–1203.

Reay, D. and Ball, S. (1998) 'Making their minds up: family dynamics of school choice', *British Educational Research Journal*, 24 (4): 431–448.

Reay, D. and Lucey, H. (2003) 'The limits of "choice": children and inner city schooling', *Sociology*, 37 (1): 121–142.

Reay, D., David, M. E. and Ball, S. (2002) '"It's taking me a long time but I'll get there in the end": mature students on access courses and higher education choice', *British Educational Research Journal*, 28 (1): 5–19.

Reay, D., David, M. E. and Ball, S. (2005) *Degrees of Choice: Social Class, Race and Gender in Higher Education.* Stoke-on-Trent: Trentham Books.

Richardson, L. (2003) 'Poetic Representations of Interviews', in J. Gubrium and J. Holstein (eds) *Postmodern Interviewing*, pp. 187–201. London: SAGE.

Ritchie, David (2001) 'One Oldham, one future', *Oldham Independent Review*, available at www.oldhamir.org.uk/OIR%20Report.pdf.

Robbins, Derek (1991) *The Work of Pierre Bourdieu*. Buckingham: Open University Press.

Rockhill, K. (1993) 'Gender, language and the politics of literacy', in B. Street (ed.) *Cross-cultural Approaches to Literacy*. Cambridge: Cambridge University Press.

Roseneil, S. and Budgeon, S. (2004) 'Cultures of intimacy and care beyond "the family": personal life and social change in the early twenty-first century', in *Current Sociology*, 52 (2): 135–159.

Roseneil, S. and Budgeon, S. (2006) 'Beyond "the family": personal life and social change', *Sociology Review*, 16 (1): 14–16.

Sandbrook, D. (2010) *'Could our first middle-class Queen save the monarchy from itself?'*, available at www.dailymail.co.uk/femail/article-1330367/Kate-Middleton-Could-middle-class-Queen-save-monarchy-itself.html.

Savage, M. (2000) *Class Analysis and Social Transformation*. Buckingham: Open University Press.

Savage, M. (2003) 'Review essay: a new class paradigm?', *British Journal of Sociology of Education*, 24 (4): 535–541.

Sayer, A. (1984) *Method in Social Science*. London: Hutchinson.

Schostak, J. F. (2002) *Understanding, Designing and Conducting Qualitative Research in Education*. Buckingham: Open University Press.

Schostak, J. F. (2006) *Interviewing and Representation in Qualitative Research Projects*. Buckingham and New York: Open University Press.

Scottish Executive (2001) *Adult Literacy in Scotland: Analysis of Data from the 1996 Adult Literacy Survey*. Edinburgh: Scottish Executive.

Shor, I. (1992) *Empowering Education: Critical Teaching for Social Change*. Chicago, IL: University of Chicago Press.

Shor, I. (1993) 'Education is politics: Paulo Freire's critical pedagogy', in P. McLaren and P. Leonard (eds) *Paulo Freire: A Critical Encounter*, pp. 25–35. London: Routledge.

Sivarajasingam, V., Wells, J. P., Moore, S., Morgan, P. and Shepherd, J. P. (2010) 'Violence in England and Wales in 2010: an accident and emergency perspective. Executive summary', available at www.vrg.cf.ac.uk/nvit/NVIT_2010.pdf.

Skeggs, B. (1997/2002) *Formations of Class and Gender*, 2nd edn, 2002. London: SAGE.

Skeggs, B. (2004) *Class, Self, Culture*. London: Routledge.

Skills for Life (2001) *The National Strategy for Improving Adult Literacy and Numeracy Skills*, available at http://rwp.excellencegateway.org.uk/resource/Skills+for+Life%3A+the+national+strategy+for+improving+adult+literacy+and+numeracy+skills%3A+delivering+the+vision+2001-2004/pdf/.

Skinner, T. and Taylor, H. (2009) '"Being shut out in the dark": young survivors' experiences of reporting a sexual offence', *Feminist Criminology*, 4 (2): 130–150.

Skinner, T., Hester, M. and Malos, E. (2005) *Researching Gender Violence: Feminist Methodology in Action*. Devon: Willan Publishing.

Smith, D. (1974) 'Women's perspective as a radical critique of sociology', *Sociological Inquiry*, 44: 7–13.

Smith, D. (1987) *The Everyday World as Problematic: A Feminist Sociology*. Boston, MA: Northeastern University Press.

Smith, D. (1989) 'Sociological theory: methods of writing patriarchy', in R. Wallace (ed.) *Feminism and Sociological Theory*. London: SAGE.

Smith, D. (1990) *The Conceptual Practice of Power: A Feminist Sociology of Knowledge*. Boston, MA: North Eastern University Press.

Smith, D. (1997) 'From the margins: women's standpoint as a method of inquiry in social sciences', *Gender, Technology and Development*, 1: 113–35.

Smith, L. J. F. (1989) 'Domestic violence', *Home Office Research Study 107*. London: HMSO.

Stanley, L. and Wise, S. (1993) *Breaking Out Again: Feminist Ontology and Epistemology*. London: Routledge.

Steedman, C. (1988) '"The mother made conscious": the historical development of primary school pedagogy', in M. Woodhead and A. McGrath (eds) *Family, School and Society*, pp. 82–95. Buckingham: The Open University.

Stone, V., Cotton, D. and Thomas, A. (2000) *Mapping Troubled Lives: Young People Not in Education, Employment or Training*. London: DfEE.

Straus, A. and Juliet, C. (1990) *Basics of Qualitative Research: Grounded Theory Procedures and Techniques*. Newbury Park, CA: SAGE.

Street, B. (1984) *Literacy in Theory and Practice*. Cambridge: Cambridge University Press.

Stuart, M. (2006) '"My friends made all the difference": getting into and succeeding at university for first-generation entrants', *Journal of Access Policy and Practice*, 3 (2): 162–184.

Teaching and Learning Research Programme (TLRP) (2008a) 'Are we witnessing the rise of a high skilled, low waged workforce?', *Research Briefing 50*, London: Institute of Education, available at www.tlrp.org/pub/documents/BrownRB53final.pdf.

Teaching and Learning Research Programme (TLRP) (2008b) 'Education, knowledge and the knowledge economy', *Research Briefing 53*, London: Institute of Education, available at www.tlrp.org/pub/documents/globalisationcomm.pdf.

Tedder, M. and Biesta, G. J. J. (2009) 'Biography, transition and learning in the lifecourse: the role of narrative', in J. Field, J. Gallacher and R. Ingram (eds) *Researching Transitions in Lifelong Learning*, pp. 76–90. London: Routledge.

Tett, L., Hall, S., Maclachlan, K., Thorpe, G., Edwards, V. and Garside, L. (2006) *Evaluation of the Scottish Adult Literacy and Numeracy (ALN) Strategy*. Edinburgh: Scottish Executive Social Research.

Thomas, L., Bland, D. and Duckworth, V. (2012) 'Teachers as advocates for widening participation', *Widening Participation and Lifelong Learning*, 14 (2): 40–58.

Thompson, E. P. (1968) *The Making of the English Working Class*. Harmondsworth: Penguin.

Tomlinson, S. (2008) *Race and Education: Policy and Politics in Britain*. Buckingham: Open University.

Tummons, J. and Duckworth, V. (2012) *Doing your Research Project in the Lifelong Learning Sector*. Buckingham: Open University Press.

Tyler, I. (2008) '"Chav mum, chav scum": class disgust in contemporary Britain', *Feminist Media Studies*, 8 (2): 17–34.

UK Commission for Employment and Skills (UKCES) (2009) *Ambition 2020: World Class Skills and Jobs for the UK*. London: UKCES.

Walby, S. and Allen, J. (2004) *Domestic Violence, Sexual Assault and Stalking: Findings from the British Crime Survey*. London: Home Office Research, Development and Statistics Directorate.

Walkerdine, V. and Lucey, H. (1989) *Democracy in the Kitchen: Regulating Mothers and Socialising Daughters*. London: Virago.

Walkerdine, V., Lucey, H., and Melody, J. (2001) *Growing up Girl: Psychosocial Explorations of Gender and Class*. London: Palgrave.

Warren, C. A. B. and Hackney, J. K. (2000) *Gender Issues in Ethnography: Qualitative Research Methods series 9*. London: SAGE.

Waterhead Academy, available at www.jigsaw.com/id4640667/breezehill.oldham.sch.uk_companywiki.xhtml.

Weiler, K. (1991) 'A feminist pedagogy of difference', *Harvard Educational Review*, 61 (4): 449–474.

Wenger, E. (1998) *Communities of Practice: Learning, Meaning and Identity*. Cambridge: Cambridge University.

Wenger, E., McDermott, R. and Snyder, W. M. (2002) *Cultivating Communities of Practice*. Boston, MA: Harvard Business School Press.

Whitty, G. (1985) *Sociology and School Knowledge: Curriculum Theory, Research and Politics*. London: Methuen.

Whitty, G., Power, S. and Halpin, D. (1998) *Devolution and Choice in Education*. Buckingham: Open University Press.

Willis, Paul (1977) *Learning to Labour: How Working Class Kids Get Working Class Jobs*. Farnborough: Saxon House.

Wolf, M. (1992) *A Thrice Told Tale*. Standford, CA: Stanford University Press.

World Health Organisation (WHO) (2000a) 'Violence against women', *Fact Sheet 239*, available at https://apps.who.int/inf-fs/en/fact239.html.

World Health Organisation (WHO) (2000b) 'Women and mental health', *Fact Sheet 248*, https://apps.who.int/inf-fs/en/fact248.html.

Wright, D. G. (1998) *Popular Radicalism: The Working-Class Experience*. London: Longman Group.

Write about . . . (2008) *Bullying*. Gate House Books: Warrington.

Write about . . . (2009) *Inspiring People*. Gate House Books: Warrington.

Wykes, M. and Welsh, K. (2009) *Violence, Gender and Justice*. London: SAGE.

Zuber-Skerritt, O. (1982) *Action Research in Higher Education*. London: Kegan.

Zuber-Skerritt, O. (ed.) (1996) *New Directions in Action Research*. London: Falmer.

Websites

Archive Awareness Campaign, *From Kitchen Table to Conference Table. Annie Kenney: Womens' Fight for the Vote*, available at: www.co-op.ac.uk/politicalwomen/cs3_2.html From Kitchen Table to Conference Table The National Co-operative Archive, the Working Class Movement Library, the Labour History Archive and Study Centre, and the Bishopsgate Foundation and Institute came together to produce this exhibition because of their complementary collections on women, labour and the left.

This online exhibition follows the progress of women from the private sphere to the public sphere through their politicisation using a series of case studies

The National Research and Development Centre for Adult Literacy and Numeracy (NRDC), available at: www.nrdc.org.uk

Through the site there is access to over 150 NRDC research reports and reviews as well as magazine features and teaching and learning resources related to adult literacy, language and numeracy.

Office for National Statistics, Neighbourhood Statistics, available at: www.neighbourhood.statistics.gov.uk
Access to detailed statistics within specific geographic areas available, which includes Education, Skills and Training

Research and Practice in Adult Literacy (RaPAL), available at: www.rapal.org.uk
RaPAL is the only UK-wide organisation that focuses on the role of literacies in adult life. Through they are members, journals, conferences, policy and advocacy work, we are active in Europe and have international links.

Index